Radical Inclusion

What I Learned About Risk, Humility, and Kindness from My Son with Autism

Andrea Moriarty

ISBN 13: 978-1721104314
ISBN: 1721104313

Cover art by José Nuñez © 2017 Creativity Explored Licensing, LLC.
Creativity Explored is an inclusive visual art program for adults with developmental
disabilities. See Chapter 12 to learn more.

Vanessa & Michael,
Thank you for all
the wonderful ways
you make the
world a better
place!
Andrea
xo

This book is dedicated to the next person who
says "yes" to an unlikely conversation.
That might be you.

Whether you are a community leader, the guy-next-door talking to your
neighbor, a mom in a waiting room, a lifeguard at your local pool, or a
guest on Reid's podcast, saying "yes" is the first step to making the world
a kinder, humbler place where everyone can take a risk and belong.

Praise for *Radical Inclusion*

"I was moved to tears by the triumphs and fell in love with Reid."
—Vincentia Schroeter, PhD, author of *Brain and Body Breakthrough Tools for Communication*

"Andrea Moriarty writes with authority, compassion, and practicality. I have watched her over the years, and her insights in this book ring true with her life experience. This book is a game changer!"
—Mark Foreman, North Coast Calvary Chapel

"*Radical Inclusion* is a feast for hope-starved families of children on the autism spectrum. Andrea Moriarty serves up creative ideas and unexpected combinations for parents who want their children to be fully immersed in life, rather than relegated to the sidelines. Moriarty's profiles of programs and businesses intentionally practicing inclusion make hearty fare. Her pairing of movie themes with lessons learned while parenting Reid, her son with autism, is delicious food for thought. The meat of *Radical Inclusion* is found in the transcripts of Reid's podcast interviews with musicians, business leaders, and celebrities like *Sesame Street's* Murray Monster, which will leave readers simultaneously satisfied and hungry for more."
—Jolene Philo, author of *A Different Dream for My Child* and *Does My Child Have PTSD*

"I'm hooked. Love the way Moriarty writes."
—Scott DiGiammarino, MovieComm

"As a mother of two children with Down syndrome, the word 'inclusion' has woven itself into our lives and become as important to our wellbeing and wholeness as food on our table. Unfortunately, this is not the case for all. This book clearly and beautifully communicates that it sure as heck should be! *Radical Inclusion* takes an idea that seems to be most important for people living with a different ability and shows why it is important for all people. I believe this book is a good news manual of sorts—showing us how inclusion benefits all people. It shows how to implement this radical idea in our daily lives in the most ordinary ways. I hope every person reads it."

—Heather Avis, author of *The Lucky Few*

"Creating possibility in the wake of resounding waves of impossibility is what this book is about. Thank you for inspiring belief and creative action toward purpose, passion, and possibility!"

—Diana Pastora Carson, author and advocate,
AbilityAwareness.com

Table of Contents

KINDNESS

Introduction

Autism was not on my radar when we adopted our twins—a boy and a girl—at birth in 1994. I was ill prepared for the diagnosis when our impish, redheaded baby boy reached two and half years old. He wasn't stringing single words together like his sister but instead exhibited "unexplained screaming" from the bushes during play dates in the park. I was thirty-one years old, and my interaction with people with disabilities was limited to just two experiences.

Growing up in northeastern Ohio, I recall twin girls who lived on my cousins' street. These girls were, in the lexicon of the day, "mongoloid." I just looked up that term because it feels so wrong. *Merriam-Webster* calls the word, "dated, offensive: of, relating to, or affected with Down syndrome." We knew to be careful of the twins on the street, although I can't recall including them in any of our kick-the-can games or frog races down my uncle's steep hill to a lake behind their homes.

My second special-needs encounter was during my junior year at the University of Wisconsin-Madison. I was getting ice cream on a study break with a guy I liked when we bumped into a woman in a wheelchair in front of Baskin-Robbins. She asked me for directions and I replied, taking a smidgeon of time. The interaction was brief at best, but notable enough for my crush to comment, "You are such a good person." He found it attractive that I had returned a common courtesy to someone who was disabled.

I didn't know any kids with special needs at my elementary school in Chesterland, Ohio. My mom taught second grade there for my entire tenure, so I went to all the staff picnics and Christmas parties. Yet I was unaware of any special educator, tutor, or reading specialist. My school had no resource room, no "pull-out" program, no accommodations, and no specialists other than a school nurse.

I am not the only one with limited exposure. According to the 2015 *Shriver Report Snapshot: Insight into Intellectual Disabilities in the 21st Century*:

> while the institutions that warehoused people in the 60s and 70s have closed, nearly half of our country's adult population still say they don't know a single person with intellectual disability. A stunning one in five don't even know what an intellectual disability is. About fifty-six percent of Americans personally know someone with an intellectual disability, but still, 42 percent report that they have had no personal contact with someone with an intellectual disability. Only 13 percent of Americans say they have a friend with an intellectual disability.[1]

Now, that has all changed for me.

Two decades after becoming a parent, I now consider myself well informed in the field of autism intervention as well as ability

1 Harris Poll for Special Olympics and Shriver Media, *Shriver Report Snapshot: Insight into Intellectual Disabilities in the 21st Century*, DisabilityScoop.com, July 24, 2015.

awareness and programming for adults with disabilities, particularly out-of-the-box approaches that identify strengths and motivate differently-abled learners to participate fully in the community and pursue lives of purpose. Experience is a fabulous teacher.

SPREADING AWARENESS

My son, Reid, is twenty-four years old now. We present together at Ability Awareness events where speakers and activities orient elementary students to the diverse experiences of people with autism, cerebral palsy, blindness, or Down syndrome. These events take "show and tell" to the next level by highlighting service dogs, assistive technology, and facilitated communication boards for all to see and touch. The special education students, many with chewy jewelry and fidgets in hand, sit front and center as the most active participants in Reid's interactive *Purple Party*—a show of original songs he wrote with his music therapist. We also speak at universities and to parent groups and provide a three-dimensional testimonial that educates the next generation and offers hope.

The latest statistics claim that one in thirty-seven boys are currently diagnosed with autism. Today when we ask for a show of hands on the question—"Who knows someone with autism?"— almost all the hands go up. Nearly everyone has a neighbor, cousin, friend, or sibling with autism spectrum disorder (ASD). But here's the good news: Boys and girls on the spectrum make significant progress with early intervention. A variety of therapies are now provided by school districts and covered by insurance, and support is readily available to develop language, social, and behavioral skills.

Beyond autism, Down syndrome impacts one in seven hundred babies in the United States. About 765,000 children and adults currently have cerebral palsy. According to the National Alliance on Mental Illness, approximately one in twenty-five adults—almost

What Constitutes an Autism Diagnosis?

Autism is diagnosed by a multi-disciplinary team of professionals including a pediatrician, psychologist, speech pathologist, and occupational therapist. When a child is between the ages of two and three, if concerns arise in the following areas or developmental milestones are not met, an early childhood development evaluation can be recommended or requested.

Early Detection Signs
- Inappropriate playing with toys
- Inability to relate to others, preference to be alone
- Hyperactivity or passiveness
- Oversensitive or under sensitive to sound
- Appears deaf or doesn't respond to own name
- Inappropriate laughing or crying
- Strange attachment to objects
- Poor speech or lack of speech
- Difficulty dealing with changes to routine
- Lack of awareness of danger

Doctors and specialists spend several hours on multiple days interacting with the child and collecting data before determining if the child exhibits these symptoms with enough severity and frequency to warrant a diagnosis of ASD. They often recommend early intervention or behavioral services to see what impact they have before confirming a diagnosis.*

* The Autism Society of America. "Diagnosis." Autism-Society.org. http://www.autism-society.org/what-is/diagnosis/ (accessed June, 2018).
Center for Disease Control and Prevention. "Screening and Diagnosis." CDC.gov. https://www.cdc.gov/ncbddd/autism/screening.html (accessed June, 2018).
Autism Speaks. "Learn the Signs." AutismSpeaks.org. https://www.autismspeaks.org/learn-signs (accessed March, 2018).

ten million—experience a serious mental illness in a given year that substantially interferes with major life activities.[2] And as the stigma around mental health issues is being removed, we are becoming more aware of those dealing with various conditions. Further, the Social Security Administration states that one in five Americans live with disabilities. The World Health Organization and Google estimate that fifteen percent of the world's population, or one billion individuals, have disabilities.[3] That is one in seven people on the planet. Without question, disability impacts almost everyone at some point.

In this book when I refer to people with "disabilities" I mean those who are not able to care for themselves for a variety of cognitive, physical, or emotional reasons. They are for example a neighbor with Tourette's syndrome whose parents have died. He may be mostly able to live alone but needs the help of in-the-know neighbors who can intervene when he goes on a tirade to an unsuspecting UPS deliveryman. They can also be for example a widowed senior who is disabled by the transition to being single. For multiple reasons, some labeled and some not, we all have neighbors who cannot thrive alone.

The main focus of this book will be on autism since I have the most life experience with it. But I believe the principles apply equally well to other diagnoses and abilities. And we need to be mindful that we are all "disabled" in some way by blind spots, limitations, or circumstances that are either temporary or permanent.

2 National Alliance on Mental Illness. "Mental Health by the Numbers." NAMI.org. https://www.nami.org/Learn-More/Mental-Health-By-the-Numbers (accessed May, 2018).

3 Google Impact Challenge: Disabilities. "About." Google.org. https://www.google.org/impactchallenge/disabilities/ (accessed May, 2018).
Social Security Administration. "Facts." SSA.gov. https://www.ssa.gov/disabilityfacts/facts.html (accessed June, 2018).

For example if you've broken your leg and hobbled around on crutches, you've noticed where the wheelchair ramps and curb cuts are in your town. Recognizing our own inabilities enables us to empathize with others.

VITAL RELATIONSHIPS
Despite the progress in awareness and services, a pressing issue continues to weigh on my mind. Understandably since Reid is now an adult, I wonder how all these young men (ASD is five times more likely in boys than girls) will live and work and socialize as they grow older? To put it bluntly: What will happen to Reid when my husband and I die?

Many people on the spectrum don't drive. A few can live independently. But most need some level of daily support for maintaining their personal hygiene, catching an Uber or bus, taking medicine, emptying the trash, shopping for groceries and making dinner, not to mention connecting with caring neighbors, communicating with friends and family, and contributing to their community. Responsible parents perform or prompt these tasks and provide the necessary scaffolding for as long as they can, but doing so is labor intensive. As parents age, who with the familiarity, training, and finesse required will step in? The Shriver report indicates that "an overwhelming majority of Americans (eighty-four percent) say that adults with intellectual disabilities should be encouraged to live independently."[4] But are the majority of Americans willing to be the kind of neighborly helpers these people need to thrive?

According to Susan Pinker in *The Village Effect*, social integration is the greatest indicator of lifespan as well as quality of life.[5]

4 Harris Poll for Special Olympics and Shriver Media. July 24, 2015.
5 Pinker, Susan. *The Village Effect: How Face-to-Face Contact Can Make Us Healthier, Happier, and Smarter.* Vintage Canada, 2015.

But money can't buy organic, naturally occurring friendship. We have been fortunate to maintain close relationships with a few of Reid's favorite therapists and keep them as family friends. But living with autism can feel like a revolving door of teachers and tutors who connect deeply with our children in therapeutic relationships, then move on as they pursue higher degrees, marriage, or their own families. These orchestrated friendships are valuable but not sustainable.

Let's face it: most of us earn relationships with our good looks, manners, or kind deeds performed according to the unwritten code of reciprocity. You scratch my back; I'll scratch yours. Invite me to dinner, and I'll pay for lunch next time we meet. Even in churches, which are built on Jesus' model of self-sacrifice and service, you have to attend before anyone will miss you or pick you up on a Sunday. Adults with disabilities, especially autism, don't trade in this currency. Their supportive friendships need to be based on something else. For now, let's call it goodness. Not unlike shut-ins, the social integration of people with autism relies on the kindness, consistency, and initiative of others.

ADULTHOOD WITH AUTISM

Families with maturing young adults on the spectrum face mediocre options as their children complete high school, many with a certificate of completion, not a diploma. They typically "graduate" into a three-year transition program within the school district. Then at age twenty-two, they choose an adult day program. These facilities can be dire; I toured one that had no lights or windows. Some are community-based, others site-based. Some even resemble senior centers complete with alarms, security gates, institutional smells, crafts, and board games.

Neither of these programs allowed my son Reid to pursue his

full potential. Responsible, devoted parents of young adults with autism are like pioneers; we do what we must to face this challenge. When programs don't meet our standards or aren't relevant for our kids, we innovate and organize. Whether we must invest every waking minute or hundreds of dollars, we fight the system for what our kids deserve—free and appropriate education and a purposeful adult life. Both stay-at-home and working parents uncover new programs and expend energy to create solutions. Unsatisfied with the available options, I customized a creative arts program for Reid that develops his passionate interest in performance and broadcasting.

In my first book, *One-Track Mind: 15 Ways to Amplify Your Child's Special Interest*, I explained how we maximized Reid's passion for music throughout his childhood. That book ends with the creation of his podcast, *Talk Time with Reid Moriarty*. Intrinsically motivating, age-appropriate, and culturally relevant, the podcast amplifies Reid's exuberant personality and penchant for performance. It has become his continuing education and a way to belong in the community.

After three years, he has more than eighty podcasts to his credit with the likes of Murray Monster of *Sesame Street*, the conductor of the Mormon Tabernacle Choir, Keith Lockhart of the Boston Pops, and tennis legend Stan Smith. In addition, Reid performs his original music several times a month either solo or with his band, Jungle Poppins. He just recorded his fourth CD and has a songwriting mentor in addition to a vocal coach and music therapist. More than money, diligence, and resourcefulness have made all of this a reality. Working with Reid's caseworker and funding options within our San Diego Regional Center government agency, we have customized a self-determination program that works for Reid. Sweat equity and creative thinking yield results.

INCLUSION CAN BE ELUSIVE

By design, Reid has more social integration in our community with neurotypicals than ever before. The shortest chapter in my first book, *One-Track Mind*, is the one on inclusion, and we have precious few examples of Reid being included with his general-education peers during his K-12 school career.[6] Though I had advocated for full inclusion since he entered preschool, he was isolated from typical peers by being placed in special classes and then in three different non-public special education schools. The public school district paid for these because they didn't have an appropriate place for Reid.

Most of Reid's interactions were with adult family friends or teachers who had the maturity, skills, or inclination to take the extra time, make allowances for his idiosyncrasy, scaffold his communication, and engage at his level. This reality often left our family with a sense of alienation, loneliness, otherness, and frustration. Reid was too self-assured to express these feelings, but we feel a burden of responsibility to be his social partners, caregivers, and consistent companions. These circumstances also create an urgency for developing and sustaining inclusion for Reid in his adult years. It is truly now or never.

STAYING OPTIMISTIC AND CREATIVE

Now that's enough about the dire problem. I much prefer talking about solutions. My outlook is a joyful celebration of possibilities. I hope this book will be a balm of hope that restores your spirit to complete the marathon of life. I have woven together a collection of stimulating stories and possibilities, rather than a despairing look at "aging out" or "falling off the cliff" (as some call the transition to adulthood for children with disabilities). If you want to laugh out loud, be amazed, and dream a little, keep reading.

6 Moriarty, Andrea. *One-Track Mind: 15 Ways to Amplify Your Child's Special Interest*. JAM Ink, 2015.

> ## Definition: Neurotypical
>
> Neurotypical is a newish word used to describe people who do not display autistic or other neurologically atypical patterns of thought or behavior. Neurodiversity frames autism, ADHD/ADD, and dyslexia as natural human variation rather than pathology. It rejects the idea that neurological differences are to be cured.

If this book seems Pollyanna-ish to you, it's intentional. I have determined that the only sustainable way for me to walk this high-maintenance road for another twenty years is to focus on the positive. I can't afford to get sucked into a downward spiral of negative thinking. My family needs me too much. I have become adamant about this; nothing bothers me more than having to listen to whining and complaining in waiting rooms or parent groups. Negative thinking is toxic. It poisons our day with fatigue and dread. Our lives may be different or require modifications, but they are still lives we can live with gusto and joy.

As parents of children like Peter Pan, who may never grow up, we need to guard our attitudes. For me, that means no comparing. No bemoaning. And never saying never. As a coping strategy as much as a reality, I need to keep a full tank of optimism, encouragement, and brainstorming fodder. So these are what I offer you.

Consider *Radical Inclusion* an invitation to get creative in your own community and make it more inclusive. You will read more than twenty impactful interactions that Reid has had with mostly strangers. Let these personal stories get under your skin and reach your heart. Enjoy the practical, educational sidebars that can equip you to take action. Consider getting involved in a model program like the ones you'll read about. Whatever your life experiences have been, I hope this book will move you to a new perspective on people with differing abilities.

Reid's presence cultivates a diverse community where everyone contributes and is welcome. He has a favorite clerk at our grocery store. He is on a first-name basis with the deli counter staff. When I call in his "usual" fast-food order, they know his name before I can say it. Because what Reid needs, he also teaches. He needs people to take a risk, laugh at themselves, and be kind. Dozens of people in the neighborhood have built a relationship with Reid by practicing these three attributes: risk, humility, and kindness. When they do, their lives improve as much as Reid's does.

OUR UNIVERSAL CRAVING TO BELONG

Perhaps even more than being loved, we all want to belong. This reality became obvious as we traveled and experienced the magic of the podcast, particularly the feel-good bits that make people smile as they are happening and again when they listen to the seven-minute edited version. Something in the human spirit of everyone is touched. We cheer for belonging. Because each podcast confirms that if there is a place for Reid, then there is a place for me. Our faith in humanity is restored by every conversation.

We all crave connection. We are hard wired as social beings, even if we have autism or you name the disability. Dallas Willard, a Christian philosopher on spiritual formation, famously said in a study on the book of Acts that: "The aim of God in history is the creation of an all-inclusive community of loving persons, with Himself included in that community as its prime sustainer and most glorious inhabitant."[7]

I believe having autism or another disability is not a matter

---

7 Dallas Willard. "If Death my Friend and Me Divide." DWillard.org. http://www.dwillard.org/about/tribute/if-death-my-friend-and-me-divide (accessed May, 2018).

of being damaged or less than, but that God has a plan to glorify himself through it. As Reid's parents, we have caught a glimpse of understanding why God allows disability. I believe that needing each other and learning from each other's differences is a radical and intentional part of His plan. Living in community with people who need help might be the best way to cultivate compassion, patience, and helpfulness.

The book in your hands spells out my deep conviction that inclusion is easier than you think. It doesn't require a master's degree or certification. I believe it starts with a willingness to embrace three life practices: risk, humility, and kindness. When everyone in the village or metropolis participates, we can all thrive.

People with disabilities can't live life alone. They need cooperative and individualized support. Cookie-cutter solutions don't work; in fact, they rob society of the unique gifts hidden just behind each disability. What's more, people with significant daily needs teach us by virtue of their need for help. I received an email recently from a student working on her master's degree in speech pathology. She saw Reid's music online and was writing to ask if he could be the same little boy she helped in a youth theater class when she was in high school. Indeed, he was. Turns out she loved being his buddy so much, helping him defined who she would become.

Does it surprise you that we learn these attitudes from the very people we tend to exclude? By interacting with differently-abled people, we learn to take risks, live humbly, and show kindness. When we do so, individuals, families, churches, communities, cities, and even our country will make room for everyone in the fabric of our lives. Adults with disabilities can then become independent and productive citizens, playing valuable roles and being allowed to benefit others through their abnormal genius.

Inclusion happens in every intentional moment of connection. Inclusion is a powerful need, a compelling motivator, and a radical idea for all of us. When individuals in the general public—not just parents, family, and trained professionals—make risk taking, humility, and kindness daily practices, the burden on society will be less and the gain for each member great. The involvement of every person is a basic human right. The fact that inclusion strikes us as radical merely indicates how long people with disabilities have been marginalized.

All it takes is a spark. The *Talk Time with Reid Moriarty* podcast began as a social experiment. We knew, at the very least, making the podcast would motivate Reid to get out of the house. Watching him in his element, we have learned some valuable lessons. We've learned about human nature, witnessed untrained professionals figure out how to interact with someone with autism, and identified the necessary ingredients for personal connection. And we've experienced the world as a radically inclusive place.

"Surviving is important. Thriving is elegant." —Maya Angelou[8]

---

8 Maya Angelou Quotes. BrainyQuote.com. https://www.brainyquote.com/quotes/maya_angelou_634520. (accessed May, 2018).

How to Read This Book

I n each chapter, I will weave together three components:

- Behind-the-scenes stories of one or two *Talk Time* podcasts
- A description of a model program for adults with disabilities
- A movie scene

Trust me, they fit together.

The chapters are organized into three sections to correlate with the attitudes and life practices each podcast guest exhibits: taking risks, humility, and kindness. These are the traits I believe we learn best from people with disabilities. To open each of the three sections, I share my personal experience learning each attitude. Usually, I give an example of how I lacked it before Reid came into my life and how it developed through my up-close and personal interaction with him.

Because I am a sucker for sidebars and resources—a wannabe librarian, actually—you'll find text boxes of tips and tools interspersed throughout the book to help you immediately apply what you are discovering in your daily life. I hope this book is one you can pick up and read when you have just a few minutes to glean a good idea or need a rejuvenating laugh.

TALK TIME WITH REID MORIARTY STORIES

I would love for you to experience the same thrills and epiphanies we have in making *Talk Time*. Reid has an uninhibited *joie de vivre*. His honesty is refreshing and disarming. You will appreciate how guests—from Aloe Blacc to Sluggerrr, the mascot for the Kansas City Royals—take off their masks with him and become vulnerable. I hope as you read our adventures, you will vicariously appreciate the pure joy it can be to spend time with differently-abled adults who are doing what they were born to do.

Listening to the seven-minute, edited podcasts online at reidmoriarty.com is also educational and amusing. People of all ages and walks of life tell us the interviews are always worth the click-through. The actual experience of taping each podcast can be completely distinct. The stories let you in on the car ride or flight beforehand, the selection of the guest, and the raw uncut bloopers. The stories of making *Talk Time with Reid Moriarty* are funny, but while you're laughing don't miss the beauty. Disability comes with gifts. Take the time to unwrap and appreciate them.

MODEL PROGRAMS

Next in each chapter, I highlight innovative programs we encountered in our podcast travels that provide possibilities for Reid and his peers. As a consumer of programs and services for twenty years, I immediately sense the difference between those created to make a buck and those that are powered by passionate beliefs.

Having a disability should not be a dead-end road. I care deeply that parents of newly diagnosed kids can find places—schools, clinics, and therapies—where they can receive help. These children deserve a champion. They will need to have their gifts acknowledged and developed to reach their full potential. Ditto as the children age: adult programs should not be a parking spot. More options emerge each day for adults who need support to thrive. The demand is there, and the supply is following.

As you read about a dozen vibrant programs across the country from Rising Tide Car Wash to Gig Buddies, your creative juices will start simmering. Be moved and inspired to replicate these successes in your community. By creating similar programs that employ the strengths of adults with disabilities, you can ensure that everyone in your town is socially integrated. The best of these programs create a place for people of all abilities to grow and belong, not just be served.

MOVIE SCENES

Each chapter wraps up with a movie scene because sometimes a single scene is the best way to encapsulate an idea. Movies are the continuous loop playing in the background of our life (and Reid's head). We go to thrift stores about three times a week to update his rotating queue of VHS tapes and DVDs. Reid understands much of the world and especially abstract thoughts through movies. The ones I've included—from *Lost in America* to *The Jungle Book*—are central to our household lexicon.

Turns out, Reid is not alone. A movie obsession is common in those with autism, and cinema therapy is a new methodology. Movies can be a catalyst for healing when viewed with conscious awareness. While nobody likes to admit it, we could all benefit from a little therapy. Movies normalize therapy by allowing for it without the stigma. Reid and I have enjoyed two books by Anna Vagin who has a PhD in speech and language pathology. In *Movie Time Social Learning* and *YouCue Feelings: Using Online Videos for Social Learning*, Vagin gives specific exercises to expand social thinking and understanding using short online videos as a springboard, like the Pixar shorts that play before the feature presentation in theaters.[9] With or without a therapist, movies create an alternative reality for the viewer that enables objectivity and an opportunity to process similar circumstances in their life.

Scott DiGiammarino, an American Express executive, discovered how movie scenes can motivate employees. His work was so effective he created MovieComm, a subscription service of movie clips isolated by theme. He explained in a TED Talk how movies work.

> As the musical score begins in a dark theater, we lose awareness of people around us, forget about our daily concerns, and are mesmerized. The prefrontal cortex shuts down since it cannot change or participate in what's happening on screen. Our brain gives itself over to the movie. The mirror neurons in our brain, responsible for empathy, start firing.
>
> Movies give us the power to summon our inner hero at the exact moment we need it the most. As we emotionally engage in a film—laugh, cry, scream—we feel as if we are in the movie itself. Watching others just like us find the courage to overcome adversity enables us to do the same. Movies have a direct impact on our thoughts, behaviors, and actions. Some scenes become part of our everyday lives and language residing in our subconscious even thirty years later.[10]

---

9 Vagin, Anna. *Movie Time Social Learning* and *YouCue Feelings: Using Online Videos for Social Learning.* CreateSpace. 2015.

10 Scott DiGiammarino, "Why Movies Move Us," filmed June 21, 2013 in Rock Creek Park, MD, TedX video, https://www.youtube.com/watch?v=Fi2c1eJAWSE 11:13.

It's no wonder that Reid's go-to question when meeting someone new is, "What's your favorite movie of all time?" Immediately he learns something about their sensibilities, and they have a connection.

Before we jump into the braided narrative, I'd like to tell you a story.

THE UNANSWERABLE QUESTION

We had a rather brusque educational advocate who represented us for a time during some adversarial individualized education plan (IEP) meetings. She was effective, like a bulldog, at procuring services, though we didn't always see eye to eye on parenting let alone interventions or school placements. At one point when Reid was about fifteen, she presented me with an ultimatum, "You have to decide whether you want him to change to fit into the world, or if

---

What Can I Do?

Maria Shriver

Have a dialogue with your children about inclusion, acceptance, and language. If you live in LA, come and watch (the Special Olympics). Reach out to someone you know with an intellectual disability or a family with a child with intellectual disabilities. If you don't know someone, as my mother (Eunice Shriver) would say, go find someone. They're here. They probably live near you. If you pass a person on the street with intellectual disabilities, instead of averting your glance and walking by, stop. Smile. Start a conversation. Share what you learn. These simple actions will begin to change the game.*

* Shriver, Maria. "We Need to Change the Game of How We Talk About Intellectual Disability." Time, July 24, 2015.

---

you're going to expect the world to change so *he* fits into it." I didn't know what to say.

The quandary stuck with me. Both seemed like impossible tasks. At the time, she was steering us toward a rigid behavioral program where Reid ended up and spent the most traumatic two years of his life. We parted ways shortly after getting him out of that place and entering a new school that felt like a detox from the soul-killing correction.

Now I have an answer for her. It has to be a little bit of both. Reid has matured and learned how to fit into the world, but not so much that the world is robbed of his unique joy. *And* I am grateful that the world—which is made up of people, after all—has become a bit more patient, forgiving, and flexible to accommodate him. I have been devoted for the better part of twenty years working on the first. This book is my attempt to tackle the second. Thank you for reading it, and thank you even more for acting it out.

Make a friend with autism. Make the world a better place for all of us.

RISK

I am not naturally a risk taker. I don't gamble or snowboard. I prefer my feet on the ground in separate skis. I do cook without a recipe, but I think that has more to do with creativity than audacity. I have learned the value of taking risks, even failing and falling, from my husband. As opposites attract, we are a complementary match. Jim skateboards and surfs, once broke his pelvis snowboarding, loves storm skiing through trees, and leans toward aggressive growth stocks. He grew up jumping a forty-foot waterfall in his hometown of Chagrin Falls, Ohio, every day of the summer. Daring action is natural to him; he firmly believes it's the best way to grow, regardless of whether you wipe out and break bones in the process.

With Jim, I can muster risk. Like bicycle racers drafting off each other, I have learned boldness by aligning with him, and maybe he has gained empathy from me. Following his lead, we moved to New York City as twenty-one-year-old newlyweds. Neither of us had a job. He found one and an apartment, then I found one. After establishing our careers, we moved every October for three years, first to San Diego, then Chicago, then San Francisco, and eventually back to San Diego. In the immortal words from *My Fair Lady*, "I've grown accustomed to his face ..." and to the adrenaline rush associated with being married to him.

Those were formative, life-changing choices. We have opportunities to take smaller chances every day. Talking to strangers is one of the things we caution children against, yet how else do friendships begin? I recall moving to Brooklyn Heights. Granted it's the nicest part of the five boroughs, but I didn't expect to meet many neighbors in this quintessentially urban environment. For the most part we didn't, but exceptions to the rule are often the richest life experiences. Our apartment was in the first-floor corner of a historic brownstone that was steps from the tree-lined Promenade. Four flights up, the building had a to-die-for roof deck that afforded an iconic view of Manhattan—South Street Seaport, the Brooklyn Bridge, and Wall Street. If you want to see it, rent *Moonstruck* with Nicolas Cage and Cher. We were intimately involved in the filming as they raised and lowered a billboard-sized crane of spotlights every night for two weeks from two a.m. 'til dawn in order to catch a genuine full moon—right outside our bedroom window.

We would come and go on Cranberry Street from the High Street subway station, barely lifting our gaze from a study of shoes and pedestrian hazards, as you do in a city. Because my maiden name was Anderson, some of my mail was mixed up with a "Jane Anderson" who lived on the third floor. I met this short, gutsy woman in her seventies in the lobby one day where we exchanged pleasantries. She skied at Hunter Mountain on the weekends and told me where to take my dry cleaning. Then one nippy November day, she invited me up for a glass of sherry.

Sherry? *Up to your apartment? Oh, I don't know. I guess.* "Okay, sure," I said.

"Come up about 4 o'clock," she said.

I guess this is a thing, like tea or crumpets, I thought.

Sitting in her lovely apartment on the third floor was like being with my grandmother. We chatted about her life and mine, and I got a glimpse of old New York, a different side of the city than I knew existed. Our friendship blossomed, and I observed another way to age gracefully. Plus, I tasted sherry.

Saying, "yes" to an unlikely conversation opens our horizons. It's a necessary first step to turning strangers into friends. I think it's a risk worth taking.

REID AND RISK

Reid is discerning when it comes to risk. Sometimes it seems like he doesn't know a stranger. Other times he has decent stranger-danger radar. He accurately detects which strangers are safe to approach. As a toddler, he often wandered off in public places, lost to us. Once I found him sidled up next to a woman at a picnic table practicing her autoharp. Often he would discover a group of musicians setting up or be on tippy-toes at the foot of a stage waiting for a show to begin.

Once when Reid was about ten, we were searching for a highly touted breakfast joint in Ocean Beach, a destination thirty minutes from home. With visitors in tow and stomachs rumbling, we had crisscrossed the neighborhood and couldn't find it. After thirty minutes of futile searching, Reid walked up to a homeless man bundled in bags with a shopping cart and asked, "Sir, where is the Rise and Shine Café?"

We caught ourselves mid-sentence correcting Reid, "Don't ..." caught in our throats.

Our jaws dropped when the man answered him directly and accurately, "Turn down this alley and go two blocks."

How hard was that? Reid had the best strategy of all. He makes little-while friends wherever he goes. He holds court in the hot tub at our pool with four-year-olds in water wings and middle-aged lap swimmers. He uses custom embossed nametags to their full advantage at the Trader Joe's and Sprouts Farmers Market near us.

"Barbara, I'll take these and may I have a balloon—please, a red one?" Reid projects as loudly and clearly as the intercom.

"Oh! Hi, Reid, how are you doing? Where's your mom?" Barbara usually works the express lane.

"I can scan it. No bag, please." Reid lets her know his preferences.

"Hi, hi, Barbara, I'm here." I scurry up with a debit card while Reid zips out to the car with his Kettle chips and pomegranate Hansen's soda.

Clerks may be taken aback for a split second, yet as quick as they can look up to see who knows their name, they are disarmed, flashing a grin, and responding in kind with super service and free balloons. Their Reid encounter becomes a high point of their day. When I go into these places without Reid, they always ask where he is.

Reid's boldness in calling people by name gets results. No one overtly taught him to do this, like we have had to do with almost every other skill that has been on his IEP for years, like carrying his wallet, counting out coins, and waiting in line. We continue to prompt and rehearse those. But I am taking a cue from Reid and copying his practice of calling people by name. Everyone loves it. Taking the courage to talk to safe strangers is almost always rewarded with a relationship that grows a little bit each time.

We experience a fuller life when we take risks. Although Reid has a myriad of social, language, and behavioral differences, he also has a clear channel to something the rest of us are missing. Experiencing life at close range with him, particularly in three years of making the *Talk Time* podcast, I have witnessed four ways that we benefit from risk.

First, we reveal our true selves when we're open to removing our masks. Once we are exposed, we actually have deeper, more authentic human-to-human interactions. Saying, "yes" to an unlikely conversation leads to unexpected blessings.

Second, accepting new challenges propels us like four-wheel drive into new personal bests. Exposure is necessary for our ongoing growth. As we raise the bar by taking small intentional risks, we open new horizons for ourselves and those around us.

Third, collaborating with others makes taking the plunge easier. Teamwork provides both a safety net and greater combined courage and strength. That's why I'm better with Jim. We are both achievers; but without his decisive push, I would be left creating harmony and keeping the peace every time.

Lastly, being different is our competitive advantage. We often think that blending in leads to belonging, but it is our uniqueness that gives us an edge and makes us indispensable in our community. We have a unique voice to add and need to be true to who we are.

THE PODCAST IS BORN

In 2014, on a dinner date at Third Corner in Encinitas, a wine bar with great food, Jim and I kicked around the question: "What is Reid going to do when he finishes high school?" At the time, he was enraptured by radio personalities and had started reciting public service announcements. We kicked around the idea of Reid starting his own podcast. No surprise, Jim was the one who said, "What do we have to lose?"

I suggested, "What if he interviewed people in the autism community … maybe his old speech therapists … music therapists. We know all the autism service providers in the city."

"No, no. Who wants to listen to that? What if he interviews Jack Johnson or Dick Van Dyke, people on his radar who *everyone* wants to meet? It would be a cross between Dick Cavett and the two-ferns guy, Zach Galifianakis." Jim had the vision for unique content.

"Would they do it?" I am more practical.

"Who's gonna say 'no' to a kid with autism?"

"I guess we'll find out. I can draft the email, and we'll send it over your signature," I said. Jim was the CEO of the Surfrider Foundation at the time.

"We can throw 'em up on SoundCloud—it doesn't cost anything—and see what happens."

"I love it! Let's do it!"

We clinked glasses of Cabernet much the same way we had thirty years prior, clinching a decision to move to New York City the week after our wedding.

Each *Talk Time* interview is a triad (Reid, the guest, and me), and all three of us have to embrace some risk. It's daring to email a total stranger. After the first few positive replies, my courage was bolstered. We approach guests who Reid finds interesting. They may be passing through our town, or they may be prominent in a town we're visiting. I email them cold and they self-select, meaning if they don't respond, we don't arm-twist or pull in favors to coerce them. If we don't hear back, they aren't a good fit. In that way, every guest Reid meets is cooperative, or at least curious.

The guest takes a leap by saying "yes" to an unlikely conversation, not knowing who this young man with autism is or what twenty minutes with him in their executive suite or musician trailer will entail. Reid steps out by going to a new place and interacting with someone he's never met before, and often their gatekeepers as well. Each of us trusts that the encounter will be short, sweet, and relatively safe.

"Never let the fear of striking out keep you from playing the game." —Babe Ruth[11]

---

11   Ruth, Babe. "Babe Ruth Quotes." BabeRuth.com (accessed June, 2018).

1

Reveal Your Authentic Self

H ave you ever noticed that we instinctively hide our true selves, as if with fig leaves from the garden? Self-preservation must be human nature. The fear of revealing who we are makes us nervous at best, paralyzed at worst. Rather than be ridiculed or rejected, we protect ourselves and stay in our own world so that no one will see who we really are. This cautionary isolation beats the rejection we convince ourselves is waiting if we risk exposure. But as much as we resist it, removing our masks to reveal our authentic self is the first step toward belonging.

We put our "best" selves forward in these digital days where most of our relating happens on social media. But our best self is often a figment of our aspirational imagination or a carefully curated presentation rather than a true reflection of our authentic self. Even the bloggers and millennials whose brand and identity revolve around simplicity, confession, and unretouched images have styled the messy hair, crumpled sheets, and disheveled posts we see. Who knows who their authentic self really is?

More than ever, we end up alienated and isolated from the very friends with whom we want to connect. To keep ourselves safe, we conform and hope to blend in. We stop taking relational risks on- and offline. We don't start conversations or introduce ourselves.

Frozen in cautious tracks, our world shrinks smaller and smaller until we are eventually isolated from new people, new experiences, and growth itself. Like partisan politics, no one leaves his or her aisle or algorithm. Fear dominates our thinking, and we cannot fathom what reward might come from venturing outside the bubbles of our own making.

We all crave true connection. We are social beings. Even my autistic son is not an island. In fact, he is an affectionate twin who has never been alone. All of us—even those with social disorders or mental health issues—crave the inclusion and sense of belonging that result from social interaction. And by social, I mean live, three-dimensional interaction, not posting online.

Reid was enamored with radio jingles and the predictable banter between deejays, but sustaining it on his own was not necessarily a skill he had when we started the podcast. He is a natural-born entertainer and an uncanny impersonator, but not a conversationalist. Starting a podcast required a little preparation. Fortunately, we were accustomed to building a scaffold of visuals and rehearsal on which Reid's could stand.

With the iTalk app newly installed on Jim's phone, we planned to have Reid practice interviewing a few family friends before we set him loose with notable strangers. Rehearsing would give him a template to follow, and we could build skills from there. What we didn't expect was how disarming, in a good way, Reid's presence would be. His raw enthusiasm, curiosity, and chutzpah caught the guests off guard just enough to cause them to reveal their true colors. Like a toddler wielding a freshly dipped paintbrush, Reid kept them in the present. His innocence mixed with the brass of Howard Cosell made for entertaining content. Picture Curious George. No matter how inappropriate he has been, at the end of each picture book he is forgiven and even more endearing.

The best parts of each recording are the unexpected, unscripted bits. Over time, we determined not to intervene too much, lest we lose that magic. Nothing can prepare Reid's guests for the encounter. Even if they start out with a mask, it soon comes off when they realize that wearing one is not an option for Reid. In reciprocity, they remove theirs, which is brilliant to behold. This process is suspenseful and a little nerve-wracking. I have often said that Reid functions as a barometer who either brings out the best or worst in people who interact with him. Our podcast guests prove that over and over.

When Reid was little, bedtime was the best time to actually connect with him in conversation. We called it "talk time" because it was one of the few times his motor idled slow enough to relate one-on-one. After, and only after, a bath, a game of "roly-poly puppies," and some hair tickles could he express his high point and low point of the day and maybe even a feeling or wish in words. So that's what we named his podcast.

We envisioned *Talk Time* as a way for Reid to engage in the community. He would be motivated to take his interests to the next level through one-to-one learning. He learned best one-on-one—whether math facts or pronouns. We needed something in lieu of going to college that could become his continuing education and be a culturally relevant way for him to continue working on his lifelong language, social, and behavior goals.

Let me tell you about two of the early podcasts.

CLIMBING A MOUNTAIN BEGINS WITH ONE STEP: CINDY OUTLAW, FRIENDLY NEIGHBOR

Reid loves Mrs. Outlaw. She is a neighbor in her fifties who goes to our church. More importantly, she has Apple TV at her house! She had always shown an interest in Reid and autism, sending me articles and tracking our journey. Cindy leads climbing trips all over the globe. We wanted to start with someone who understood Reid, and I knew she would let Reid ask her anything. I also knew if she came to our house, Reid would have stayed upstairs in his bed rolled up in his cozy plush blankie like Linus with a virus. If we had gone to her house, he would have jumped down the rabbit hole that Apple TV is for him. So we planned to meet on neutral ground: Panera Bread.

Besides attending the same church, we had gotten to know Mrs. Outlaw when—a few too many times—Reid had wandered unannounced into her living room three suburban cul-de-sacs away. One time after school, I was on a northbound train and got a text from Cindy, "Reid is here. Are you looking for him?" *Oy vay.* My heart skipped a beat before I texted the babysitter to clarify. Reid was about ten years old that time. He was a flight risk at home and at school, and this eloping (as the terminology goes) was disconcertingly common for a season. I had found him more than once sorting through the Outlaw's video drawer or demonstrating the features of their entertainment center that was twice as big as ours. Thank God he picked *her* house. She was gracious about it. So was her husband when he came home to find Reid camped in the glow of their liquid-crystal display. Let's just say, Cindy had seen me in my pajamas with morning hair. Our masks had already been removed.

A trip to Panera is an ace in the hole for motivating Reid; he will do anything for those pecan braids. Still, the day we choose was a rough one with a lot of stimming—an autistic tendency to zone out through repetitive behavior to the exclusion of all else. Sometimes this behavior is anxiety driven, other times there is just nothing better going on. Probably anticipating this new endeavor drove Reid to self-soothe by rocking his head and fast-forwarding a familiar movie in his head.

We found a table outside across the parking lot from the tantalizing pastry that would come *after* Reid completed the interview. I had written a handful of questions on both sides of a blue three-by-five card. Jim and I sat close by redirecting and prompting. Cindy obliged, trusting us for assistance and looking up at all three of us in turn to take her cues. As Reid asked about her favorite movie or who climbed Mt. Kilimanjaro with her, the thought bubble over her head asked, *Should I tell him what he wants to hear? How much detail do you want? Was that too long?* It's funny how much you can communicate non-verbally when you turn on a recorder. We answered her inquiries with a wink or nod. Reid took it away like a natural-born anchorman.

Reid: Welcome to Panera Bread! Today, we have a very special guest, Mrs. Outlaw. I'd like to answer a couple questions with her tonight. So, first, where are we, Mrs. Outlaw?

Mrs. Outlaw: We are at Panera Bread.

Reid: Okay, and where is Mount 'Kimajaro'?

Mrs. Outlaw: Kilimanjaro that is in Africa.

Reid: That's in Africa. What was your high point of climbing to Mt. 'Kimajaro'?

Mrs. Outlaw: My high point was 19,000 feet.

Reid: What was your low point?

I started to clarify that we meant low point in the figurative sense, not elevation, but realized they would figure it out. Jim shushed me putting his finger over his lips. He wanted the natural slip-ups and contextual noise for authenticity. Still, my impulse was to coach Reid and Cindy to clarify this point for listeners and reasoned that we could edit me out later.

Mrs. Outlaw: My low point was 6,000 feet. That's where we started walking.

Reid: And what's your favorite movie? *They both spoke loudly as if addressing a live audience.*

Mrs. Outlaw: My favorite movie is *Mary Poppins*.

Reid: Me too!

"Did you hear that, Reid? Same as yours," I said. He wanted that pecan braid and was standing up again to dance a little step-in-time jig. I wanted the podcast to last longer than two nanoseconds.

Reid: Did you have dinner on Mount 'Kimalajaro'?

Mrs. Outlaw: I had eight dinners.

Reid: So, your high point was climbing to the top of the mountain, and your low point was climbing lower, from the mountain, climbing a couple feet?

Mrs. Outlaw: Well, I have another low point.

Reid: What's another low point?

Mrs. Outlaw: Someone got sick, and they couldn't walk anymore. That was sad for me.

Reid: Someone couldn't walk? Someone was sick from walking? *Reid laughed nervously, almost excited to have gotten beneath the surface.*

Mrs. Outlaw: Yep. They were throwing up, and they had to turn around and go back home.

Reid stood and looked longingly across the parking lot. He had no precedent for how long a podcast or an interview was. In his ideal world, conversations amounted to two greetings and maybe a high five or bear hug. His attention was fleeting.

"Reid, stay here," I said, "Mrs. Outlaw is still talking. Turn the card over; there are more questions on the back." Reid went on.

Reid: What do you like to go for dinner?

Mrs. Outlaw: Uh, well, two places. I like to go to Panera. Do you like Panera?

Reid: Hey, you're always at Panera! *They laughed.*

Mrs. Outlaw: I know. And I like Pizza Port.

Reid: Me too. But we're getting Leucadia Pizzeria and bringing it to George's Beach.

Mrs. Outlaw: When, today?

Reid: Today. You know there's a Leucadia Pizzeria by the Community Resource Center and the La 'Palonium' Theater. That's the closest one. And there's another location by Helen Woodward Animal Center. Those are the two locations I could only think of.

Now Reid was revealing his incredible sense of direction and comprehension which is usually hidden behind the mask of his diagnosis. Not everyone is privy to his intelligence.

Mrs. Outlaw: Is that your favorite pizza?

Reid: We're gonna go to the one by the one by La 'Palomium' Theater because it's closer to the beach, and it's much quicker. We can't do the one by Helen Woodward because it's much too far, and we'll never make it to the beach on time. Isn't that right, Dad?

Dad: That's right.

Mrs. Outlaw: Is that your favorite pizza?

Reid: Yea, I like Leucadia Pizza. I do have a high point. What is today's high point, Mrs. Outlaw?

Mrs. Outlaw: This interview. I really like it!

I wasn't sure who was mirroring whom, but they had established a clear rapport enhancing each other's sense of self.

Reid: And what is your low point ... not going to a thrift store.

Mrs. Outlaw: I have a sore leg. It hurts.
Reid: You have a sore leg?
Mrs. Outlaw: I do. Hopefully, it will be better tomorrow.
Reid: It'll be better tomorrow?

I could tell he didn't have the vocabulary to respond to the bad news and wasn't sure how to handle her honesty. After a long pause, he opted for the hopeful outlook for recovery.

Reid: That's awesome! And now ...

Reid turned toward the recording device, slid into his wheelhouse, and composed his own outro on the spot.

Reid: That's all for today. Hope you enjoyed our fun interview with Mrs. Outlaw. Until then, see you next time.

I smiled, proud and relieved. It had gone well for a first.

We came home after the pecan braid. Jim edited the audio in GarageBand, teaching me the shortcut commands as he learned them. We created a SoundCloud profile and shared it on Facebook. Then we held our breath a little, nervous to reveal our family's authentic self. It was imperfect but real: an interaction between two people who cared about each other and had interesting lives. That made it perfectly imperfect. Unaffected.

Still I wondered: *Would Cindy Outlaw share the link once it was online? Would anyone listen? Had Reid learned anything?* Jim reminded me that it didn't matter. We had engaged him for more than an hour on a Sunday with an activity that didn't involve electronics and expanded his world beyond the four walls of our family room. That was a success for now.

There is pure power in simply listening. Psychiatrist Karl Menninger wrote, "Listening is a magnetic and strange thing, a creative force. The friends who listen to us are the ones we move toward. When we are listened to, it creates us, makes us unfold and expand."[12] It is transformative to have someone attend to and care about what you have to say, no matter how rambling or mundane it might be. Cindy modeled that. She said "yes" to an unlikely conversation, revealed her authentic self, and, in turn received Reid's authentic self.

Listening to their conversation now—three years later—reveals to me the progress Reid has made in listening to other guests. In fact Joey Mazzarino, the head writer of *Sesame Street*, gave Reid that advice as an interviewing tip: "listen to what the other person is saying and try to respond based on that." Reid has heeded that advice.

WHEN IN ROME, OR CLEVELAND: GREG HARRIS OF THE ROCK AND ROLL HALL OF FAME

Later that summer of 2014, we were traveling to Cleveland to visit family. We didn't go often because the only thing worse than wrangling Reid away from our television and remotes is doing so at my in-laws. We aren't great houseguests; we know it, so we avoid it. Yet we love our family, and it's a long way from Cleveland to California. Someone has to make the trek.

This was our chance to continue our podcast venture. We asked ourselves who we could interview in Cleveland. It would give us a new activity while we were visiting, and give Reid a reason—outside of searching for the Dumbo VHS he insists he left—to stay focused and engaged on the destination. Without a schedule, a week away can be a long unplug for Reid. Normally he would check out while

---

12 Menninger, Karl M.D., *Love Against Hate.* Harcourt, Brace and Company, 1942.

the grownups chatter, make meals, play cards, and otherwise talk over his head. To him, that's an all-access pass to hours of unsupervised viewing. Who can blame him for staying glued to the set?

We took another risk. I drafted an email to Greg Harris, the CEO of the Rock and Roll Hall of Fame, Cleveland's biggest sight-seeing draw. Jim sent it over his CEO of Surfrider Foundation auto-signature that carried clout. Our style was bold and honest. "We have a son with autism who'd like to interview you …" There were no masks, just our stated desire.

Within an hour of hitting send, Harris replied with a one-liner I've memorized: "Absolutely! Sharon will schedule it."

God love that man. He didn't know us from Adam, but something possessed him to respond immediately with a "yes" to this unlikely conversation. With no façade or lengthy explanation, he was completely willing to welcome this "twenty-year-old man who plays in a band and happens to have autism" into his corner office. We promised it'd be quick—twenty minutes max—and fun.

Buckled into my brother's minivan, we cruised down the shores of Lake Erie to the landmark that puts Cleveland on the map for most people. The huge glass triangle, designed by I. M. Pei, is hard to miss. It looks like the Louvre on a lake. We pulled around back to a loading dock large enough for concert memorabilia and stacks of Marshall amps. Reid, Jim, and I—host, director, and producer—made a lean crew. We had previewed the museum the day before, absorbing its psychedelic exhibits, and "sensurround" gallery spaces chronicling the Beatles, Neil Young, and Lynyrd Skynyrd on the walls that treated them with more dignity than my mom ever gave them.

Gift shops are always a black hole for us. We had lost Reid in more than one, including the Tate Modern in London. This one was deeper than any Sam Goody or Tower Records I'd seen. Reid and Jim both could have spent a full day in this gift shop browsing vinyl and CDs in large quantities. We promised Reid he could make a purchase the next day *after* the interview ... and, ever so carefully coaxed him through the exhibitions with us. My daughter, Allie, was with us the first day, on break from Berklee College of Music. She loved seeing her music history classes played out in documentary photos, audiotapes, and all sorts of graphic detail. I loved walking through Motown and Memphis in the "Cities and Sounds" exhibit. They have a tower you climb up into that pays tribute to arena concerts—the biggest and loudest of them all. Loud Jimi Hendrix music pours out from all four sides.

For weeks prior we had been plugging Harris, explaining his job to Reid, looking at their webpage, and preparing questions. Harris had been recruited from the National Baseball Hall of Fame in Cooperstown, NY, and was admired for his storytelling, passion, and ability to connect with people. He was approaching the stature of Mick Jagger in Reid's mind. As we entered through a staff loading dock from the VIP parking lot, Reid inquired of every male passerby, "Are you Mr. Greg Harris?" One exiting man ignored him.

We signed in with a sturdy security guard. Reid asked him, "Are you, Mr. Greg Harris?" Perhaps we had overemphasized the protocol of addressing him by his full name.

He chuckled, "No, no, I'm not him."

In we went to the dramatic, edgy décor of the executive suites. Reid even asked a female receptionist, "Are you, Mr. Greg Harris?" Reid hadn't been to many business suites I realized, as he sneaked up to a candy bowl and into a few open doors. A man in a conservative suit selling insurance or printer ink came out. "Are you Mr. Greg Harris?" *Oh no.*

We were as nervous as Reid was but had more experience acting calm in waiting rooms. I used my soothing hushed voice, "It'll just be a minute, Reid. They'll come to get us when he's ready. Let's look at this magazine."

From a partial staircase came a trim executive assistant. *Could it be Sharon, who had scheduled us?* I wondered.

"Hello, Reid." She had us pegged.

"Are you Mr. Greg Harris?"

"No, no, but I know where he is," she rolled with it.

We followed her up the half flight past her office to one at the end with a window overlooking the museum atrium. *Oh my, gosh, this was happening.* Jim and I caught each other's eye and raised our eyebrows expectantly. We were playing it cool though we had no idea how this might go.

Reid: Mr. Greg Harris!!

Reid's volume reached 120 decibels now that we had found the real deal. Medium height, Greg had with dark hair streaked with gray, thick eyebrows, and a gap-toothed grin. He was warm and focused and looked like a clean-cut Lou Reed.

Greg Harris: Hello! Hello, Reid.

After a little impromptu musical chairs and quick shaking of hands, Reid dove in with characteristic aplomb. Jim had already hit record on the phone app; we were rolling.

Greg Harris: Wow, Reid, you are getting right off the ground running.
Reid: Wide off the ground, Mr. Greg Harris.

We all laughed, venting a little nervous steam. Reid didn't know that expression, but he could echo.

Greg Harris: You're jumping right into it.
Reid: I'm here to interview you, Mr. Greg Harris.
Greg Harris: I understand that. What've you been doing in Ohio, Reid?
Reid: Well, we have been to the Rock and Roll Hall of Fame Museum with Allie.
Greg Harris: What do you think of this place?
Reid: I like this place.
Greg Harris: It's got a lot in this building doesn't it?

Not one to dilly-dally, Reid got to the point.

Reid: Here are the questions, Mr. Greg Harris. I like to sit down if that's alright with you, Mr. Greg Harris.
Greg Harris: Absolutely, there's plenty of chairs. Pick the one you like best.
Reid: Have you ever heard of B. B. King? He does do the blues.
Greg Harris: I have.
Reid: Have you ever met Alison Krauss or B. B. King?
Greg Harris: I have met Alison Krauss.
Reid: Hey, I know a song from Alison Krauss, which is a good song. It's called, "Ghosts in the House" or "Let Me Touch You for Awhile."
Greg Harris: Uh huh.

He was smiling, not able to get a word in edgewise.

Reid: And she sings it live in front of an audience. I used to be afraid of the applause on albums, but now I'm starting to like it, Mr. Greg Harris.
Greg Harris: There's a lot of energy in that applause.

They had captured it in the psychedelic tower exhibit, I thought. Who else would admit to a fear of live albums but Reid? I duly noted that Mr. Greg Harris was the first one to understand why. I interrupted like an associate producer with a prompt.

"Reid, I think he has a story to tell you about that," I said.

Reid: Do you have a story, Mr. Greg Harris, about Alison Kraus? Tell us a story about Alison Kraus, Mr. Greg Harris.

Reid's mask of courtesy was down and his natural leadership was showing. He was as commanding as any CEO.

Greg Harris: Well, I'll tell you a story about Alison Krauss. She came to the Rock and Roll Hall of Fame when we did a tribute to a blues singer named Lead Belly, and she performed with Robert Plant on our stage. They met at our show, and seventeen months later they had a Grammy together.

Reid: They had a Grammy award together ... "Raising Sand." Isn't that the album?

As if it were common knowledge.

Greg Harris: Yup.

His facial expression revealed a definite surprise at the detail.

Reid: The next question is: What is the best concert you've ever attended, Mr. Greg Harris?

Greg Harris: Wow! I've been lucky enough to go to a lot of them. I think a Bruce Springsteen concert is probably the best one I've attended.

Reid: Bruce Springsteen concert, you've ever been to.

Greg Harris: Yup. He really puts on a great, great show. There's something magical about three hours of great music ... four hours of great music.

Reid: Okay. The last question is: We play deejay in the car. What would
   you pick for your songpick for your kids to listen to?
Greg Harris: Either the Rolling Stones ....
Reid: Okay.
Greg Harris: Or maybe Otis Redding. We like old blues and soul stuff.
Reid: Otis Redding!? Maybe that's what we'll play in the car. That's what I
   would pick, and you pick Otis Redding, me too!
Greg Harris: Well, you have good taste.

They had discovered their common passion as Reid revealed his
deep subject-matter expertise and mined Mr. Greg Harris.' These
facts were way over my head, but they were the kind that gave Reid
credibility to podcast guests and listeners alike. He was bonding
with Mr. Greg Harris as he demonstrated encyclopedic memory
for details within their shared special interest.

Reid: Well, it was nice talking to you, Mr. Greg Harris, and CUT!

It was over faster than it had begun. Reid headed out the way he
had entered. We stopped at Sharon's door when Mr. Greg Harris
asked us, "Does Reid wear ball caps?" and offered one.
   Jim said, "I do." We thanked him profusely.
   Waving goodbye to the security guard on our way out the loading dock exit, Jim checked the time and whispered, "Twenty minutes exactly."
   Slyly, I made a fist and bent my elbow, "Yes!" We felt like we
had pulled off a heist. We high fived each other in the privacy of
the car. Reid posed for a snapshot in the back seat sporting the new
Rock Hall ball cap from Mr. Greg Harris.
   Jim was proud and relieved. It had gone off without incident.
"That was awesome, Reid," he said. "You rocked it!"

Reid loves meeting new people. His true self is affectionate, gregarious, and magnanimous. All that is hidden just beneath the mask of autism. This encounter and many that followed revealed Reid's true self. The conversations also invited others to take off their masks if only for fifteen minutes and show their true self to a young man who was listening.

"Alright Reid, who's next? Who else would you like to interview?" I asked. Reid is a movie buff, as you know. *All Dogs Go to Heaven* is frequently in his queue. What you may not know is that a lot of famous actors were voice talent for the animated dog characters in that film. Burt Reynolds is Charlie Barkin. Sheena

---

Ten Things Every Child with Autism Wishes You Knew

*from Ellen Notbohm**

1. I am a whole child. My autism is a part of who I am, not all of who I am.
2. My senses are out of sync.
3. Distinguish between won't and can't.
4. I interpret language literally.
5. Listen to *all* the ways I'm trying to communicate.
6. Picture this. I am visually oriented.
7. Focus and build on what I can do rather than what I can't do.
8. Help me with thinking and being social.
9. Identify what triggers my meltdowns.
10. Love me unconditionally.

* Notbohm, Ellen. *Ten Things Every Child with Autism Wishes You Knew.* Future Horizons, 2012.

Easton plays Sasha Lafleur. Dom DeLuise is the voice of Itchy the Mutt.

One day, as our podcast planning continued, Reid came out with a zinger: "Mom, is Dom DeLuise living or dead?"

"Oh boy, let me Google that. I'm not sure, Reid. I think he … yep, he died in 2009."

"Well, we can't interview him then."

"Nope, you'll have to wait 'til you get to heaven for that one."

"What about Eddie Murphy? He's living."

"Well, I can email him. Let me check."

Reid's limitless thinking is exhilarating; he doesn't have filters for realism. In his mind, if we reached Mr. Greg Harris, we could reach Eddie Murphy. Hanging with Reid emboldens me to take risks. He is the underdog who needs an advocate and knows no bounds. I am thrilled to come alongside and help with the mechanics. I'd ask for the sun, moon, and stars on his behalf. Why wouldn't I email Eddie Murphy?

I love that the sky is Reid's limit. Even death doesn't separate him from his ambition. If a person is dead, then we'll give them a bye. Otherwise, they're fair game. Then and only then will Reid have to exercise some delayed gratification and wait until he gets to heaven. They better be there.

"Acting is largely about putting on masks,
and music is about removing them."[13]
—Hugh Laurie, British actor

---

13 NPR Music. "Hugh Laurie Puts Blues in the House." NPR.org. https://www.npr.org/2013/08/18/213144473/hugh-laurie-puts-blues-in-the-house (accessed June, 2018).

CELEBRATE EDU
Boulder, Colorado
CelebrateEDU.org

I am going to give away my best-kept secret, the model program I recommend most often to other families. Celebrate EDU is a truly fabulous program run by a sort-of extended family you get to choose. They appreciate the awesomeness of autism and know what it takes for people with autism to pursue self-employment. They know from the inside out how to develop potential and encourage progress in visual learners of all abilities. By their estimates, eighty-five percent of people with disabilities are underemployed. What's more, they are two times more likely to be self-employed than the general population. So this nonprofit is investing in the next generation of entrepreneurs. Their programs simultaneously challenge young adults with disabilities to take risks and support them in being successful.

We met the staff of Celebrate EDU at their daylong Kindling Workshop offered in San Diego in 2016. This was one of the first times I dropped Reid off for a full day, trusting that the instructors, founder, Jenny Anderson, and her mom, Linda, could meet his needs on the fly without a behavior support plan or a lot of background information.

Reid was twenty-one at the time and spending his weekdays in the pathetic adult transition program our school district offered. The overworked staff did the best they could, but Reid already had more going on than this or any other program I researched had planned for him to do. I could not in good conscience let him spend idle day after idle day when he has so many skills and gifts.

I was pleasantly surprised when the new experience of the Kindling Workshop went well. Sadly, I had come to expect aborted efforts and failures. But this program was different. They had participants break into teams and plan a popcorn business. Then they walked the teams through presenting an abbreviated business plan to their peers and generally gave them a taste of what being an entrepreneur involves.

Instead of underselling young adults with autism, who often look like they're not listening, and insulting them with diluted materials, Celebrate EDU programs take age-level content and present it in simple, concrete ways. They presume competence and stretch the edge of their clients' comprehension, expecting that they can grasp new information. They present the participants with a challenge and raise the bar for them.

I was smitten! The experience was kinesthetic, relevant, and high octane. Reid, while not a popcorn fan per se, enjoyed the workshop and seemed attentive enough that I registered him for their next step: The Spark Program. Spark is an eight-week online program that defines exactly what an entrepreneur is and why some find it preferable to a traditional job. Suddenly, we were seeing examples all around us.

"Hey Reid, Jaime (who cuts our grass) has his own business." I pointed out.

"He is an entrepreneur!" Reid was getting it.

"Does he give us a product or a service when he comes on Tuesdays?" I asked.

There might be silence; this was all new. So I prompted him, "It's a service when Jaime trims the bushes. Now, Uncle David, he owns his own business, and they sell machines. That's a product."

A new vocabulary unfolded like a red carpet. When Reid got his haircut, I asked, "Who is the customer?" And when Reid had a gig to perform, I asked, "Who are your competitors?" The concepts were applicable, relevant, and within his grasp.

Next, Celebrate EDU explored Reid's aptitude for being an entrepreneur with a career assessment by industry. Their adapted assessment asked questions like: Do you like to bake or paint? Are you creative or technical? They tabulated the results to determine and rank categories of work that Reid would find motivating.

Week by week, Reid watched short videos of entrepreneurs like him who did voiceover work, or sold pastries, or wrote books. Reid determined he was cut out to be an entrepreneur. I refer to Celebrate EDU as Business 101 for visual learners. Their program is sequenced in digestible portions that Reid can understand and includes video lessons, curated homework to watch on YouTube, and worksheets in fillable forms that are self-paced. This is a model to follow whether your craft is writing or marketing or animation or videography or baking. Every master should take on apprentices. There is a knack to simplifying content, and they've mastered it.

As we examined Reid's competitors and competitive advantage and applied the principles of cost, revenue, and margin to his music business, we set the goal of having more paying gigs than unpaid. My eyes had glazed over in college economics class, but suddenly a chart for Reid's music business costs, revenue, and margin made perfect sense. Cost is what you pay for the CDs and tee shirts he sells; revenue is what you collect in the moneybag; and margin is what you take to the bank.

Reid also made baby steps toward representing himself. After a gig, he would thank the host and say, "I would love to perform here again." When he was in the library, which is three times a week, he would take his business card and ask the librarians, "Could I perform here?"

Our friends at Celebrate EDU use the term "supported

entrepreneurship." And they definitely teach it. Entrepreneurs are risk takers. Something—a sense of adventure or the need to set their own hours—compels them to define their own parameters and overcome whatever hurdles stand in their way. Ambition, invention, or circumstance drives them to carve out a niche in the face of unknowns.

Many individuals with ASD have an independent mindset, and their frequently exceptional interest in a specific area makes them great candidates for entrepreneurship. As entrepreneurs, they can pursue a chosen topic with fervor and avoid social office dynamics and other challenges inherent in a traditional workplace. Still, they need training and support to learn the aspects of running a business that don't come naturally and to be successful.

Celebrate EDU founder, Jenny Anderson, grew up knowing both the limitations and potential that her brother who is on the autism spectrum faced. Here's Jenny's story from the Celebrate EDU website:

> I was watching him, as I had for years, but this time I saw something entirely different. Brent was able to express how it feels to be living on the spectrum and not just to my mom and me, to an entire audience. I watched relief on the faces of the parents who had gathered there that night. After watching their own children respond in ways that were confounding, here was this young man on the spectrum—my own brother—shedding a positive and humorous light on living with autism.
>
> There are moments when you are watching and, suddenly, you see. You see the brother you've known your whole life, you see his purpose and,

perhaps, even your own. I knew, then and there, what I had to do.[14]

Celebrate EDU is dedicated to giving self-advocates with disabilities the tools they need to build a productive path forward in the world." Anderson's nonprofit is teaching thousands like her brother to express their needs, follow their passions, and define their career paths. Her risk has become their reward.

Reid completed the Spark Program with a one-page business model that he can now present independently. In it, he articulates the problem his business is solving as well as describing his competitors and competitive advantage. He defines the members of his support staff and concludes with an elevator pitch that he continues to deliver with improving business etiquette. Spark empowered Reid to be taken seriously as a self-advocate. They legitimized the vocation we created for Reid that uses his unique gifts and equipped him to understand various aspects of his business and be increasingly involved in running it.

Reid interacted primarily with the Celebrate EDU curriculum specialist Melissa Nieber. She and the Celebrate EDU team know their craft and their clientele well enough to distill high-level principles into an approachable format for people who learn differently. Every Tuesday and Thursday for the last year, Reid has logged onto Zoom.us for his video check-in with Melissa.

This engaging challenge continues as Reid is now working through a pilot of Celebrate EDU's Ignite Program. Teaching brand and identity fundamentals, the program is structured for how he learns and sets him up for success with repetition, relevant examples, and accessible sequential steps. Using their clear-cut process,

---

14 Celebrate EDU. "Founder Story." CelebrateEDU.org. https://celebrateedu.org/founder-story/ (accessed May, 2018)

Reid has defined the core values of his business and can state his mission and vision. We've completed sections on brand messaging, creative direction, marketing materials, web design, and social media, all culminating in Reid presenting his own brand book—even choosing the fonts and colors and brand statements—because they believe he can! And they are able to engage him in the process.

Why don't they use this program in adult transitions programs like the one Reid was in? Some states do: Colorado and Nevada are on board. Celebrate EDU just received two significant grants from Chick-fil-A and the Kauffman Foundation to train local leaders to take more differently-abled students through their outstanding "Discover Your Awesome" curriculum that empowers students with the dignity of using their gifts in real work as supported entrepreneurs. Ask your day program or agency to offer it or tell them about it.

Visual Learning

Many people with autism are visual learners. Early language can be supported by PECS (Picture Exchange Communication System) cards—laminated images students use to convey their wants and needs as well as expand their vocabulary. Teachers can also use visual supports including visual timers, calendars, illustrated steps for hand washing, and daily schedules.

When you are starting a new friendship or want to interact more, using visuals can help. Bring a photo album of pictures or a magazine with you. Writing a plan or next steps on a three by five card or a napkin can be more effective than talking. Looking together at visuals is often easier than carrying on a conversation that includes eye contact.

One of these entrepreneurs may be in your backyard, sculpting soaps that could go in your Christmas stockings or baking biscotti for your next party. I have a friend who is an occupational therapist. Every holiday, she makes a point of buying small handmade items from supported entrepreneurs to give as gifts. Keep an eye out for them so you can support a local business with your dollars or on your social media feed. Better yet, take a real risk and mentor someone who is uniquely built for self-employment.

WILLY WONKA & THE CHOCOLATE FACTORY[15]

One of my favorite scenes on risk is from this movie. I think you might know it. Willy Wonka, the eccentric chocolatier, has decided to reveal his authentic self and invite five golden ticket winners into his chocolate factory. Nearing the end of his life, he has no heir and wants to identify a successor, a special someone who is honest, pure of heart, and shares his passion. His factory tour will narrow the field and test the candidate's mettle.

Myths about Wonka (Gene Wilder) abound, but he surprises even the children as he somersaults out to greet the lucky winners and their chaperones. Inside the gates, automated coat hooks snatch the hats from their heads. The first stop on the tour is a giant, legal contract wallpapered to the wall. Wonka asks Violet to sign it first.

Her dad, Sam Beauregard, is a used car salesman. He's not so protective of Violet, but he does want to flaunt his expertise. An expert in fine print, he takes a gander. Wonka tells him it's all standard, but no one is sure how far they can trust this eccentric character. Everything seems a lark to the candy man in a purple velvet suit and cocoa top hat.

In turn, each of the escorting parents voices concerns. One wants a lawyer. They're all in a tizzy, which is compounded by the fact that they're locked in, at this guy's mercy. Dismissing her dad, Veruca grabs the pen from Violet. Wonka congratulates her sassy defiance. He is a confirmed bachelor with no interest in parenting.

Little Charlie (Peter Ostrum) is last. His Grandpa Joe donated his tobacco money so Charlie could buy just one Wonka bar. Cooperative and respectful, Charlie looks to his grandpa for permission to proceed. None of the other children did this. Grandpa

---

15 *Willy Wonka & the Chocolate Factory.* Directed by Mel Stuart. Hollywood: Paramount, 1971.

Joe loves this boy and dreams for his future. Knowing his days are few, he gives him the go-ahead, "Sign away, Charlie; we got nothing to lose."

Spoiler alert: Wonka gives Charlie the whole factory. Despite stealing fizzy lifting drinks, Charlie is the one with the purest heart who Wonka can trust with his legacy. They both took a leap of faith and won!

WRAPPING UP CHAPTER 1

I'm an introvert, so under stress my reflex is to protect myself and stay in my own world. I'm aware that if I do this too much, no one sees who I really am. My self-preservation can turn to isolation if it goes on too long. We all need connection, even if at times we reject it.

Reid may have autism, but he is a human first. He craves connection too. No matter how awkward he may be at connecting, Reid loves meeting new people. His true self is affectionate, gregarious, and magnanimous. That is just hidden behind the mask of autism. *Talk Time* has become a way for him to engage with the community. The pre-planned, one-on-one conversations, the anticipation of questions, and choosing guests grant him enough control over the connection to feel secure.

Each encounter is imperfect but completely real. We began practicing with family friends like Cindy Outlaw who we knew were safe to Reid. They wouldn't laugh at him or embarrass him. They'd be patient. As we began to ask strangers who had some celebrity, we learned something new.

Mr. Greg Harris at the Rock and Roll Hall of Fame took a chance and said, "yes" to an unlikely conversation. He had to let down his guard and reveal his authentic self. Reid might have laughed at him or ask him embarrassing questions. To our great delight, Greg Harris shared of himself and received Reid's authentic self, which encouraged us to ask even more total strangers.

The very best parts of each recording came in the unexpected bits when both parties revealed their authentic true self—on purpose or by accident. As the podcast gained traction, we added it as a new dimension to Reid's business. Our new friends at Celebrate EDU took Reid seriously and developed his business sense as an entrepreneur. They are investing in the next generation of young adults with disabilities by challenging them to identify their authentic selves, develop their talents, and define a career path as self-advocates.

The quintessential chocolatier, Wonka, revealed his true self when he invited visitors into his factory. He saw in Charlie Bucket a purity that may have reflected his younger self. Charlie wasn't perfect, but he was honest and good. Wonka invested in little Charlie's future, believing he would run the business. It was chancy, speculative, and bold, but grounded in their connection—the connection of their real selves.

Would you believe a guy obsessed with pastry could run a small business selling his own baked goods at farmers' markets? Could a boy who knows everything about reptiles be a docent at a wildlife museum? Charlie Bucket is a good example that anything is possible. Grandpa Joe encouraged him to take a chance, and what happened was unimaginable. Charlie ended up running the whole Wonka Chocolate factory. What risk would you take—to remove your mask, connect in community, or change your corner of the world—if you had nothing to lose?

2

Raise the Bar on Your Personal Best

Taking risks—either becoming an entrepreneur or running a chocolate factory—requires a mix of optimism, boldness, and resilience. You won't find despairing pessimists hanging shingles on their front doors or inventing new products. Risk taking requires vision, some hope of seeing your idea come to fruition, and a lot of hustle. A hefty portion of resilience also comes in handy because risk takers are likely to fail a few times on their way to getting things just right. Hope keeps them raising the bar on their own performance and surprising their detractors as they surpass their own personal best with each reiteration or improvement.

Reid is good at this type of aspirational, imaginary thinking. He engages in it regularly with anyone who is willing. He is also the most resilient person I know, waking with a positive outlook each new morning no matter how grueling the school year or how ineffective an intervention has been.

For years, my mom wanted to take the whole family to New York City after Thanksgiving. Dreamy as that sounds, it was physically impossible for us for years. My husband and I had a major expectation of traveling as a family. The adoption book we created to describe ourselves to birthparents was a pictorial resume that touted the adventures we'd had and how we wanted to share more adventures with our prospective children and see the world through their eyes. Sappy I know, but such were our aspirations.

Reid's autism made travel difficult at best. Many days we dared not leave the house. Having to wear shoes and pants could be a deal breaker for Reid. Unpredictable things set him off, like a gooey sticker over the barcode on a library book or random stray noises like a dog barking. We managed his volcanic eruption-like reactions to little things with a sophisticated combination of prevention, diversion, and attentiveness. Reid's episodic non-compliance was disruptive. I preferred to manage a noisy outburst or tirade of slamming doors in the privacy of my home rather than out in public. Navigating New York City traffic, dense and bustling crowds, and sensory overload felt insurmountable.

I had read a novel about a man with autism who sets out to solve the murder of a neighbor's dog, *The Curious Incident of the Dog at Nighttime.*[16] On a harrowing journey far from home, he dodges police and nearly gets hit by a train. I knew just how plausible the story was.

Although we were hard pressed on every side, we were not crushed (2 Cor. 4:8). And when Reid approached twenty, we moved into a new season. With age he experienced the freedom of being able to make adult choices rather than being told what to do in school. He got better about "staying with the group," not bolting out into traffic, and regulating his emotions. So I wondered if the prospect of meeting some big names in New York would be enough motivation for us all to tough out the subway and barrage of city smells. Reid was a man on a mission. He might not be able to anticipate all the logistics, yet we believed he could plow through anything given a goal. And Jim and I knew the city well

---

16   Haddon, Mark. *The Curious Incident of the Dog at Nighttime.* Doubleday, 2003.

enough to choose judiciously between a cab and subway. We also decided that if we had to weather a meltdown and peel him off the concrete, we could do that on a trip as easily as we could at home.

Thus the podcast hit the refresh button on some of our dreams. Having a few interviews set up in advance gave us a new structure for traveling with Reid. It motivated him—and us—to take the chance and go. Suddenly, a trip to New York seemed feasible. We carefully chose a hotel that was away from the most stressful neighborhoods and traveled with the entire extended family. So if necessary, we could form a human shield for Reid within our gang of nine who love him and talk him off an irrational ledge or communicate with police if necessary.

But our first question was *who to ask for an interview?* Autism Speaks was just launching their "See Amazing in All Children" initiative with *Sesame Street*. The character Julia, a Muppet with autism, had not been introduced to the world, but she was in development. I sleuthed around and found an email for the director of marketing at Sesame Workshop. Then I drafted a direct and true email about how much we appreciated *Sesame Street* and how formative the show was in Reid's life. He would be thrilled to interview anyone there. Carol Spinney, Big Bird, Cookie Monster? We were flexible.

The best thing ever is receiving email replies within an hour. It's an awesome pattern I've noticed with some of the most receptive people we have interviewed. Affirmative responses came immediately from Greg Harris of the Rock and Roll Hall of Fame, Ladysmith Black Mambazo (the South African male choral group), Grammy-award winning blues singer Keb' Mo', and Chef Michael of Chuao Chocolatier. If the decision maker agrees to an interview, they don't deliberate too long, and we see an immediate willingness. Sometimes we learn after the fact that they have a family member with autism. Other times, they're just adrenaline junkies who are thrill-seeking.

Whatever the reason, their reflex is to say "yes." Just yesterday, Benjamin Franklin (actually one of his best interpreters in Philadelphia) replied within minutes, "I'd be delighted to be interviewed."

The vice president of marketing at Sesame Workshop replied the same day, "I hope we can make this work" and delegated a colleague to do just that. In short order, I heard from that person who offered, "We could schedule an interview with our head writer and voice of Murray. Would that be okay?" *That would more than okay!*

For the interviews he really cares about, Reid makes the long flight, deals with the hotel's weird shower and strange pillows, and clutches my elbow as we brave the city streets to make his aspirations reality. For someone who likes things to stay the same, the idea of traveling is antithetical. Why bother? But if that someone had watched *Sesame Street* reruns on YouTube for hours at a time over two decades, meeting Murray, the big, red, furry roving reporter was worth walking on hot coals.

Our hotel in New York had a spacious lobby where Reid held court greeting his sister, Allie, who took the train from college in Boston to join us, and other family members as they arrived. He even spontaneously interviewed Aunt Beth as a precursor to the morning agenda. Serendipitously, the restaurant in the lobby served Reid's favorite "three-course meal:" steak, mashed potatoes, and French fries. Things were off swimmingly! Then we walked to the nearest Starbucks to check if they had the same apple fritters as at home (they did), and taxied to the Sesame Workshop offices across from Lincoln Center.

ROVING REPORTER MEETS ROVING REPORTER: MURRAY MONSTER OF *SESAME STREET*

As the elevator doors opened, we were all six-year-olds again. Jim and I began snapping pictures of everything from the furry call bell to the interactive digital portraits of every monster on *Sesame Street*. The copier, the tables, and even the rugs were all on brand—bright colors matching the monsters' distinctive fur. It was as if the television set had come to life. Reid was out of his skin.

After playing with everything in the lobby, we were ushered back to Joey Mazzarino's small, nondescript office. Well, nondescript except for the Emmy award on his desk, a colorful clutter of gag toys on the shelves, and movie musical posters on the walls. After shaking our quavering hands all around, Joey took Murray out of a duffel bag near his feet.

Jim was already recording: the niceties, the handshakes, the duffel bag zipper. We wanted to remember it all.

Reid: Red light is on.

Was he confirming his crew was on pointe?

Murray: Hi, how are you?

Murray greeted in his familiar, distinctively high-cartoonish voice.

Reid: I'm fine.
Murray: It's so nice to meet you, Reid.
Reid: Hey Murray, what's the 'word on the street?'
Murray: Today's 'word on the street' is transportation. How did you get here today?
Reid: I got here by walking.
Murray: Walking, that's a transportation method!

Murray lisped slightly and was nearly spitting with enthusiasm.

Reid: Or by taxi.

Reid was tentative, experiencing a little cognitive dissonance from seeing this onscreen character in the flesh, or fur. Understandable.

Murray: You took a taxi too! That's another transportation! And how'd
      you get here from California?
Reid: I t-t-took a plane.
Murray: That's yet another transportation!
Reid: That's awesome, Murray!
Murray: You know all about transportation, sir.

I don't think Reid even needed his trusty printout of questions. Joey as Murray could have done a twenty-minute monologue, and we all would have applauded. Still, Reid knew his part and strived to take the lead from this master of masters.

Reid: Have you ever had a sleepover at Bert and Ernie's?
Murray: You know, I did. I did. But Bert, he mistook me for a throw rug. I
      was down on the floor for a while, then Ernie said, "Oh hey, buddy,
      Bert that's not a throw rug, that's our friend, Murray." So then Bert felt
      bad, and he offered me some oatmeal.
Reid: That's, that's a bummer. Have you ever met Miss Piggy?
Murray: You know, I have not. I'm a big fan. I love all pigs, but she seems
      like a nice pig in particular, and I would like to meet her. Have you
      met her?
Reid: I ha – – did I… No.
Murray: I would like to. We should write to her.
Reid: Okay.
Murray: Are you a fan of hers?
Reid: I'm a fan of hers. She's in the *Muppet Show*.

Murray: She is in the *Muppet Show*. I love the *Muppet Show*! What's your favorite episode of the *Muppet Show*?

Reid: I love the sketch with Julie Andrews. She does the Lonely Goatherd.

Murray: I love that sketch!

This was all rapid fire. Like ice on a skillet, Reid was sputtering and having trouble keeping up. Students with ADHD would learn so much if their teachers could keep this compelling pace. I also half expected Reid to tell Murray to use an inside voice.

Reid: Okay, and do you have a favorite movie of all time?

Murray: My ALL-TIME FAVORITE MOVIE IS *RAIDERS OF THE LOST ARK* because I want to be LIKE INDIANA JONES!!!

Reid: Mine ...

Murray: Except I don't want to be chased by a giant boulder!

Reid: Mine is *Mary Poppins*.

Murray: I love that movie too! I think we should sing a little something from it.

Reid: I don't think so, no. What do you want to be when you grow up?

Murray: Ohhhh, that's a good question. I would like. To. Pursue. A career in engineering.

Reid: That's amazing!

Murray: I think we have to learn how things work and how to build 'em. I don't know anything about it, but I wanna learn! I'm willing to learn!!!

Joey as Murray stayed on brand, setting such a good example of Sesame Workshop's mission to help kids grow smarter and stronger while entertaining us to the hilt. Instead of "Supercalifragilisticexpialidocious," they stuck to Reid's plan and closed by singing the *Sesame Street* theme song together and imagined a new band called Furry Reid or Reid and the Monster.

Murray: Fist bump!

He did it and said it.

Reid: And now it's your turn, Joey Mazzarino.
Murray: Okay, I'm gonna go. I don't wanna be here for this. I'm gonna leave. I'm leaving.

Murray scrambled back into his duffel bag.

Reid: Bye, Murray.
Murray: Bye, Reid. See ya later!!

THE MAN BEHIND THE MUPPET: JOEY MAZZARINO OF SESAME WORKSHOP
Now Joey took over, whispering in contrast to his voice as the excitable vermillion puppet.

Joey: Hey, Reid.
Reid: You were amazing!
Joey: You were amazing, sir. It's awesome to meet you.

Oddly, Reid only then acclimated to the room, shifting his focus away from the masterful voice talent. As if we had just unplugged a talking television set, he looked around at the cartoon prints on the walls. Joey keyed into the distraction and told Reid about Jack Davis of MAD magazine.

Reid: Alright, and now our next interview is with Joey Mazzarino!

Joey: Hello!!!
Reid: I'd like to ask him a couple of questions, if you don't mind.
Joey: I am ready to answer your questions, Reid.

They compared favorite letters of the alphabet and Bible stories. After expertly answering each personal question, Joey reciprocated and asked Reid questions. After all, he played a roving reporter who interviewed children all over Manhattan.

Reid: What was your first job as a kid?
Joey: I worked at a balloon shop blowing up balloons.
Reid: Can you tell me how you got to *Sesame Street?*
Joey: So, I started going to acting school. I wanted to be an actor. Then I met a puppeteer, and I didn't even know it was a job. I was like, "that seems awesome." I went to visit the set, and I met Jim Henson. Then I became obsessed with wanting to do that. I said to somebody at the costume shop, "can I borrow some fabric and stuff?" I started making very bad puppets that were terrible, but I was proud of them. Then I started practicing in front of a camera how to do it. And eventually, I began writing ....

Joey had taken some risks in life. I was so glad he shared them authentically. He was also showing how failure should be ultimately educational.

Reid: And, did you know, we have the same birthday?
Joey: Are you a June fourth?!?
Reid: Yes.
Joey: June fourth in the house!!! June fourth all around! You're my first June fourth I've ever met.

High fives started flying.

Reid: And, and, we already talked about your favorite movie ... which was *Raiders of the Lost Ark*.

Joey: That was Murray's favorite movie. You didn't ask me.

Reid: Alright, what's your favorite movie of all time, Mur ... Joey?

Joey: My favorite movie is probably *The Godfather*, which you probably haven't seen yet. It's an R-rated movie but it's my favorite.

Reid: Yea?

Joey: Thank you so much for coming out to talk to me today. That was so nice of you.

Reid: You're welcome. Oh! Can we say, "this podcast was brought to you by the letter M" together?

Joey: Okay, so as Murray or as me?

Reid: For Murray ....

Joey: For Murray, here we go! This podcast was brought to you by, uh, the letter — what letter?

Reid: M

Joey: And that stands for?

Reid: Murray, Mazzarino, and Moriarty!

Joey: Murray, Mazzarino, and Moriarty!!

Reid: That's awesome!

Joey: Thank you so MUCH! That's another M word.

Reid: Okay, CUT!

Joey: Cut!

Wearing an orange- and pink-striped sweater and with an Emmy on his desk, Joey Mazzarino in this private performance made the podcast all about Reid. Let me tell you: I love that man! For his gift to my son. For his skill as a performer, comedian, and conversationalist. For his father's heart.

I used to think no one could match Reid's energy level, but Joey Mazzarino surpassed it. That's hard to do while maintaining perfect control and intentionality. Joey was exceptional at leaning into the imaginary thinking that creatives, entrepreneurs, and Reid share in common. They have bold confidence in spades. Joey is a master at turning anything into a teachable moment. He took the challenge placed before him and gave it his absolute best. I like to think that by interacting with Reid, Joey learned something he could use in the "See Amazing in All Children" campaign. It certainly gave him firsthand experience in appreciating someone with autism.

By saying "yes" to the unlikely conversation, Joey Mazzarino also presented Reid with a challenge and raised the bar on his ability to travel, navigate new experiences, make conversation, act appropriately, and even keep a winter coat and mittens on. (We go without those in southern California.) And all in one take.

Once we got home and started editing, we realized we had enough for two podcasts, one with Joey in character as Murray and the other with Joey the man. The podcast with Murray was one straight take. I didn't edit out a thing. The man is a master at his trade. He demonstrated the trifecta of attitudes and life practices that people with disabilities need from others and teach us: risk taking, humility, and kindness. Perhaps Joey had learned them by kneeling on the ground to bring an alter ego to life on camera.

Joey Mazzarino restored my faith in humanity. In a city of nearly nine million people, it took just one to singlehandedly make our trip worth the effort. Heck, he even made decades of *Sesame Street* viewing worthwhile. Joey and the staff at Sesame Workshop also gave us swag bags full of Elmo journals, tumblers, and video documentaries about their international efforts. They showed us that the world could be a safe place for Reid and all children. They invest themselves internationally to creating a welcoming dialogue where everyone is invited in, given a place at the table, and even celebrated. Joey knows how to laugh at himself and make others laugh. He does it freely and generously for thousands of children on the airwaves. He took risks and wasn't afraid to fail. If one line wasn't funny, he'd roll out another one. His mastery raises the bar for staff writers and character actors everywhere.

Whether we are writers, moms, or carwash attendants, we need to get out there, try new material, take chances, and rise to a challenge—or we will never know what we are truly capable of. Our potential is hidden like a seed below the surface of the soil. We don't even know it's there until we reach for water and the sun.

"Work is about a search for daily meaning as well
as daily bread, for recognition as well as cash, for
astonishment rather than torpor; in short, for a sort of
life rather than a Monday through Friday sort of dying."
—Studs Terkel, American author[17]

---

17 Terkel, Studs. *Working: People Talk About What They Do All Day and How They Feel About What They Do.* The New Press, 1997.

RISING TIDE CAR WASH AND RISING TIDE U
Parkland, Florida
RisingTideU.com

Parents will do a lot for their children. I will write total strangers or celebrities, fly to New York from California in a middle seat, and walk forty blocks back to a hotel when the subway is not bearable. Love motivates us to extremes. In Florida, a father and son, John and Tom D'Eri, have gone the distance to help their son and brother Andrew reach his potential.

Rising Tide Car Wash was created to employ adults with autism and serve the community with excellence. The significant thing about their brand and identity as well as their decision-making process is that they are not a charitable endeavor. Instead, they have flipped the script by focusing on the competitive advantage that their employees with autism bring to a business. Rising Tide is a social enterprise that makes money. And they're teaching others around the country how to do the same.

Tom, like his dad, is a natural-born entrepreneur who wanted to make a difference for his brother Andrew who has autism. So Tom and John envisioned a place where Andrew and his friends could work. They researched the types of businesses that would be sustainable, profitable, and suited to their skills and preferences. I love that one of their parameters was inclusion for their employees. They looked for a business that requires skills in which employees on the spectrum have a competitive advantage. A car wash fits the bill because it requires proficiency in a very specific production process that can be taught. Tom and John also prioritized a community service in which social interaction was embedded. Everyone likes a clean car, and with a loyalty app, customers come back consistently and become friends with the employees.

People with autism have exceptional attention to detail, follow processes and safety rules to the letter, and prefer consistent routinized tasks, all of which make them ideally suited to work at a car wash. Employing these innate skills in a supportive work environment enables them to raise the standard on their personal best and excel. This work improves their lives by helping them develop an area of expertise and work in the community rather than sitting at home wallowing in untapped potential.

Rising Tide has been featured on social media and the press, so we wanted to check it out for ourselves. We also thought this would be a good *Talk Time* podcast. We were going to be in Jupiter, Florida, over spring break when Reid would sing at the Els Center for Excellence annual Awe in Autism event. South African pro-golfer Ernie Els founded this state-of-the-art school and service provider for his son and the community. While we were there, we also visited both sets of grandparents, interviewed a NASA astronaut, and spoke at a few churches to boot. Reid is not one to lie on a beach.

We set up the interview with Tom D'Eri, and bright and early, we pulled up to the Parkland, Florida location of Rising Tide Carwash. Car washes are loud even at 8:00 a.m. before they opened. But Reid walked right into the glass-viewing tunnel where you can track your car's progress through the machinery. He also investigated the vending machines and brochure racks that always catch his eye. Tom introduced himself, and we followed him to the offices upstairs for the interview. We met Andrew in the break room and jockeyed for chairs around a kitchen table. Reid, Tom and Andrew were close in age, all three of them were twenty-something.

INTERVIEWING TOM D'ERI OF RISING TIDE CAR WASH

Reid: I'll be the master of ceremonies.

Reid took a seat at the head of the table.

Tom: There we go!

Tom was comfortable with Reid's mannerisms and brass. It was all familiar.

Reid: Tom, what is the best way to motivate employees?
Tom: Well, every employee is different so I'm not sure if there's a golden rule there. But it is to try and find out what they are passionate about. Some of our guys are passionate about learning new skills. Some of our employees just want positive reinforcement. Some want to be heard about their ideas or want to be listened to about their personal life. I think that listening to your employees and trying to understand what motivates them is the answer there.
Reid: What's your favorite part of the Rising Tide story to tell?
Tom: I love telling the stories of personal change of our employees. So, getting to tell the story of Matt who worked for two years to try and get his driver's license. And Kevin, our general manager, worked with Matt weekly to get him ready for that test—over and over, and, over again, until he finally passed. Those types of stories of the community kind of rallying around itself. Now that Matt has his license, there are three more guys who want Kevin's driving school to get their licenses. That's a special part of this business.
Reid: Tom, what do you mean when you say, "Customers evangelize our brand"?
Tom: So, when I say that, I mean that we've got customers who come here

not just because it's a great car wash but also because they believe in what we do.

Whether we like it or not, our culture values people for what they do. Work is also how we value ourselves and is part of our identity. I recently met a gentleman and promptly asked him, "What do you do?" As much as I meant, *tell me about yourself; let's get acquainted,* my question implied that his work defined him. We work primarily to make money but also gain value from having a job. Being unemployed, well, that implies someone is worthless.

But the value of work goes beyond making money and impressing others. In the same sense that being creative reflects being made in the image of God, I believe we are "called" to work. Pope Francis says, "Work is fundamental to the dignity of a person. Work, to use an image, 'anoints' us with dignity, fills us with dignity, makes us similar to God, who has worked and still works, who always acts."[18] When we work, we become worthy of honor and respect. Working is a human right. And honest work done well brings glory to God. Okay, my righteous anger is stoked. Why should my son and his peers with special needs, who are made in the image of God and are able to work, be excluded from this dignity, right, and opportunity? Don't Reid and young people like him deserve these things? We need more places where people with autism can be supported to work.

The founders of Rising Tide report that unemployment among adults with autism is 80 percent. "This figure has nothing to do with the capabilities of people with autism and everything to do with the way society views autism, as a disability requiring

18 America The Jesuit Review. "In All Things: Pope Francis on the Dignity of Work." AmericaMagazine.org. https://www.americamagazine.org/content/all-things-pope-francis-dignity-labor (accessed March, 2018).

sympathy, rather than valuing diversity."[19] So Rising Tide is setting an example of how to capitalize on individual strengths and utilize them in a culture of service, to build customer loyalty, and to promote word-of-mouth advertising. Their thriving business employs seventy individuals with autism and serves more than 300,000 customers a year. Their concept is so viable that families and business people flock to them for advice on how to replicate their business model in other communities. Businesses including Blue Star Recyclers, Walgreens, UltraTesting, AutonomyWorks, and Extraordinary Ventures are adapting the model.

RISING TIDE U

When the car wash turned a profit, Tom and his dad, John, created Rising Tide U. Their mission is to provide roadmaps for other entrepreneurs who wish to start businesses that empower individuals with autism through gainful employment. Tom and John did a TED Talk on their big idea. Through Rising Tide U, they offer a podcast called the Autism Advantage, several webinars, free "Cheatsheet" resources, and a two-day immersion workshop for creating a business that can sustainably employ your loved one with autism. The workshop has modules on training, recruitment, workplace design, culture design, and building an autism empowerment brand. They want to see the concept multiply.

As we see saw with Celebrate EDU in Chapter 1, siblings rule. Jenny Anderson knew her brother's potential was greater than the world would acknowledge. Her kindness and conviction grew legs in the Celebrate EDU nonprofit. Tom D'Eri is an awesome brother who was also motivated to correct the injustice and inequity he saw

---

19 The Mighty. "7 Ways Employees With Autism Can Make Businesses Better." TheMighty. com. https://themighty.com/2018/03/7-ways-employees-with-autism-make-businesses-better/ (accessed June, 2018).

Advance Notice as a Strategy

Many people on the spectrum respond to repetition, ritual, and advance notice. When trying anything new, we often commit to doing it three times because we know it will take that long to evaluate and determine if it is worthwhile. Reid likes to understand the whole overview, so the first two times are about getting the lay of the land, figuring out logistics, and feeling comfortable, whether the activity is going to a new dentist or a new movie venue or working with a new caregiver. Third time's a charm. In your interactions with differently abled adults, don't take it personally if you don't get a positive reaction at first. Try and try again. And again. Your persistence will pay off.

his brother and other people with autism experience. They channeled their righteous anger into social change and took bold risks, and in the process demonstrated humility and kindness in thinking beyond themselves. Both of these siblings started something new because they believed that their siblings' personal best was greater than others perceived. And they expanded their own personal best by learning new skills and gaining business acumen.

Of course, I believe my daughter, Allie, is another exceptional sibling. She recently completed a double major from Berklee College of Music in music education and music therapy. She is using that education and the experiences of growing up with Reid in her work at Berkshire Hills Music Academy, a two-year college experience for adults with autism and Williams syndrome. Allie's bond with Reid led her to not only develop her own talent but also use it professionally to help others. Whether you are a sibling to a person with autism or not, you can raise the bar on your own personal best by helping others employ their skills.

ELF [20]

When we aren't in New York City to see the tree in Rockefeller Center and the Rockettes, we kick off every Christmas season by watching *Elf, Christmas with the Kranks*, and *Charlie Brown Christmas* among other classics. (Reid also watches *Elf* at other times in the year.) More than a silly holiday movie, *Elf* strikes close to home because it is a story of adoption and special needs. Watching Papa Elf (Bob Newhart) find a baby boy in his bag as a stowaway from the orphanage melts my heart. They may not look alike, but Papa Elf is compelled to make Buddy his own and teach him everything he knows.

My parents divorced when I was only six, my dad disappeared from my life, and my mom didn't remarry until I was in high school. So for most of my childhood, I took notes and compared other people's dads to fill the void in my experience. I also watched *The Bob Newhart Show* every Wednesday night and fantasized about having a dad as attentive, understanding, and dry-witted as he was.

When Buddy the Elf (Will Ferrell) grows up, he decides to search for his birth father in New York City, which is a long way from the North Pole where he has been raised. Can he get there by himself? Will he survive in the city? What will his father be like? Everything about the idea involves risk and presents a challenge that will expand Buddy's personal best.

Besides being adopted, Buddy the Elf has some issues that resemble autism, at least in my experience. Like so many with ASD, he takes things literally, which gets repeatedly him into trouble. Once he purchases a slinky red negligee for his dad because he is prompted by the "For Someone Special" tag. He has limited job options. Elves are either cobblers, cookie bakers, or—the

---

20 *Elf.* Directed by Jon Favreau. Burbank: New Line Cinema/Warner Bros., 2003.

ultimate— toymakers in Santa's workshop. Buddy also has a passionate special interest in elf culture and is learning to self-advocate.

The character of Buddy the Elf reminds me of Reid who is ecstatic about little things like butter beans, a Netflix in the mail, or a garage sale on the way to church. Reid is accustomed to being different, like Buddy who doesn't fit in the elfin shower stalls and is the only baritone in the elfin choir. Eating cookies and ice cream with maple sausage for breakfast would be perfect for Reid. Like Buddy, he might eat a piece of gum he found on the street, and he has run in front of cabs. Our social norms are as inexplicable to Reid as New York City is to Buddy.

Both are also unstoppably driven when fixed on a mission. Buddy and Reid share the indefatigable spirit, optimism, and boldness required for risk-taking. Their personal best never plateaus; curiosity and a craving for the next challenge are forever raising the bar. Buddy discovers that his elfin training has value in the great big city. He ends up saving Christmas as well as his cold-hearted birthfather by employing his competitive advantage. Buddy the Elf convinces everyone in the city of the power of believing. And that's why I well up every time I see the closing scene.

WRAPPING UP CHAPTER 2

While I may not have been born with a bold, risk-taking temperament, I have learned to be both from being a parent. Advocating for a special needs child in school, at church, and in the community presented a challenge that raised the bar on my personal skill set. Some new traits come out of us naturally, and others we can cultivate to be better parents as well as better neighbors and citizens. Wanting to supply what your children need motivates parents to acquire new skills such as assertiveness, patience, or time management to name a few. Love is a great motivator.

It helps me to acknowledge that when I step out in faith to do new things, I might fail, but that failure is okay. I don't like it, but remembering that failure is not the end of the world helps me endure it until I finally succeed. Like surfing or snowboarding (not that I do either, but imagine with me), falling off the board is part of the experience. You're likely to fall a bunch of times before you catch a real ride. Falling and getting back up is the definition of resilience, which is another trait that those with disabilities embody and teach us. Because many things are harder for them, they sometimes develop more character than the rest of us ever do.

Creating a podcast with an autistic host was a new challenge for us. Every single episode raised the bar as we asked a new guest, wrote new questions, went to new places, and encouraged fresh conversation. The podcast motivated Reid and me to practice and master new skills. Taking risks is a way to grow at any age. I learned audio editing skills while he learned to write thank you notes. At any age or ability are risks you can take that will improve your personal best.

The makers of *Sesame Street* know this, and it is at the heart of their "See Amazing in All Children" initiative. What makes them a progressive educational agent for world change is that they believe in trying new things and taking risks and do so across all levels—from marketing to writing to continually inventive shows. They enter new countries and tackle issues others won't touch from race relations to girls' health. They create new Muppets like Julia. They push the envelope and constantly improve, which we can see in their product, their brand, and their employees.

A similar pursuit of excellence motivated Tom D'Eri and his dad to found Rising Tide. Their boldness to flip the script by focusing on the competitive advantage that employees with autism bring has led to countless stories of personal change in their business and around the country as others follow their model. They believe in what they are doing, so their ideas are catching on with others who have loved ones with autism. Like Buddy the Elf, a competitive advantage may come from a unique perspective, quirky habits, and unquenchable curiosity. Certainly being determined and persistent are gifts to be harnessed and channeled.

While doing new things can be frightening and make us uncomfortable, taking risks has rewards. Take a situation you face right now and imagine the potential for new growth that it offers. Then lean into risk and watch new skills develop. Love motivates us to seek the best for each other. People with autism are employable and have a desire to work. Can we create a society that views them as capable and supports their pursuits?

3

Collaborate with Others

As bold and driven as Reid can be, he doesn't love trying new things. Obviously, we have devised ways of introducing him to new things by pairing the novel with the familiar, giving him advance notice, and making lots of visual schedules. We have learned it works best to prime his brain for cooperation by letting him know what we have planned for the week ahead. We even do this in shorter time increments. For example if I want him to turn the car radio off, I ask him to do it at the next traffic light. We also give Reid space to say "no," understanding that he often changes his mind later. His erudite response is now a family joke.

"Reid, would you like to go to the IMAX headquarters in Los Angeles and see the premiere of *America's Musical Journey*? You're in it with Aloe Blacc," I cajoled.

"I'll consider it," he offered reluctantly. That beats a "no."

By far the best strategy to motivate Reid to do the new activity is with a preferred person. Best of all with a familiar person who is passionate about that new, non-preferred activity. For example as Reid has become an adult, we have wanted him to acquire independent living skills like meal prep and light housekeeping. While there are protocols and specific agencies that teach these skills, we've discovered that for Reid, personal chemistry is a "must have."

He has absolutely no interest in learning to sweep a floor or mash potatoes with a random recruit who has an agenda.

However, he's all about doing those tasks with his songwriting coach, Paul Eddy. Everything is fun with Paul. Reid trusts him, and they enjoy each other's company. With Paul, Reid is perfectly willing to practice depositing money in the bank or starting a load of laundry. The chemistry of collaboration can be the antidote to resistance. Making a task relational propels Reid to learning new skills.

Strong collaborators make us better and stretch us to learn new skills. Steven Crowle is an exceptional musician who facilitates Reid's band, Jungle Poppins. Steven teaches almost every instrument and plays guitar, banjo, and mandolin professionally in three other bands. Our strategy of pairing him with Reid and Ethan the drummer is intentional. Reid plays keyboard with a distinctively strong percussive style. He learns the chords and pounds them out almost like a second drummer. While we work with Reid to vary his chord patterns, Steven plays lead guitar and throws in more than his usual share of the melody line. This not only sounds better to the audience but also scaffolds Reid's emerging skill. As he hears the song in its ultimate form, he moves that much closer to playing it himself. Strategic pairing makes for great fidelity.

Over the last sixteen years, Reid has done many new things with his longtime music therapist, Angela Neve Meier. Their trusting, therapeutic relationship enables Reid to develop new skills and take calculated risks. More than once he has refused a performance when I proposed it, then agreed when Angela suggested it. She has been alongside Reid as a master collaborator for many "firsts." His legs quaked like leaves on an aspen at his first public performance; he was eight years old and singing next to her at the NBC health fair. When he was twelve, she suggested that he be in a band and then supported him by creating one.

For Christmas when he was sixteen, Angela gave Reid his first recording session; then they wrote an original song to record together. She invited him to speak with her to her American Music Therapy Association colleagues—his first "conference gig"—and challenged him to write an impromptu song before a live audience. Reid and Angela have recorded two CDs and performed countless times at coffeehouses, fundraisers, conferences, music venues, preschools, and senior centers. Last summer, Reid sang "Come Thou Fount" at Angela's wedding.

Most recently, Angela recommended Reid to MacGillivray Freeman Films. They wanted to include a segment about music therapy in their fortieth IMAX film, *America's Musical Journey*. We drove up to Laguna Beach for a day of filming with chart-topping soul sensation Aloe Blacc. Aloe's parents are from Panama, and he has an international hip-hop vibe. No doubt you would recognize "Wake Me Up," the eighth-most downloaded song in the United Kingdom. Aloe wrote that with the Swedish musician Avicii.

We might all have a little risk aversion as part of our human nature. But we are more willing to risk in partnership with others. A question about collaborators has come up in several podcasts, maybe because we are hyper-aware of helpers. Reid will always need one.

ON AND OFF THE GIANT SCREEN: ALOE BLACC

For the IMAX film, Reid and Aloe performed each other's hit singles—"I Need a Dollar" and "Purple Party"—before a live audience of Angela's preschool-age clients dressed in their favorite colors. The plan was for Reid to interview Aloe afterward. I thought we'd sneak off to a vacant room in the Laguna Beach Boys and Girls Club. But before I knew it, the MacGillivray film crew were prompting Reid themselves and filming the whole interview from multiple angles on their professional cameras. Knowing it is "now or never" with Reid, because he would never repeat it later when I was ready with my handheld recorder, I scurried to be sure we could have access to their far superior audio files. Both Reid and Aloe were rigged with lapel mics and battery packs. "Sure, sure," they assured me they would share everything.

The room was rapt as Reid nervously took over as director, host, and fanboy. I'm not sure what was more unusual to him, standing for the whole thing or having spectators. Aloe was as cool as a So Cal surfer. He had slipped in through a side door precisely when he was needed and reassured everyone around him with a suave smile.

Reid: How did you get your name, Aloe?

Aloe: As an artist, I wanted to choose a name that I felt described my style. So, I chose Aloe because I felt my style was smooth like lotion.

Reid: Of course. You seem to do a lot of collaborations, why do you think that is?

Aloe: Well, I do a lot of collaborations because interacting with other people making music is really fun. It helps to build the excitement and the energy and the inspiration for the songs.

Reid: What makes a good collaborator?

Aloe: A good collaborator is someone who is talented in what they do— whether writing lyrics, creating melodies, or playing an instrument. Uh, but some people don't have to actually do any of the music. They just have to have a great personality, and that can make for a really cool piece of art.

When preparing for the film shoot, we were surprised to learn that Aloe actually doesn't play keyboard. In fact, he learned trumpet as a child. Reid learned the chords to Aloe's song, but singing with them in tempo is harder than it looks. So Angela brought two keyboards. In a real way, all three of them collaborated: Angela on keys, Reid on supplemental keys and vocals, and Aloe on vocals.

Reid: Alright. What do remember about recording with Avicii?

Aloe: Well, in recording with Avicii, we tried a couple of different things. What really worked was a song that mixed together some country music elements with pop and dance music elements called, "Wake Me Up."

Reid: Of course! What's been a most memorable performance?

Aloe: My most memorable performance was in London at a TV show where I got to perform on a stage alongside Paul McCartney.

Reid: Of course. So, Aloe, "Three Little Birds" is one of my favorite songs. What can you tell me about your project with Ziggy and Stephen Marley?

Aloe: Well, really soon, we'll be performing, and it's a commemoration of Bob Marley, their father's, *Exodus* album. It's forty-years-old, and it's a great celebration of his music and his life.

Reid: Alright. Who's at the top of your listening playlist?

Aloe: Well, I think now at the top of my listening playlist is Reid.

Reid: Yeah! I'm really awesome.

The roomful of grips, directors, and gaffers erupted in laughter.

Reid: So, is there anything you want to ask Reid?

Those pesky pronouns still trip him up.

Aloe: Yea, I have a question for you, Reid. Okay, when you start writing a song, what gives you the inspiration, like for "Purple Party"?

Reid: Well, I come up with some words and I play the keyboard and sing those words, with Angela.

He made it sound effortless.

Aloe: So, do you write songs only about colors?
Reid: What if I write songs about animals? Maybe after the soundtracks album. In fact, Jungle Poppins is releasing a soundtracks album.
Aloe: Jungle Poppins, who's that?
Reid: Jungle Poppins, it's the name of my new band. And we named it after two movies.
Aloe: Wait a minute, you have a band?!
Reid: Yea, *Mary Poppins*, and *Jungle Book*.
Aloe: Of course! And do you guys have names in your band? Are you Mowgli or is there a Bagheera?
Reid: No, no there's no Mowgli or Bagheera or Bert or Mary Poppins. It's Reid, Ethan, Steven, and maybe Paul. Oh, and Greg on bass.
Aloe: Okay, and Greg's on bass. What ... do you do vocals?
Reid: I play keyboards and vocals.
Aloe: That's great. Who do you write the songs for?
Reid: I write my songs for everybody.

Reid spread his hand across the room in a gesture of universal inclusion.

Aloe: Why do you like to write songs?
Reid: Because writing songs makes me feel awesome inside.
Aloe: How do you think it makes everybody else feel?
Reid: I think happy!

Another spontaneous chorus of "Yes! Yeah. Yay!" burst from the moms, children, film crew, and other spectators.

Aloe: So, you like to make people happy?

Reid: Yes.

Aloe: That's pretty awesome. That's the best part about music. You can use it to make people feel good.

Reid: Of course. Well, thank you, Aloe. It was very nice talking to you. I'm glad I could do this interview.

Aloe: Yeah, I'm glad too!

Aloe and Reid were collaborators now. They had created a scene together for the giant IMAX screen that will educate thousands of schoolchildren about the history of music in America. Reid gave Aloe a big bear hug that rolls in the credits of *America's Musical Journey*. You can feel the little-while love that was fueled by playing music together. They made each other happy.

All of us will always have a list of things we cannot do alone. But the list of things we can do with support should be even longer. We make progress and learn new things by taking itty-bitty steps with others into something new and risky. We take risks better together, which makes needing help an asset for someone like Reid. His need for collaborators ensures that he is always learning something new from someone new and experiments and expands in ways he couldn't do by himself.

> *"Alone we can do so little, together we*
> *can do so much."* —Helen Keller[21]

---

21 Lash, Joseph P. *Helen and Teacher: The Story of Helen Keller and Anne Sullivan Macy.* Delacorte Pr., 1980.

THE MIRACLE PROJECT
Santa Monica, CA
TheMiracleProject.org

Teens and young adults with special needs can create original work. This is best seen in the performing arts when creative expression, rather than conformity, is encouraged and supported. *Autism: The Musical* was all the rage in 2007 when it came out. The documentary follows innovative acting Coach E, Elaine Hall, and the lives of five autistic children and their parents as she helps the children write and perform their own original, hour-long musical based on preferred interests and life experiences. Elaine was known as "the child whisperer" who coached child actors on set before adopting her son with autism, Neal, from Russia.

I watched the documentary intently, feeling envious that Reid could not be in a program like hers. Perhaps you're having those feelings now reading about programs that aren't in your town. The Miracle Project grew out of the documentary. They now offer a full docket of inclusive classes in theater, film, and expressive arts for children, teens, and adults with autism and all abilities. They understand that theater is an effective tool for building communication, social skills, job skills, and friendships. They are also intentional about developing a unique, neurodiverse community.

Through shared social experiences, participants find their voice, develop their talents, and rehearse for life. Enlisting actors and other young performers with a passion for the arts, they enable a synergy that raises the bar for everyone because the truth is that we risk better together. This apprenticeship model proves to be highly effective. They perform their shows at the acclaimed Wallis Annenberg Center for the Performing Arts in Beverly Hills. With so many contacts in Los Angeles, the Miracle Project is also becoming a talent source that has placed students in TV shows *Parenthood*, *Speechless*, *The Good Doctor*, and *Atypical*, and the film *Please Stand By!*

I read *Now I See the Moon*, Elaine's beautiful memoir, and felt we had parallel lives. Although she is Jewish and was divorced, we had a lot of other experiences in common. We shared a spiritual perspective on our life's work, and our boys were similar in age, behavior, and interests. Reid was writing his own baptism song as Neal was preparing for his bar mitzvah. I even emailed Elaine in the middle of an adolescent crisis with Reid's medication to ask if she'd had any related experiences. She replied. She is a maker of everyday miracles.

Imagine my delight in 2010 when I learned that the Miracle Project had funding for expansion programs in San Diego. I emailed Elaine and offered to help in any way possible. She called *me* her angel then when I connected her with schools, teachers, and arts programs here. We collaborated on our shared passion of making the arts more accessible to kids in special education. I couldn't wait to help Elaine extend her reach in circles that intersected mine. In due time, her team chose three pilot sites to launch training. One was the little hippie oasis—a nonpublic, special-ed school in Ocean Beach where Reid was detoxing from the rigid behavioral program.

Elaine came down and led a group session. I wasn't present, but afterward she told me Reid was an eagle in the exercise. Elaine is like a tiny butterfly (she stands about 4' 10") that lands on your shoulder and makes you feel chosen. An ethereal magic follows her, and you're not sure how to get it back after she leaves. She carries it like an anointing. Reid overtook her in a bear hug at the end of the day after a short assembly in which he sang with his unorthodox principal.

The Miracle Project has now expanded to New Jersey, San Francisco, and New England and conducts professional development workshops, camps, and staff training at like-minded organizations. Operating in conjunction with the Vista Del Mar Jewish Community Center, Elaine has also developed a groundbreaking bar and bat mitzvah program of inclusive religious programming for individuals with a disability. It's called Nes Gadol, which means "a great miracle."

About five years later, when my husband began commuting to Marina del Rey in Los Angeles for a new job as director of brand citizenship at 72andSunny, I got a bright idea. Reid and I could crash his hotel room and do some fun stuff up in LA over the summer. Namely, the Miracle Project was offering their "Improv for Interaction" on Wednesday nights in Santa Monica. Reid was ready for a new challenge with some new people. He had done some improvisation with a local actress, Samantha Ginn (more on that in the next chapter). Going on the road to a new location would be an opportunity to generalize his skills and see if they transferred to new people. We would drive up for class, spend the night with Jim, and then poke around the next day before returning home. Reid was willing to give it a whirl.

Boy, did he impress me. The first night of class we arrived early, having allowed ample time for the long commute. We met the unfamiliar teacher in the unfamiliar parking lot behind an unfamiliar church hall, and Reid took it from there.

Elaine has trained most of the Miracle Project staff, and they all seem to have the Coach E anointing—a passion for people and theater. It rubs off. All the participants can sense it and respond favorably. They introduce themselves with a fun name game that includes stepping forward into a circle and are affirmed at every attempt. Reid can sense intention and authenticity like a trained

German shepherd on drug detection. He was hooked on the staff's scent from the first interaction. Rubbing his hands together in elation, and doing his signature freestanding kick-the-butt jumps, he declared, "They love theater. I love them!"

The next week, Reid got a seat between the two magnetic teachers, Geno and Hannah. They were cut of the same cloth and they shared exuberance, a flair for flamboyance, and an ear for a good pun. They had been mutually won over by generosity, spontaneity, and a willingness to jump into a circle to do unscripted comedic socializing.

I watched a lot of guys like Reid file in. They were mostly older than him at twenty-one, and I was one of the few parents who stayed. Some were more street savvy, using their phones and being dropped off on the curb. One or two arrived by Uber. This was a fresh slice of the LA lifestyle. One used a wheelchair. A couple had personal care assistants. One was vocally distressed by the largess of the circle, so he took a break outside on a patio with one of the teachers. The teachers skillfully nurtured each participant, accurately sensing which behaviors to ignore and which warranted a response.

The teachers closed an accordion divider promptly at 6:30 p.m. to contain the group and intentionally give improvisers independence from their nosy parents. I got it. Behaviors famously change when parents are watching. I was appreciative of the teachers' competence and the break they gave me from having to provide copious CliffsNotes.

The scene of parents coming and going was similar to a night at our Banding Together Jam Sessions in San Diego. Collaborating with each other, some are preparing for an upcoming IEP meeting. Others are comparing notes on how to file for conservatorship or asking about ABLE accounts. Parents navigating the special needs world need each other. And they know the best resource is always another parent. In addition to the incredible arts program, Elaine has created a community in Santa Monica of people—families, caregivers, professionals, and creatives—with shared experiences, needs, and interests. They uphold each other turning everyday life into a wonderfully creative, expressive, joyful piece of work. A miracle.

Reid didn't need much help from me for the rest of the eight-week sessions. He made new friends who supported him. He learned to trust others, take new risks, and lean on new shoulders. Before we left the last night, I got a snapshot of him arm in arm with Geno and Hannah who were no longer strangers but now his biggest fans and best buds. We were privileged to enter into

Ten Tips for Interacting in Public with a Distressed Person with Autism

1. Humor can help shift gears.
2. Back off rather than move in.
3. Use a matter-of-fact tone. Your emotion can escalate theirs.
4. Offer empathy without confrontation or judgment.
5. State the desired action rather than repeating what they're doing that needs to stop.
6. Use simple, quiet directions. Auditory processing decreases under stress.
7. Explain "why" so they understand your plan.
8. Ask for a phone number of someone who knows them.
9. Sit at a distance and create a human shield from crowding.
10. Don't force anything; a caregiver will likely arrive before you need to.

their camaraderie for those memorable summer evenings. We miss them and appreciate the confidence and competence they evoked. A shared affinity is powerfully motivating and fulfilling at the same time.

This was the beginning of my new recruitment policy. I would keep an eye out for more people like these Miracle Project teachers: creative, passionate, and helpful mentors and collaborators. We need to surround ourselves with helpers, mentors, and colleagues who will bring out our best. By walking alongside, they help us make progress.

THIRD MAN ON THE MOUNTAIN[22]

I think we happened upon this obscure Disney release back in the day when libraries had VHS tapes to borrow. Based on a true story, *Third Man on the Mountain* was filmed in Zermatt, Switzerland, in the shadow of the Matterhorn. The movie inspired the bobsled ride at Disneyland, which I'll ride rather than the Finding Nemo Submarine Voyage any day of the year.

We have made a study of Walt Disney and are fond of his visionary passion and creative legacy. As the story goes, Walt had a knack for identifying talented child actors. He was known to say, "Just go to a school playground. In a few seconds, you can spot one or two in the crowd who captivate your attention. You just can't stop watching them."[23] Those are the children he recruited and put on contract. Cheerful, indefatigable Janet Munro had "it"—that unmistakable quality Disney sought and packaged in his early films like *Third Man on the Mountain*.

Rudi Matt (James MacArthur) is an adventurous lad whose ambition is to conquer the mountain that killed his father rather than wash dishes in a local restaurant. His mother and uncle forbid him to climb ever again, wanting to protect him from his father's fate. He died in an avalanche after giving his coat and eventually his shirt to save another man's life.

Three people are necessary collaborators for Rudi to fulfill his destiny: Captain John Winter, an Englishman Rudi rescues from a crevasse, Lizbeth who is smitten by his conviction, and old Theo who was with Rudi's father the day he died. Theo can't climb anymore with his lame leg, but he can shout out directions and cover for the boy at the restaurant.

---

22 *Third Man on the Mountain.* Directed by Ken Annakin. Burbank: Walt Disney, 1959.

23 Williams, Pat and Denney, Jim. *How to Be Like Walt: Capturing the Disney Magic Every Day of Your Life.* HCI, 2004.

Theo helps Rudi master the finer points of climbing and prepares him for every adversity by loading his pack full of rocks and setting up obstacles. He also teaches Rudi that a good guide leads others and puts others before himself, reminding Rudi of his father who was the greatest climber—and guide—of all. Theo passes this torch to Rudi by calling him to the higher ground of sacrifice over personal glory.

The movie ends after a perilous journey and some intense rivalry. Quintessential Swiss revelers with cowbells and flower garlands greet Captain Winter's climbing party in a triumphal entry into the town square. The hotelier reads a proclamation naming the mountain after them. Captain Winter stops the celebration to correct the announcement and give Rudi the credit. Although Rudi descended prematurely with an injured man, he discovered his father's fabled "chimney route" to the top. Calling Rudi forward to the telescope, Winter shows him his father's red shirt posted at the top of the mountain. Winter carried it up the final ascent and staked the claim on Rudi's behalf, knowing he could have been the first. The town cheers for the dishwasher!

Rudi needed Theo, Lizbeth, and Captain Winter as mentors, conspirers, and confidantes to fully risk and achieve his destiny—both as a climber and a man of honor. Similarly, Walt Disney needed his brother, Roy, to run the business and make his dream a reality. Ryan Seacrest and Ellen DeGeneres have producers and writers who create the material they deliver from teleprompters. Musicians and artists have spouses or partners who handle their marketing and administrative tasks. In creating the podcast, I like to think I am Reid's "third man on the mountain" by writing thought-provoking questions in his voice. And I need my writing coach to get any words down at all. We are made to complement each other. We risk better together.

I named Reid's creative arts program "Strength Collective" to reflect the importance of partnerships. When we combine our strengths and shore up the ones we don't possess, our teamwork creates a rich tapestry of interwoven accomplishments we can celebrate together. Success in life is not overcoming disability any more than it is possessing exceptional ability. It is camaraderie with others. We are not designed to function in isolation. We are social beings who can be a sounding board for each other's ideas and shoulders to stand on to see our next steps.

WRAPPING UP CHAPTER 3

A little aversion to risk is part of human nature. At least, it's part of mine. But doing new or hard things with a companion is usually a good strategy. Collaboration can offset our resistance and make a new venture more fruitful and rewarding. Reid defies a lot of myths about autism. And he's not alone. No two people with the diagnosis are alike. Despite the literature suggesting that he might be in a world of his own or asocial, Reid is gregarious, affectionate, and deeply attached to the people in his life. As a twin, he has actually never been alone. He trusts and relies on his support staff and mentors, some who he has known for decades. These collaborations make it possible for him to take risks and continue to make progress. He has assistance from people who genuinely care about him, share his passions, and push him to develop his potential. Their enthusiasm and camaraderie motivate him.

Collaboration often comes up when Reid interviews interesting musicians and creatives. In fact, some people make a living by collaborating well. Reid grew in self-awareness as he heard Aloe Blacc talk about what makes a good collaborator. Aloe reminded him that everyone makes a contribution in his collaborations whether through their attitude or musicianship. Filming a scene for a movie together made that point in real time. Each of us has something to add.

Collaboration is an art, not a science because people are unique, emotional beings, not machines. We learn dynamically from each other and can make beautiful progress together when we take supported leaps. The Miracle Project is a community of actors and performers of all abilities. They support each other in creative expression, rather than conformity, through original classes and dramatic productions. The resulting neurodiverse community raises the bar for everyone. A shared affinity for singing, dancing, or acting is motivating and fulfilling at the same time. Students in Miracle Project programs learn social skills and gain confidence and self-esteem because they are surrounded by helpers, colleagues, and peers who bring out their best.

Third Man on the Mountain dramatically illustrates how necessary collaborators are for young people in particular. Rudi's safety as well as his success depends on others. His collaborators challenge, heckle, encourage, and call his bluff to ensure he is equipped for mountain climbing as a professional guide. They teach him that a guide doesn't climb alone. He is responsible for others, and to achieve his full potential, he must trust others and be trustworthy.

None of us live this life alone. As much as we revere self-sufficiency and independence, we are at our best when we are in a community. We thrive together. We all need help at times, or to do certain things, let alone to tackle new things and grow. Who are the collaborators who help you take risks or achieve success? Who could benefit from your camaraderie and expertise? Where can you come alongside and collaborate with someone to help them reach their destiny?

4

Embrace Your Competitive Advantage

As we collaborated with our friends at Celebrate EDU, Reid and I internalized basic business principles. One was identifying his competitors: Who were other children's performers in the area? Who had special interest podcasts? Why would a library hire Reid instead of Miss Ladybug or another children's performer? Answering these questions was a fantastic exercise that also revealed the demand and some new places to promote Reid's services.

The next question was: What sets your business apart? Celebrate EDU gave us a choice of six competitive advantage options: price, speed of service, ease of use, quality, customer experience, and specialty. Reid and I talked about why we go to Staples instead of FedEx to copy chord charts. The obvious answer here is price. Why does Dad prefer Blue Ribbon pizza to Leucadia's? Blue Ribbon has a better gluten-free crust; their competitive advantage is quality. As a musician and podcast host, Reid's competitive advantage is his personality that guarantees a customer experience like no other. Defining Reid's competitive advantage shaped our marketing.

As individuals, we each have some quality that sets us apart from other members of the human race. This quality might be the result of a childhood experience, or a passion for a cause, or some special ability. We don't necessarily compete for customers, but our "competitive advantage" equips us for some purpose on this planet. We are unique in infinite ways, and our uniqueness is a complex combination of qualities and formative influences. However, embracing what makes us different from our peers can be daunting. We may not fit in at first, and everyone may feel awkward. But when we lean into how we are distinct, we can experience the greatest rewards.

The next podcast guest is a leader in her field. Quirky and narrow as the genre may be, she owns and excels in it. What sets her apart has become her niche. Temple Grandin reminds us that we don't have to match others, sound the same, or look the same to succeed. In fact, as we lean into the originality of how we are made, the world benefits.

ONE OF A KIND: TEMPLE GRANDIN

A person whose intellect is her competitive advantage is Temple Grandin. Arguably the most accomplished adult with autism, she proves that an "abnormal brain" can be genius. Temple spends time helping others address the challenges she experienced as a child with ASD. She not only remembers her sensory defensiveness and social struggles but also articulates them to help the next generation of parents better understand their children. Temple is also an advocate who has changed the course of autism intervention.

When we show the slide of Temple and Reid in our presentations, Reid asks the audience, "Who knows who this is?" Always a hand goes up. Temple is often on NPR (National Public Radio) talking about the humane cattle slaughterhouses she designs. Temple is revered in the field of animal science because her empathy for animals and ability to think in pictures enabled her to invent and design machines that revolutionized the livestock industry thirty years ago. Perhaps you've seen *Temple*, the movie about her life;

Claire Danes portrays her masterfully. Temple did not have an easy path in autism or animal science, yet she has embraced her competitive advantage without question. Now she is helping thousands of young adults on the spectrum do the same in her characteristically gruff way. She found her niche and challenges them to find theirs.

A friend landed this interview with Temple Grandin for Reid. She knew the host of a fundraiser in Los Angeles where Temple was the keynote speaker. Allie, home from college, drove two hours with Reid and me to what was then the Nokia Theater in downtown LA. We would have fifteen minutes in the greenroom with Grandin before the event started.

Reid didn't know much about Temple Grandin, other than what he had gleaned from a juvenile biography and some pictures online. She was a little outside his sweet spot for musicians and entertainers. But at this point, he could lean on his professional chops rather than just relying on the adrenaline rush of meeting a personal hero. I convinced him that Temple is a big name and interviewing her would be an honor.

Questions in hand, he clutched my arm all the way up a two-story escalator. I could feel his panic of being swallowed by the serrated edges of each step folding unto itself. His defenses were kicking in. The organizers were frantic with pre-show jitters. I took deep breaths and waited for instructions.

We were set loose through the bowels of the Nokia Theater to find Grandin's spacious greenroom. She looked just like her pictures. She was near seventy, a tall, masculine woman with no product in her hair. She wore her signature cowgirl uniform. That day, it was almost all black: black jeans, black lace-up boots, big belt buckle, a black western shirt with turquoise embroidery on the yoke, and a red bolo tie. Her outfit made a striking combination with the red leather sectional and zebra rug. Reid sat "criss-cross applesauce" with an end table between them. Temple's travel companion sat at a distance and said nothing. Allie kept her distance too, taking pictures with her phone. I sat on the ottoman piece of the sectional. Up close, Grandin's face showed signs of age, but not her expression. In contrast, Reid's adrenaline and exuberance had kicked in. He was all smiles when "on the air."

Reid: Hi, Temple! We're here in LA interviewing Temple Grandin. So, Temple, how did your parents choose your name?

Temple: It's an old family surname.

Reid: That's amazing.

Temple coughed. Coughing and throat clearing are bugaboos for Reid who can obsess on the timbre and source of odd sounds. I worried that the sound might interfere.

Reid: Oh, sorry. *Reid apologized for her cough.* So, what were your favorite books as a child?

Temple: I had a book about famous inventors. That was one of my favorite books 'cuz my grandfather, on the mother's side of the family, was the co-inventor of the automatic pilot for airplanes. And when I'd go visit granny and grandfather, I would ask questions about, "Why is the sky blue?" Things like that ....

Reid: Why is the sky blue? Okay. So, what movie have you watched the most times?

Temple: Well, I really like *Avatar*. I watched that. Also, I have to admit, that I really liked *Monsters, Inc.*, and I've watched a whole bunch of times on planes. I'm embarrassed to say how many times I've watched it on a plane. *Her voice had a forced animation at this memory, then returned to fact.* But, recent movies, *Gravity* and *Avatar* .... There's certain movies you *have* to see in a theater, in a *decent* theater. *Avatar* and *Gravity* are not ones to look at on a plane. And they were great movies. On a plane, people told me they were boring. You're not *getting* the whole view of it on a plane.

Reid: Soo, Temple, the movie I have watched the most times was *Mary Poppins*.

Temple: Oh. Okay.

Reid: What was the high point and low point of having the movie made about you?

Temple: Well, I really liked the fact that they recreated all my projects, and really showed the work stuff. This is the thing I'm so concerned about today. Too many people aren't learning basic skills. I talked to one mom of an eighteen-year-old honor student who'd never grocery shopped. I never thought, in these autism talks, I would have to talk about grocery shopping. *Her voice showed the expression, that her face did not. She was annoyed.* But, I'm finding that I need to talk about that—learning how to shake hands .... One advantage of growing up in the '50s is they *pounded* in the social skills. *All* children ... saying please and thank you, taking turns while playing games. And that's not being done today. That more rigid way of bringing the kids up, actually, was the best thing that ever happened to me. On the other hand, plenty of time for creativity and making things. But, when you come in for dinner, you had to have manners.

Reid: Yeah, well, I always go grocery shopping with Joe and my mom.

Joe was Reid's one-on-one behavioral aide.

Temple: You need to learn how to grocery shop by yourself.

A classic achiever, Temple took everything to the next step.

Reid: Mmhmm.

Reid wasn't going to argue with her.

Temple: You've gotta learn how to handle budgets.

Reid: Yeah, budgets. Yes.

Temple: You gotta make sure that somebody doesn't rip you off. That's the other thing. There's a lot of scams out there, now. *Fake.* All kinds of fake people calling you up, saying they represent car insurance. I've gotten that call a whole bunch of times. And I like to bother those people. I go, "Where is your physical address? Who do you work for? Who is your boss? Because you're a fraud and *goodbye!*

She was savvy; ASD did not leave her defenseless.

Reid: Can you tell me when you realized that "thinking in pictures" was a unique gift?

Temple: Well, I always knew I thought in the pictures, but it's been interesting for me to find out how people think differently. You have a mathematician mind, the visual thinking mind, the verbal mind. And in my book *The Autistic Brain*, I go into detail about the different kinds of minds and different jobs for the different types of minds. Like my mind is the visual thinker, which would be art, design, industrial design. The mathematician is engineering, physics, computer programming. And the word thinkers, a lot of them are really good at retail jobs, writing ....

Reid: Okay. When was the happiest time in your life?

Temple: Well, I've had a lot of happy times. People are always looking a single turning point. It's much more, kind of a gradual, learning more and more ....

Reid: Okay?

I knew Reid could handle this. But at the moment, I was willing him to go on to the next question.

Temple: I wanna ... I'm gonna interview you. What are you doing now?

Reid: I'm here to interview you.

He was being factual, not fresh. They took each other's questions literally.

Temple: No. What ... I wanna ask *you* some questions.
Reid: Okay.

His voice was breathless now with nerves. He looked to me for help, but I felt helpless too. Temple was a feisty one. I didn't dare intervene because she wouldn't tolerate any assistance from "mommy."

Temple: And where are .... Are you in college? Are you in school?
Reid: I am in school.
Temple: What are you studying?
Reid: Oh, I'm st ... I go to ATP. It's adult transition program.
Temple: And have you had any work experience?
Reid: Yes.
Temple: Good.
Reid: I am working at Roundtable Pizza Tuesday and Thursdays.
Temple: What's that, a restaurant?
Reid: It's a restaurant.
Temple: And what do you do there?
Reid: Fold pizza boxes.
Temple: See, this where you've gotta learn discipline and the responsibility of a job. What are you doing in music?
Reid: Well, I did a lot of gigs.
Temple: Music, well, that's good.
Reid: And you can order my CD for $10.

He had his pitch ready and didn't offer her any freebies. Don't worry; we gave her one.

Temple: And have you put any... do you have music up on YouTube to
    show it off?

Reid: Of course.

Temple: Are you getting any hits on it?

Reid: Okay. Yes.

Temple: Yeah, 'cuz a lot of music today, the way it gets started is it gets
    started on YouTube. That's where they're finding all the new artists
    these days.

Reid: That's amazing. Temple Grandin. I self-talk to Allie-in-the-tummy, who
    is like my twin sister, Allie. Who is your closest companion, Temple?

Reid was doing what those in the radio business call "taking back
the mic."

Temple: Well, I have ... I'm friends with a lot of people.

Reid: Okay, a lot?

Temple: Yup. What I'm the most interested in is your future, that you make
    a good career in music. That's more interesting than asking about me.

When it got personal, she changed the subject. She could be as
insistent as Reid.

Reid: All right.

Temple: Yeapp, alright. Let's go ... high five on that. *They high fived.* I want
    you to have a good career music. What do you sing about your music?

Reid told her about his green song and that being green means
taking care of the earth. She grilled him on how many recordings
he had sold, and he asked what music was on her playlist. She is a
fan of *Phantom of the Opera*. Then she recapped her recent trip to
China and explained the diversification of crops.

Reid: Alright, Temple. What could you stay up all night talking about?

Temple: Well, I can't sleep. I'm usually up, looking up stuff online. When I did my book *The Autistic Brain*, I found the scientific research is backed up by visual thinking and mathematical thinking. I found that at three o'clock in the morning in the reference list of a rather boring paper on visual perception.

Reid: Okay, Temple. We're gonna wrap it up to one more question: What dreams do you have for the future?

Temple: Well, I wanna see a lot of kids that are like me get out and get great careers and great jobs. 'Cuz when I was working in construction, and I worked in construction for twenty years, I'd design a job, supervise its construction, start it up. And when I was out there on those construction sites, there were a lot of people in skilled trades that I know were on the spectrum. They took welding in school and that saved 'em.

She was on a rant, like an angry citizen speaking before city council. You would want her on your side. In fairness, I think this speech was part of her sound bite for the keynote later. Perhaps she was practicing her delivery. Clearly this topic was her hot button, her competitive advantage. She used her passion to be persuasive and an effective advocate for kids like her.

Temple: I think one of the big problems today is the schools are taking out all those things. How are you gonna know you're gonna like music if you never get exposed to an instrument? How are you going know if you like theater if you never get exposed to a school play? That's what saved Patrick Stewart of *Star Trek*. You've got to expose kids to interesting things to get 'em interested.

We were getting a high sign from the wings. Temple didn't notice, but I gave Reid a signal.

Reid: We're gonna have to wrap it up, Temple. It was nice talking to you.
Temple: Okay, nice talking to you. *Okay.* I've got the CD. *Okay.*

I felt torn between respect for the handlers who were hustling us out and for Grandin who needed enough time to transition. But she is all grown up and managed it. Reid proved he was now, too. He handled everything she threw at him.

Whoosh, we did it. Relieved and giddy, we stopped in front of the Grammy Museum to dance to the music they piped over the sidewalk at their entrance. Belting out Taylor Swift's "Shake It Off," we decided to cancel our room for the night and drive home.

The interview with Temple was one podcast Reid asked me not to put online. He did not enjoy it. Temple was ruthless in grilling him with questions. Their control issues collided mid-sentence, and the interview was tricky as it was happening. After Reid listened to the edited version, I convinced him that lots of people would want to hear the podcast, and he eventually agreed.

Temple Grandin has a competitive advantage that could isolate her. Instead, people flock to her to learn. People trust her perspective on a myriad of topics because she has identified what sets her apart, maximized these qualities in her professional life, and channeled them for the good of others like her. She has changed the landscape for her generation and many to come.

> *"Sometimes freedom from normal rules is what gives you competitive advantage."* —Reid Hoffman, founder of LinkedIn[24]

---

24 Harvard Business Review. "Blitzscaling." HBR.org. https://hbr.org/2016/04/blitzscaling (accessed July, 2018).

SPECIALISTERNE FOUNDATION
International
SpecialisterneFoundation.com

Specialisterne Foundation is an international, award-winning social enterprise that sets the "gold standard" for neurodiversity employment. Founded in Denmark in 2014 by Thorkil Sonne, whose young son was diagnosed with ASD, Specialisterne has created one million jobs for people with autism. They have done this through social entrepreneurship, corporate sector engagement, and changing the global mindset. In Danish, Specialisterne means "The Specialists."

Sonne resolved to focus on the abilities of neurodiverse people rather than on "disability." This focus has a familiar ring to it now, but in 2014, it was a new bell. Recognizing that attention to detail, high accuracy, innovative thinking, loyalty, and honesty are the competitive advantages of those with autism was radical.

The staff of Specialisterne hold a vision of a world where people are given equal opportunities in the labor market and work with stakeholders like SAP, Microsoft, and Cisco. Specialisterne is a socially innovative company in which the majority of employees have been diagnosed with autism. They work as business consultants on tasks such as software testing, programming, and data entry for the public and private sectors.

Specialisterne harnesses these special characteristics to secure meaningful employment and now has operations in thirteen countries from Brazil to Singapore. In 2012, Specialisterne USA began the Autism Advantage movement in the highly successful SAP and Microsoft autism employment programs and assist smart business leaders in tapping into the neurodiversity talent pool. Working with Specialisterne USA is one of the best ways companies can benefit from neurodiversity. They are also pioneering online training and credentials to help the supply side keep up with corporate demand, and their goal is to enable one-hundred thousand jobs for neurodiverse people in the United States by 2025.

In Northern Ireland, Specialisterne uses Lego Mindstorms Robots to identify the skills of people on the spectrum and discover their support needs. As small teams build Lego robots, the staff is able to assess task completion and team management skills. Observations are shared with participants and used to match them with the best jobs for them. This assessment and matching helps employees perform at their best in the workplace.

The Dandelion Metaphor in Specialisterne's logo espouses their core values and mission.

> Context is key. Many of us view the dandelion as a weed—something to be rooted out of our lawns and flowerbeds. What a lot of people don't realize is that, when cultivated, the dandelion is one of the most valuable and useful plants in nature—known for its nutritional, healing, and medicinal properties. The value of a dandelion is very much dependent on our knowledge and perception of its value.
>
> A dandelion is only a weed in an environment where it is not welcomed. If the dandelion is in an environment where it is valued and nurtured, it turns into an herb. People with autism often struggle to feel welcome in the labor market. Specialisterne strives to create an environment where each individual can thrive and provides support both for the individual and the employer to maintain this comfort zone.[25]

---

25 Specialisterne. "The Dandelion Metaphor." Ca.Specialisterne.com http://ca.specialisterne.com/about-specialisterne/our-logo-the-dandelion-seed/ (accessed June, 2018).

I've mentioned that we moved every October for three years. Each time was for a job offer that was too good to refuse. Jim has had several of these over his career. Allie and Reid were two and just stringing words together when he got the first irresistible offer. They said "jump," and he asked "how high?" Before I could pack up the trikes, we were off to Chicago for a year. And then the next October, it was San Francisco.

Such is life in the fast lane with corporate entities like SAP and Intel. In that first move to Chicago, Jim headed up marketing for Pandesic, a strategic joint venture between these two companies. That's how I learned a bit about how the German software leader

How Can My Business Benefit by Including Employees with Autism?

1. Call your local school district or regional center to learn about their programs for young adults with different abilities.
2. Offer your site as a place for people on the spectrum to learn certain tasks such as shredding, filing, dusting, or making copies.
3. Employ people with differences part-time, even one hour a week, to enable them and you to gain experience.
4. Encourage your employees to mentor individuals with challenges.
5. Purchase and display artwork by local artists with autism.
6. Host an inclusive special event showcasing your trade to adults in special education.
7. Give a workshop on autism to your employees.
8. Provide Strengthsfinder (gallupstrengthscenter.com) training to help your employees learn and appreciate their competitive advantage.

SAP works. They're innovative, efficient, and move quickly. They embrace change. It's no surprise that they are leading the way in creating job opportunities for adults with autism based on their competitive advantage rather than as a sympathetic act of charity. Doing so makes good sense for the bottom line.

Are you a business owner, or do you work for a corporation? Do you have an inclusive workplace that reflects the diversity of our culture in terms of gender and race as well as ability? How can you or your company capitalize on the competitive advantage that adults with autism offer?

NATIONAL VELVET[26]

Allie went through a definite horsey stage as a girl. We read all the Marguerite Henry books, visited Chincoteague Island, and half-leased a dapple gray horse named Marshmallow until Jim saw the first vet bill. *National Velvet* was Allie's favorite movie of all time until *The Count of Monte Cristo* replaced it. She has good taste; *National Velvet* was preserved in the National Film Registry of the Library of Congress in 2013 for being culturally, historically, or aesthetically significant.

One of the highest compliments I have received was when Jim and Allie said I reminded them of the mom, Mrs. Brown, in the movie. Stoic and wise like Yoda, she delivers sage advice that stops the rest of the family in their tracks, especially the fretful, pessimistic father. Mrs. Brown sits knitting or darning socks while they spiral around in a tizzy, then levels them all with a one-liner that convicts, corrects, and lays down a summary statement with loving kindness.

A young girl named Velvet Brown (Elizabeth Taylor) wants a horse badly. Against all odds, she wins a wild chestnut horse named The Pie (short for Pirate) in a town lottery. Riding The Pie across oceanside cliffs, Velvet dreams of entering the Grand National horse race. But to her father, this seems ridiculous, far-fetched, and expensive.

It seems Velvet has inherited her mother's ambitious, competitive streak. They understand each other, which enables Mrs. Brown to recognize and support Velvet's goals, however lofty. In fact, Mrs. Brown seems to have been waiting for this moment to come.

Before bed one evening, Mrs. Brown pulls some gold sovereigns out of a treasured box. They are her prize money from swimming

---

26 *National Velvet*. Directed by Clarence Brown. Culver City: Metro Goldwyn Mayer, 1944.

the English Channel when she was twenty, and she offers them to Velvet as the entry money she needs. Not one to rest on her laurels, Mrs. Brown warns Velvet that character matters more than winning or losing. Always thinking on a higher plane, Mrs. Brown also counsels Velvet that there is a time for everything under the sun.

The last question on Velvet's mind is, "Who will tell father?" Mr. Brown does not appreciate the importance of folly, as they call it. So Mrs. Brown will "do the telling." She is aware that the ability to take risks is a gift that not everyone understands naturally or embraces easily.

Whether Mrs. Brown means folly as funny and laughter or ambition against all odds — I admire her. We need more of both in the world. The younger the child, the more likely they seem to take risks naturally. All of twelve years old, Velvet trains extensively with Mi (Mickey Rooney). Her competitive advantages are determination and riding skill.

The actresses Elizabeth Taylor and Angela Lansbury, who plays Velvet's older sister, are compelling to watch. They are both vested in these breakout roles that prepared them for lifetimes before the camera. *National Velvet* makes an exhilarating pairing with *Seabiscuit* (detailed in Chapter 9) if you're up for a horse-movie marathon weekend.

WRAPPING UP CHAPTER 4

Successful businesses know their competitive advantage and what sets them apart from their competitors. They communicate both in their marketing. As individuals, we also have strengths and passions that make us unique. And when we find a niche for using our competitive advantage, we find the most satisfaction.

Embracing our competitive advantage can feel risky because doing so can go against the ideas and expectations of others. Also, educational systems set up conformity and standardization as markers of success. When we become adults, we are freer to take the opportunities to do what we do best and let go of unfair expectations. But what might happen if we gave children in their formative years opportunities to embrace their competitive advantage? If they discovered their "genius zone" and pursued it fully, they might change the course of history. Historical figures like Albert Einstein and Thomas Edison are cases that support this point. As quirky and narrow as their competitive advantages may have been, they owned them and excelled in ways that made history.

Temple Grandin is a woman who has changed history for generations of women inventors as well as individuals with autism. Her accomplishments are unequaled. She took uncomfortable risks to get her education and be heard in a male-dominated industry. But she allowed nothing to deter her. As she embraced the traits that set her apart, she changed a major industry and became the most articulate advocate for kids like her.

Building on the foundation Temple Grandin poured, Specialisterne harnesses the competitive advantages that people with autism offer in the workplace. As a liaison between talented individuals and large corporations, they are redefining environments where neurodiverse employees can be productive and thrive. As with a dandelion, being valued and nurtured turns a weed into a valuable herb.

I admire young Velvet Brown and her mother in *National Velvet*. They hope and train against all odds, embracing a challenge because it builds character. Young Velvet has an intuition about horses and riding skill, and she has unbounded determination. Her moxie and spunk are a competitive advantage that her mother recognizes and nurtures. What if we did the same for more young people in our culture? What might they achieve if we let them be different from the norm?

HUMILITY

My arc as a parent has been from a self-conscious control freak breaking a sweat to look good to one who leaves the house without mascara most days and can't be bothered with what people think. Jim and I both credit the experience of parenting Reid through adolescence with breaking our supersized pride. Before that, we thought we knew everything and could do anything. Now we know God is in charge and we are learning all the time. This is a gift that has come from disability even if it was wrapped in recycled tissue.

In a sense Reid has no pride, if walking to the mailbox in the buff is any indication. We have had to teach him self-consciousness (or self-awareness as the jargon goes), which is surely an offshoot of pride. I think humility is the opposite of pride, and one way to define humility is the ability to laugh at yourself.

Humility elevates others. I've watched our podcast guests respond to Reid with no ego. I've watched them enter the room tentatively, scanning for clues, slightly nervous about how it will go. They quickly detect that we are not seeking perfection and the podcast isn't about them. Reid's brazen innocence sets them at ease. Before you know it, they are sharing with Reid what they wouldn't dare tell a typical reporter. They confide stories from childhood they have never shared. If they misunderstand a question or Reid mispronounces a word, they are free to laugh. Laughter is evidence that pride has been dispelled. If we can laugh at ourselves after a fall or flub up, we are truly rid of the self-seeking pride that says, "I need to look important."

When was the last time you laughed at yourself?

Jim and I traveled a lot before we had children. It gave us something to do while we couldn't get pregnant for eight years. We took an idyllic ski trip to Zermatt, Switzerland—long before we watched *Third Man on the Mountain*. Nothing charms like old men pulling sleighs carrying children and silver milk jugs home at dusk through a car-free alpine village. Pedestrians stop in the falling snow to gaze upon a game of curling before commencing up the mountain trails. Night after night we crashed, exhausted from exertion, the freshest alpine air, and consumption of raclette, the fondue-like cheese specialty.

Zermatt boasts a challenging ski area under the looming shadow of the Matterhorn. The highest ski area in Europe, it is interconnected across a glacier paradise to the top of another ski area in Cervinia, Italy. Remember, we are an explorer married to a risk taker, so of course, we wanted to experience this mountain pass and ski in two countries on the same day.

The first day we ventured up to the crossing, it was closed due to high winds. No biggie; the next day it was open. We set off from the top of the highest lift, and followed a group of five Italian men who obviously knew the way. They were friendly enough, but they weren't exactly waiting for us on the cross-country traverse. *Why are they in such a hurry,* we wondered? Gradually, the wind picked up and the visibility dropped to the ski pole in front of your face. These men became vital as our unofficial guides. We couldn't see a thing, and my morning coffee was catching up with me. Ever strategizing, Jim said, "I'll keep up with them, so we don't lose sight of the trail. Just make sure you can see me."

In a matter of minutes, this jaunt through a winter wonderland became a harrowing, life or death adventure. Thank God, one of the five Italians had on a highlighter lime cap; it was all we could see in the whiteout conditions. Jim followed that fluorescent cap, and I hustled my buns as fast as I could to keep up with him. Of course, he was calling back to me too, which is more than we could say of the Italians.

After an hour, the elevation dropped, and we came in sight of what we could only assume was the town of Cervinia, Italy. Turns out, Italy at that altitude looks a lot like Switzerland. I relaxed my white knuckles and thigh muscles. We weren't going to die. We stopped to take a deep breath, and I realized I could not wait for another second to go to the bathroom. I told Jim, "I'm not going to make it into that town. I've gotta go now."

"Are you sure?"

"Yes. I really don't want to wet my ski pants."

"You can't wait?"

"I've been holding it since Switzerland."

"Okay, just follow that chairlift straight down. I'll meet you at the bottom of it."

He floated out of sight down a powdery and steep ungroomed slope. I skied on to find some modicum of privacy in the snowy wilderness. Like the proverbial bear in the woods, I squatted in a snow bank mooning the Matterhorn. What a relief. Now I was ready for a beer and some orecchiette. I swished down the rest of the groomed hill and waited by the lift. *Where was Jim?* I waited and waited, shuffling over to another lift in case I had overshot the target. No Jim.

I had no lira, no wallet, and little reserve after the grueling crossing. The rest is a blur like a black-and-white Fellini film with no subtitles. At least I didn't have to go to the bathroom. I was so excited when I spotted the orange lapel trim of Jim's Marmot ski coat in the distance. On foot, lugging his skis and poles over weary shoulders, he was a welcome sight after another hour of being separated. We lumbered into the first half-timbered chalet restaurant that was open. It was full of Italians at the end of their lunch break having chilled mugs of birra all around. Bleary-eyed, we clomped up some stairs in our heavy ski boots. As I dragged myself toward an empty booth, I skid across the slushy floor. In slow motion, I went down with a THUD! landing spread eagle on my rump in front of the foreign revelers.

The whole restaurant roared in unison, "YETI!!!"

What? Are they talking to me? What'd they call me? I scrambled for composure, crawling over to a chair to hoist myself onto. Yeti was a new word in any language. I learned the next morning, over muesli with our Swiss hotelier, that it means abominable snowman. It's an insult like yelling "BIGFOOT!" at a woman in size eleven ski boots. Now YETI is a retailer selling durable coolers for outdoor adventurers and using the tagline "Built for the Wild." But the original word is from a Tibetan legend. And in Italy that day, it was not a compliment.

At twenty-six, I was offended and looked around nervously for a delete key to erase what had just happened. I cared what other people thought of me, even if they didn't speak my language or live next door. For me, being embarrassed is connected to learning humility. It had to happen enough times to break down my pride and convince me that life isn't really about me.

Buckling at the knees from humiliation changed my baseline from pride to humility. Now I've let go of my self-consciousness to embrace a common humanity with others. Imperfect is my new perfect.

LEARNING HUMILITY THROUGH PARENTING

Numerous embarrassing moments with Reid have mashed down my pride. Humility has developed in me like the protective calluses that form on the fingers of a seasoned guitarist. Slowly and consistently, experience has trained me to care more about his welfare than how I look.

Being a mom is about self-sacrifice. Some moms begin the journey to humility at childbirth. Recounting the birth of her firstborn, a close friend told me, "They could've rolled me out in the hallway. You just don't care after a certain point." The pain and the urgency of delivering displace self-consciousness. Moving on to with sleepless nights and spit up, mothers are forced to embrace humility as part of the job description, and exponentially when special needs are involved.

For me growth in humility didn't start with childbirth, but it developed exponentially through hundreds of other moments—funny smirks, stink eyes, sideways glares, and bite marks. The realization that a child needs more of you than you have to give makes you wonder, *Am I even capable of this?* and relegates pride to the back burner. So does facing the reality that you are part of something greater than yourself and need to live for someone else's growth and development.

When I say embarrassing moments, I see Reid in his birthday suit at nine years old running down Genesee Avenue a block from the La Jolla Jewish Community Center pool. I remember a police car swerving diagonally to cross the intersection to intercept him. I was booking it on foot with a towel from our swim bag, having let go of Allie's hand and telling her to wait on the grass. I wasn't laughing then, but this is an example of the frequent events that each chipped away at my pride. Fear also has a tendency to drive out pride.

Having been humbled like this multiple times, I've become unflappable as well as empathetic. The benefit of hindsight is that I am determined not to give shame a foothold. Surviving enough tenuous moments yields humility. Like the rabbit in *The Velveteen*

Rabbit who became "real" by having all his fur rubbed off, I've *become* humble. It has happened gradually as my need to look like I had things under control was ground to a pulp and died a slow death. I'm left with enough humility to laugh at myself, which is actually a good thing. Maybe the best thing.

SPOTTING HUMILITY ON *TALK TIME*

Along the way of our *Talk Time* journey, I have noticed four benefits of humility that both Reid and his willing guests exhibit. The first benefit is surprising. Our vulnerability wins people over. Reid needs help with many things. He doesn't always want it, but it's part of his life to receive it. He needs help washing his hair, remembering to put on clothes, and cutting his meat. These needs have trained him—and me—in vulnerability. Needing help has developed a childlike humility in Reid that makes him likable and joyful.

The same can be true for us. By acknowledging our inner child and needs, we allow for laughter and growth. I believe we all can find childlike joy, humor, and curiosity. Acknowledging that we are beginners rather than experts keeps our brain nimble, curious, and eager to take on new information. We can better absorb something new and enjoy it if we are in a playful posture.

The second benefit I have seen through the podcast journey is that laughing improves our quality of life. Especially laughing at ourselves, which is proof positive of being humble. Removing our masks and being vulnerable makes us more likable and leads to deeper relationships. Let's face it, who likes a know it all? Pride and ego damage relationships. We are much more attractive when we are interested in others and accept help from them. Humble people laugh easily and often with others, at themselves, and at circumstances. As the characters Mike and Sully discovered in the movie *Monsters Inc.*, "Laughter has ten times the energy of scream."

The third benefit I have seen through the podcast journey is that humility is a function of life experience. As our world has expanded, our pride has shrunk. Traveling to new places, meeting different people, and plugging into something bigger than ourselves reveals how small we are as individuals. The older we get, the less pride we have left. After working, parenting, and seeing more of the world, our hubris has been whittled away and revealed as just baggage. We often see this life-grown humility when we interact with older adults who are wise but not pushy, gracious not demanding, and attentive rather than distracted. They have amassed both years and humility.

Lastly, putting others first is heroic. Classic heroes like George Washington, who risked his life and fortune in the Revolution and refused to be crowned king, or Harriet Tubman who risked her life to save escaped slaves through the underground railroad inspire even more than fictional superheroes. The superpower of real, modern heroes is their willingness to step into harm's way and even sacrifice themselves for others. They choose to make themselves vulnerable in dangerous situations to benefit others. But after they save the day, they may be elusive, disappearing before they even get credit. In the end, we revere humility because it is radical and countercultural. It goes against the grain of our self-seeking human nature.

> *"When we quit thinking primarily about ourselves and our own self-preservation, we undergo a truly heroic transformation of consciousness."*
> —Joseph Campbell, American professor[27]

---

27 Campbell, Joseph. *The Power of Myth*. Anchor, 1991.

5

Win People Over with Vulnerability

I felt vulnerable as we arrived at the Del Mar Fairgrounds—only two miles from our house—to interview pop star Andy Grammer. It was the summer heyday of his "Honey, I'm Good" hit. Andy's feel-good single "Keep Your Head Up" was playing on every radio station across the nation. Taylor Swift even invited him to do it as a duet on her tour. Andy was one of the big-name acts in the concert series at the San Diego County Fair.

Ordinarily, Reid doesn't care for the fair. It's too loud and crowded, and although he performed there once in the sticky Kids Zone, he didn't want to return. The entertainer's entrance requires passing through an arcade tunnel and the Scream Zone of rickety rides where they have a scream track piped over the hundreds of actual screaming teens. We were not fans. But for an interview with Andy Grammer, Reid would brave the fair.

IN THE TRAILER WITH A POP STAR: ANDY GRAMMER

Grammer's "people" had said "yes" to the unlikely conversation, so I packed up my iPhone with iTalk app and camera included because we were intentionally keeping this simple.

I enlisted help from one of Allie's childhood friends, Amber, who was studying speech pathology and was home for the summer.

She knew Reid and was willing to help me out. In fact, Amber and her family had a history of participating in our hair-brain ideas, from owling at midnight as part of our kindergarten homeschooling curriculum to dressing in red-carpet Grammy attire for a movie night. Amber had been to all of the kids' themed birthday parties—ballet, bats, cats, Mary Poppins. Jim couldn't be there, and I anticipated needing an extra pair of hands, or rather legs if Reid got lost among the many hawkers, food vendors, and exhibits. I hadn't been to the fair once without losing him. Amber said sure, she'd go to the fair with us to meet Andy Grammer!

I stepped up to the ticket booth marked "Press" and announced ourselves.

"We have an interview with Andy Grammer." The attendant looked at me with slight surprise and after talking to another agent behind her, made a few calls. Entry was not immediate.

"How many in your crew?"

"Uh, three," I looked over my shoulder. Reid was still with us.

"Do you have any equipment?" *Was she taunting me now?* I wondered.

"No, well, it's just audio. All right here," I patted my cross-body Baggalini pouch.

"Okay, go through this first gate."

The three of us—Reid, Amber, and me—donned press lanyards and set out through the throngs of fairgoers and funnel-cake eaters toward the infield. I had to laugh, "Oh, Amber, if they only knew." We were a humble troupe, not your ordinary press corps. I felt like an imposter until I saw the blogger ahead of us in the "meet and greet" line. She was all of twelve. We got this!

We were vulnerable, but who isn't? Humility follows taking a risk because when you're doing something new, it's natural (even accurate) to feel exposed and inexperienced. I was learning how to make a podcast by doing it. I did a lot of self-talk. *We're all human. You have to start somewhere.* Even the old standby came out. I thought if the interview totally flopped, *I'll never see these people again.*

Reid was all business. He flips on a "professional" switch when he steps into his role as a podcast host. This is common for people with ASD when they engage in preferred activities and is just another of the many reasons we do it. With exaggerated posture, he race-walked like a policeman in pursuit. Reid was on task, motivated, and in his element, as if impersonating Ryan Seacrest or one of the many emcees that capture Reid's attention. Amber and I jogged to keep up. After asking a few security guards and texting the manager, we found the right ramp down to the infield where the star's trailer was parked. We waited in plastic patio chairs for a teenage blogger to exit. Then it was our turn.

Reid snuggled in beside Andy Grammer on a sofa in the makeshift greenroom. Andy was not yet thirty. Fit and trim, he looked as buoyant as his songs sound. I had read about his new wife, and how much he missed his mom who died of cancer. Amber and I sat in the three-room trailer at a table covered with munchies. We could hear bandmates fraternizing behind a closed door.

When Reid and Allie were toddlers, we listened to cassettes by Ella Jenkins; Peter, Paul and Mommy (Peter, Paul and Mary's first children's album); and Red Grammer. Full of good virtue and the catchiest tunes, Grammer's *Teaching Peace* and *Hello, World* were two of our favorites. When researching the questions for this interview, I realized that Red Grammer is in fact Andy Grammer's dad. What a full-circle moment.

Our equipment intrigued Grammer. After clarifying that it was just "mom's phone," Reid launched into the first question.

Reid: So, what's the weirdest venue you've ever played, Andy?

Andy: The weirdest?

Reid: Yes.

Andy: Hmmm. I did—for a radio station—they were giving away toys, so I played in the produce aisle of Walmart ... in Kentucky or something.

Weird was the operative word, still Andy was not too proud to reference his humble hard work playing wherever he could. This was a musician who got his start busking on street corners.

Reid: In Kentucky? Okaay! How many songs have you written?

Andy: That is a great question. I don't even know the answer to that ... I would say ... somewhere ... like ever? I would say four hundred, five hundred something like that.

Reid: Okaay. How did you get started writing a new song?

Andy: Uh, you just kinda start swinging in the dark, throwing out chords and ideas, and singing something 'til something sounds good.

Reid: That is amazing.

Rather than spouting off fancy theory or pedagogy, Andy made songwriting approachable. You just do it. I appreciated his modest simplicity. It meant Reid could enter in.

Reid: Hey, do you have any songwriting tips for me on writing catchy hooks?

Andy: *He pondered this one with a hum.* Simple is always the best. But simple is really hard, so you gotta try hard, and you have to try a bunch of different options. To get something simple, that hasn't been done before, is difficult.

Reid: It is difficult. *Reid knew difficult. He did all his songwriting with assistance.* What do you look for in bandmates?

Andy: I look for great musicians that are also a really good hang 'cuz they're kinda like your roommates. They should be your best friends, hopefully, as you travel around the whole country.

Reid told Andy all about his bandmates from The Kingsmen and Jungle Poppins. They talked about the multiple instruments Grammer plays—trumpet, piano, and guitar. Near the end of the questions on his printout, Reid went off the board creating his own question.

Reid: So, I'm gonna make up a question just for you, Andy. Did you write *(long pause)* a new song? Did you write a new song … for me?

I wondered if he was doing this because he couldn't read my writing.

Andy: For you? Uh. Not yet, but I could.

What gracious ad-libbing on both their parts. They were winning each other over by virtue of the awkward vulnerability. Connecting through the uncoordinated parts of the conversation. This only happens one on one.

Reid: Hey, did you do, "Honey, I'm Good?
Andy: I did write that one.
Reid: Hey, I listen to it on the radio, in my mom's car.
Andy: That's perfect.

Andy grinned ear to ear at the thought of being on the airwaves. After a few more questions about hip-hop and the beat that runs, Reid brought it to a close.

Reid: Is there anything you'd like to ask me, Andy?

His invitation to reciprocity sometimes catches guests by surprise. They aren't prepared to learn from him.

Andy: Yeah. Uh, let me get something good. 'Cuz I've got a lot of questions for you. You are a fascinating individual.

I burst out in nervous laughter thinking his first question might be for the publicist who booked this. I don't think celebrities get briefed on the details I provide in the request. Although I tell them Reid has autism in the first line of the email, that detail doesn't always trickle down through the managers and handlers.

Andy: What makes you the most happy?
Reid: What makes me most happy is seeing you on stage!
Andy: You stop it! Is that real?!
Reid: Yeah, it is real.
Andy: Alright.
Reid: High five!
Andy: BOOM! High five it!
Reid: It was nice talking to you. That's the interview with Andy Grammer. Cut!
Andy: Thank you so much. Great job, man! That was amazing. Wow, you just made my day!

Andy Grammer hasn't forgotten what it's like to stand in the cold and play your heart out before passersby who won't give you a nickel. That suffering might even be the root of his humility. His vulnerability makes him likable to Reid, to me, and to the thousands on the airwaves who love his heartening lyrics: "You gotta keep your head up, Oh, oh! So you can let your hair down, hey, eh!" I love that song.

Reid has a humility all his own. Without the self-consciousness that is human nature to most of us, his expressions have the innocence and purity of a child's. He isn't embarrassed when he passes gas. He picks his nose without shame. He has what some call "social blindness." The beauty of it is that when he gives a compliment, it is one hundred percent honest. He doesn't lie to be polite. He gives genuine praise. Andy was most important to Reid at that point, and he was free to tell him so.

Reid is vulnerable to a lot of things in life, from ridicule to abuse. But as tough as we pretend to be, we all have weaknesses. When we admit these and let them show, we bond with others through a common denominator. Admitting vulnerability can even be endearing. I bet you could sidle up to swap stories of embarrassing moments. Instead of trying to impress your neighbor or date this weekend, experiment with being forthright. My prediction is that your humility and vulnerability will win them over.

"Humility is not thinking less of yourself but thinking of yourself less." —Rick Warren[28]

---

28   Warren, Rick. *The Purpose Driven Life: What on Earth Am I Here For?* Zondervan, 2002.

MIRACLE LEAGUE BASEBALL
Rockland, Georgia
MiracleLeague.com

Humility is on mega-watt display at a Miracle League baseball game. We happily spend our Saturdays at a fully accessible baseball diamond that is within walking distance from our house. In between the fall and spring seasons, we lament the loss and spend Saturdays missing it terribly. Jim wrote the last chapter of *One-Track Mind* titled, "It's Not about Me" and explains how Miracle League Saturday crystallized his transition from a self-centered to a servant father.[29] Let me tell you how the league was born.

In 1998 in Rockdale, Georgia, coach Eddie Bagwell invited a seven-year-old child in a wheelchair to play baseball on his team. Michael had attended every game to cheer on his younger brother but hadn't been able to play himself. Then more children with disabilities were invited until a new league began that had thirty-five players on four teams the first year.

Now Miracle League is in more than three hundred cities around the country serving more than 200,000 individuals with disabilities. I am sure each location has its own flavor, but the guiding principle remains the same—everyone gets to play. This inclusive league ensures that players with cognitive and physical disabilities can enjoy the great American pastime. Every player gets a buddy. These volunteers bat, run, and sit in the dugout with their player. Every game is two innings. Short and simple and without the strain of a practice schedule. Every player gets a hit. Every game is a tie. Everyone plays. Everyone is a winner.

---

29 Moriarty, Andrea. *One-Track Mind: 15 Ways to Amplify Your Child's Special Interest.* JAM Ink., 2015.

In our town, an exceptional man named Dan Engel was looking to leave a legacy and to divert his attention from melanoma treatments to something positive. So he started the Miracle League of San Diego. We now have two fields running a dozen games each Saturday. It brings tears to your eyes to see these families gathering. Otherwise marginalized during the week, our subculture is suddenly not a minority but the majority as we infiltrate San Dieguito County Park. All manner of wheelchairs roll up the paved trails, and service dogs abound, taking their spot in the dugout or stands.

A notable subtext is the reprieve parents feel in having a care-free hour in the stands where they can simply cheer for their child. They sit laughing and chatting, celebrating each other's kids, and tapping a knee in the midst of rapid-fire conversation and saying, "Wait, Billy is up to bat." Miraculously, the clear expectations and structure of this activity ensure success. The volunteer coaches and buddies keep it all copacetic. Rarely have I witnessed any melt-downs or issues. It's like the one-hour experience is suspended as a gift to just pluck and savor like ripe fruit from a tree.

The buddies capture my attention by their displays of humility. Many of them are high school students from nearby public and private schools. The local chapter of the National Charity League has adopted Miracle League and sends mother-daughter members to complete their community service hours. Siblings sign up to be buddies, and college kids return on breaks to reunite with their players. Heartwarming just doesn't do it justice. It is a family that revels in its diversity.

Buddies invest attention in their players. Many of them have their own passions either for sports or academics. They may start being a buddy for the community service credit. But once they are there, they shift their focus from themselves to another person in an intense, concentrated effort of humility. Choosing to be a friend is an unselfish act. These buddies create the miracle that empowers the players to believe they matter, and they make playing the games possible for many players.

For years Allie's best friend, Haley, was Reid's buddy. When Haley left for college, her younger sister, Molly, took over. Reid was pushing twenty years old—and was older than Molly—by the time she was his buddy. He was fully able to bat and run independently, so she was more of a social companion than a physical assistant. Neither Molly nor Reid cared much for fielding balls in the traditional sense. They loved the outfield though. They stood under the scoreboard making up cheers and dance moves.

Reid preferred being up to bat. Molly stood a few paces behind him to the side. Local radio announcer Ernie Martinez would commentate:

> *There's Reider Speeder with his chopper-style hit right down the center of the field ... He's off to first base. Doesn't look like they'll be able to stop him ... Wait, he's going all the way .... It'll be another home run for Reider Speeder.*

Molly would jog halfheartedly behind him and back to the dugout for high fives and shenanigans. One week something dawned on Reid. Standing side by side at home plate, he turned and whispered discretely in Molly's ear, "Molly, don't run with me. Wait here. I'll be right back."

"No problem, Reid." Molly, a beautiful young lady with a long curly mane like Rapunzel, was only too happy not to break a sweat. Reid's confidence became chivalry of a sort.

In her junior year of high school, Molly began writing college

How Can My School Be More Inclusive?

Your school parent teacher association can host an Ability Awareness Week where students can learn more about living with a disability. Invite guest speakers to show and tell about their service dog, prosthetic leg, or facilitated communication board. Children should be encouraged to ask questions and experience how we are all the same and different. For example at activity centers, students might wear a blindfold or gloves, walk with a cane, or type on a Braille reader to simulate sensory differences. Teachers can challenge a wheelchair basketball team to a game. Diana Pastora Carson's site AbilityAwareness.com offers many more suggestions.

entrance essays, and you guessed it, she wrote about the best part of her week. "Saturday mornings are the one day I love waking up early and going to be a Miracle League buddy." People of all ages can find purpose through humility. Learning there's more to life than ourselves broadens our horizons, lifts our spirits, and opens us up to develop new skills. Humility also pays dividends in joy.

Through Miracle League, a whole community has formed. Buddies stay in touch, and parents write recommendations. Sadly players die and tributes are given. Our kids don't just have mom and dad as their champions. They have a whole village looking out for them, creating opportunities, and opening doors. Announcer Ernie Martinez opened a door for Reid to visit him at his radio station, and to interview him one Saturday before game time. Their conversation is a home run worth checking out online.[30]

Having attended these Miracle League games when she visits, my mom often calls on a Saturday morning and asks, "Did you

30 Talk Time with Reid Moriarty. Podcast with Ernie Martinez. Reidmoriarty.com. https://www.reidmoriarty.com/podcast (accessed August, 2018).

have 'Magic Baseball' today?" Her Freudian slip is pretty accurate. We seem to live in a magical land between the Miracle League and the Miracle Project, don't we? Not a bad place at all. In fact, San Diego Miracle League founder Dan Engel calls the field he built the "happiest place on earth."

AS IT IS IN HEAVEN[31]

Unaffected, unselfconscious people who become vulnerable on stage are compelling to watch. Kate was a single friend who sang in the choir at our Presbyterian church. The director put her front and center for obvious reasons. She sang in a full voice with exaggerated facial gestures and dramatic flair that rippled through the other robed singers and took worship to a new emotional level for the congregation. The choir at that time was more like a society; they lingered over a potluck brunch each Sunday and had their own newsletter, social events, and mission trips. Kate was the one who told me to watch *As It Is in Heaven*. "Everyone in choir is recommending it," she said, "There's a character that reminds me of Reid. You'll love it." She was right.

A Swedish film nominated for Best Foreign Film at the 2005 Academy Awards, *As It Is in Heaven* is about an internationally renowned conductor named Daniel who returns to live in his childhood home. A small town choir invites him to help improve their rag-tag group of characters including the pastor's wife, an enterprising shopkeeper, and a battered wife. Good 'ol pride, church politics, and traumatic memories stand in his way. Director Kay Pollack wrote, "I gradually realized what a metaphor for humanity a choir is. I did not know then that this is the largest cultural movement in Sweden—close to 700,000 people take part in choir practice every week."[32]

What touched me about the choir in the movie is their inclusion of a young man with cognitive challenges. Tore is the nephew of the most ambitious choir booster. As curious as everyone is about Daniel, Tore notices everything that is happening with the new

---

31 *As It Is in Heaven.* Directed by Kay Pollak. New York: Lorber Films. 2004.

32 Michael Nyqvist Archives. "As It is in Heaven." Michael-Nyqvist.com. http://www.michael-nyqvist.com/heaven.html (accessed May, 2018).

conductor. His unorthodox methods include shouting, throwing air punches, and gyrating their hips. Tore giggles watching the choristers lay on the floor in a circle that turns into a dog pile to find their tone and tune into each other's breathing.

As the choir members dance in a circle stomping in time in the center, then out with a clap, Tore passes by the door grinning. It looks fun. He takes off his coat and stomps more like a marionette into the center of the circle grunting loudly. His behavior communicates clearly; he wants to join them. His uncle shoos him away, and another woman patronizes him by offering cookies to keep him busy. They don't want Tore to reveal their flaws and ruin their plans to compete in the big city. Ambition stands in the way of their relationships; illusions of grandeur cloud their vision. But others in the group include Tore. Sounding his tone immediately, he becomes the baritone they needed.

Inclusion can be messy, but it is worth it. Confused by their bickering, Tore wets his pants. In a beautifully awkward scene, Lena, a beautiful young blonde, cleans Tore up, which is humbling for Tore and the viewer. While some might watch the scene with pity, my own life experiences bring it close to home. It brings tears to my eyes that someone who is not Tore's mom finds within herself the tenderness and respect to help Tore. Without words, she convinces him of her helpful intentions and stands in the gap between what he needs and what he can do for himself. She suspends a number of emotions that would be understandable—ridicule, being grossed out, avoidance, vulnerability, temptation to mistreat—to serve him. He trusts her. She humbles herself to dignify him.

Almost done, Tore stands wearing just a shirt. In garbled inarticulate speech, he asks Lena to say those three words. She looks right in his eyes, nose to nose as if they're siblings. He wants to hear "I love you," perhaps recalling his mom in this role. They rub foreheads in a gleeful, platonic, significant moment.

My mom used to say, "But for the grace of God, there go I," when she saw someone struggling. She meant that any one of us could be homeless, battered, hungry, or depressed. Her expression was a reminder to treat our neighbor as we would like them to treat us. Jean Vanier, the French philosopher who founded L'Arche, writes about how living with disabled people put him in touch with his own humanity. Our humanity is visceral and involves some bodily fluids that make all this risk, humility, and kindness more tangible. To need help with daily living skills develops the ultimate trusting relationships.

I remember my Nana who aged so gracefully and reached 101 years old. I visited a few times in her last years. She needed help clasping bracelets and pulling up socks, as well as many other things I can only imagine. Once, she asked me to put her socks on for her. Why wait for the usual nurse who did it, since I was right there?

I loved her dearly and had grown up spending time with her. As a girl, I would sit on her lap begging her to tickle my arm. Still, it was awkward to be that intimate and exposed, for me and maybe more so for her. But she had amassed a lot of experience being vulnerable by needing assistance for more than ten years. It's amazingly difficult to "scooch" socks up on someone else's leg. But I could bend over and move my fingers, which she could not. She modeled humility as she served others throughout her life and then had to be served. Both build character in ways that nothing else can.

At the end of the *As It Is in Heaven* when the country choir arrives at a choral competition in Austria, Daniel greets a familiar older maestro who asks whether he has accomplished all that he dreamed of. Daniel has an epiphany right then and answers

"Yes." The simple, mixed-up bunch loves him, and he loves them, which is what happens when we each find our individual tone and harmonize.

WRAPPING UP CHAPTER 5

We are all vulnerable. Some of us are just better at hiding it than others. Whether we are swinging in the dark writing lyrics to a song that doesn't exist or making a podcast with a crew that doesn't exist, we need to start somewhere. Like taking risks, we avoid exposing vulnerability for fear of looking weak. But the reality is that when we let our awkwardness and weakness show, we win people over because doing so reveals what we have in common—our humanity.

I see this winning over often in Reid's interactions with others. His childlike innocence is endearing. A store clerk grins when Reid sits down cross-legged to browse a DVD rack or to eat a bag of Kettle chips in the snack aisle. Total strangers identify with Reid's lack of pretense and comment, "I wish I could do that," or "Boy, that looks comfortable. I'd like to join him." His lack of pride is an invitation.

Pop star Andy Grammer started as a humble busker; now he can't be out in public without being mobbed. The reasons for our vulnerability change, but it unites us as human beings. He and Reid made each other's day in different ways.

In an inclusive reality like Miracle League baseball where cognitive and physical needs are the norm, everyone lets their guard down and makes cooperation the new standard. It takes courage to let our ideals of perfection go floating down the river. But when we do, the relief is beautiful.

Whether you're on a team or in a choir, like the one in *As It Is in Heaven*, there is probably someone near you who is more vulnerable than you. Have they won you over already with their courage?

Could you be a buddy and run alongside them? Or wait until they round the bases and cheer for their success? Is there someone you could include who is watching and waiting to belong? Some people become helpers by necessity. Others do so by choice. However it happens, it is a sight to see, and people can't help but notice because it shows the world a miraculous other way.

"Need is the most beautiful compact between humans." —Brené Brown, author[33]

---

33 Brené Brown. "Everyone Has a Story." BrenéBrown.com. https://brenebrown.com/blog/2018/06/07/everyone-has-a-story/ (accessed July, 2018).

6

Laughing Improves Your Quality of Life

When I was a young teen, my brother and I were goofing around in the kitchen. He had a firm hold of my ankle and was pulling my foot above his waist. I had to hop across the linoleum floor to keep up with his tugging so I didn't tip over. Don't try this at home. It wasn't safe, but we found it hilariously funny. My mom stopped us with an odd rationale, "That's how people go crazy." I think we laughed more at her preposterous claim than at the gymnastic stunt. Scientific evidence actually reveals the opposite. Silliness is an effective coping strategy. I know; it's the reason I watch *The Late Show with Stephen Colbert*.

Laughing is good for our health according to both the Mayo Clinic and the Bible. Proverbs 17:22 says, "A cheerful heart is good medicine" (NIV). An old Yiddish proverb says, "What soap is to the body, laughter is to the soul." Whether you're chortling at an old episode of *Seinfeld* or giggling at a *Peanuts'* cartoon, laughter relieves stress, releases endorphins, and stimulates many organs. In the short term, laughter soothes tension. Over the long term, laughter improves your immune system, relieves pain, improves your mood, and helps you connect with other people.

Dr. Lee Berk and Dr. Stanley Tan at Loma Linda University in California researched the benefits of laughter, and in their landmark studies, they found that laughter lowers blood pressure, works your abs, and improves cardiac health.[34] A study by researchers at the Johns Hopkins University Medical School showed that humor and laughter can also improve memory and mental performance.[35] So I have decided that I am going to make laughter the cornerstone of my fitness program. Humor has certainly helped us through many awkward moments with Reid. I recommend it as a way to break down resistance to learning, diffuse power struggles, and reframe awkward situations in public. It is truly more blessed to laugh than to cry.

Reid's obsession with *Mary Poppins* extends to all the songs on the soundtrack. Jungle Poppins just recorded a contagiously giddy version of "I Love to Laugh" on their first CD. Mary Poppins herself can't resist the total abandonment of Uncle Albert's bender. Like Uncle Albert on the ceiling, Reid loves laughing even when he doesn't know why. Once he gets started, it can be hard to stop. Laughter spreads like a virus you want to catch.

However this tendency was a problem for Reid in school. When another student acted up—let's say took off their shirt and were reprimanded by a teacher—Reid would burst out laughing. I believe this was a nervous release of tension for him. He was not laughing at the person but at the dramatic quality of the situation, as if it were a good scene in a sitcom. Reid sits on the edge of his seat anticipating the canned laughter on the old *Andy Griffith Show*. In real life if laughter doesn't kick in at the right moment, he provides the laugh track. This creates an awkward social conundrum, as you can imagine.

One school put a mini-campaign in motion and lectured Reid

---

34 American Physiological Society. "Laughter Remains Good Medicine." ScienceDaily. www.sciencedaily.com/releases/2009/04/090417084115.htm (accessed April, 2018).

35 American Psychological Association. "How Laughing Leads to Learning." APA.org. https://www.apa.org/monitor/jun06/learning.aspx (accessed April, 2018).

on bullying. They treated his untimely laughter as meanness to others. I believe they misinterpreted it. I think the first rule in interacting with Reid, and many other adults with different abilities, is don't take it personally. Most atypical behaviors can be explained in another way, and laughter serves many functions. Reid wasn't laughing *at* anyone; he was releasing tension, and, maybe trying to connect.

Recently, the back window of my convertible-top Volkswagen Beetle crunched into a thousand particles of shattered glass when we accidentally folded a new, factory-rolled Ikea rug into it. I heard a loud "POP" and "crunch," and let out a repetitive flow of choice swear words that Reid has rarely heard. He burst out laughing and couldn't stop.

Later when I apologized for cursing, Reid seemed to have missed that part and instead reenacted the scene by imitating me with a long extended, "Noooooooooooo!"

I explained the traumatic consequence of how much this accident would likely cost (a whole new roof, not just the window), and having to tell Dad. Reid listened and responded with a movie line: "I'd like to tell you … Unfortunately, this wire is already too expensive. Stop."

I recognized that his reply was a movie reference but needed help attributing it. "Wait. What's that from, Reid?"

"Rolf in *The Sound of Music*," he shot back.

"Ah, right," I remembered. "Exactly! You're exactly right, bud. Expensive. It's going to be expensive."

Reid had picked up on the key word—expensive—and linked it to something he had heard in a movie. Money concepts and consequences are often outside his grasp. But imagining the incident from his perspective, I must've been funnier than Dick Van Dyke and his classic pratfall over his living room divan.

End scene.

EVERY BOY NEEDS A FUNNY GIRL:
SAMANTHA GINN, LOCAL ACTRESS

You're likely seeing the pattern here; Reid connects with people who share his passion. We all do. Musicians, worship leaders, and actors are the ones Reid finds or who find him. As we began his adult program, I looked forward to replacing the behavioral specialists and tutors he was used to with people who shared his spirit as a performer. I just wasn't sure where to find them.

It was kismet when we reconnected with local actress Samantha Ginn. She had directed a Christian Youth Theater (CYT) production of *California Gold* when Reid was ten years old. It was his one and only experience with their demanding rehearsal and performance schedule which worked because of Sam and several parents who prioritized people over programs.

Sam has two passions: theater and special education. Her mom was a sought-after special education teacher in our district, so Sam came by that passion naturally. Sam had recently married her passions by launching Monday Night Live! (MNL!)—a new program you'll read all about in the next section. Let's just say that we were seeing her more often, and Reid wanted to interview her.

Nobody loves to laugh more than Samantha Ginn. In her twenties, picture a cross between Carol Burnett doing her mop-and-bucket shtick and the intensity of Meryl Streep. Up close and personal, Sam is attentive, caring, and animated. She will do anything for a laugh, and it's often at her own expense. Her Instagram handle is "girls-don't-fart."

We met Sam to do the interview at the New Village Arts Theater twenty minutes before her Improv class was to start. As she unlocked the lobby door to let us in, she mirrored Reid's energy. Sam is a hugger. She plants her feet and puts all her might into a connection that leaves no regrets. After they let go of each other, she and Reid bounded back to the costume room like Tigger and Kanga. Then they sat on a well-worn leather sofa under a rack of cowboy vests and gowns hanging overhead. I opened a folding chair and held the recorder.

Sam: Reid Moriarty! I'm so excited!

She hit her fever pitch of enthusiasm immediately.

Reid: We're at the New Village Arts Theater interviewing Sam Ginn. So, Samantha, of all the roles you've acted, do you have a favorite one?
Sam: Yes. I have two favorite roles.
Reid: Tell them to me.

He was mirroring Sam now with a dramatic formal flair.

Sam: My first favorite role was playing Sylvia, the dog. I got to be a dog. 'Hey Hey. Hey. I smell a cat. I smell a cat in here. Hey. Hey. Hey. Hey.' Instead of barking, she would go like this: Hey. Hey, hey, hey.
Reid: What role are you *dying* to play?

Reid adds expression and intonation in his questions with someone as familiar as Sam. No nerves stifled him here.

Sam: Do you know the play *Annie*? I wanna play Miss Hannigan. *She broke into song:* 'Little girls, little girls ....'
Reid: You *wanna* play Miss Hannigan?
Sam: 'Little girls, little girls ... everywhere ....' Do you know that song?
Reid: I think Miss Hannigan is mean. She's really mean.
Sam: Oh, yeah. *This apparently hadn't dawned on her before.* She's not very nice to those kids, sometimes right? But sometimes, in a way,

she's funny. You know? You're like, g'all this woman's so mean, sometimes she's actually kinda funny.

Reid: Hahaha! *He joined in laughing, just 'cuz Sam was laughing.* That's
really funny. I have a funny question. Can you tell me a funny memory of one of your auditions as a kid, Samantha?

Sam: *(Gasp)* That is a great question. I sang this song called, "I Feel
Pretty" from *West Side Story*.

Reid: I Feel Pretty ... *West Side Story*?

Sam: You know what I did, Reid?

She knew how to capture attention by varying her dynamics and
using a question.

Reid: What?

Sam: I blacked out my tooth *(gasp from Reid)*, and I put on silly glasses,
and a *(another gasp)* crazy dress, and I sang, "I feel pretty ... oh so
pretty ...."

She sang it like a drunken sailor or Carol Burnett with a flask of
bourbon.

Reid: Of course, Samantha!

Sam: And it was kind of a joke because ...'cuz ya' know? I felt pretty inside,
but on the outside, I could've used a little trip to the nail salon or
somethin'.

I was choking back laughter; Reid was onto the next question on
his list.

Reid: Remember when you directed *California Gold*? I was in it. That was
fun, Samantha.

Sam: That was so much fun! That was when our friendship started. Do you remember what you sang for your audition?

Reid: "Ways to Say Hello." Actually, I sang it with Angela at Coors Amphitheater.

Sam: You sang at Coors Amphitheater? You're big time.

Reid: It was awesome!

Sam: Can you sing a little for me right now?

Reid: Uh, no, no, no, no.

Sam: Maybe another time ... You were so good in *California Gold*, Reid. You knew all the lyrics to the songs. You knew the choreography. You were amazing in that show.

Reid: *(Sigh)* ... and I didn't have a hoarse throat when I did this play.

Sam: That's right. Sometimes I get hoarse, and I'm like "Oh man, I need some lemon and some honey. I sound deep."

This was becoming an improv game of "yes, and" as they responded and encouraged each other with each comment.

Reid: Or water or tea could help.

Sam: That definitely helps. Or a spoonful of sugar ....

Advanced improvisation skills now.

Reid: That's from *Mary Poppins*!

Sam: That's right! I love that movie.

Reid: I like you as a director, Sam.

Sam: Thank you, and I love directing you.

Reid brought the interview back on track by asking if Sam preferred acting or directing. They talked about how she got into teaching.

Reid: What's your high point of your career?
Sam: Oooo, these are really making me think here.
Reid: Think, think, think, Samantha.

Reid referenced Winnie the Pooh's classic line by tapping his forehead.

Sam: I would actually say one of my high points of my career is actually starting this improv class.
Reid: Of course! And there's lots of students.

Sometimes the "yes, and" was a bit obtuse. Sam made it all work, rolling in, acknowledging, and affirming every suggestion made by her improv partner, as it were, using both nonverbal and spoken cues. The principles of improvisation are built on humility, mutual respect, and encouragement. In order for it to be successful, you have to think of the other person and respond accordingly. It's a cooperative art form.

Sam: Lots of students. And how much do we laugh?
Reid: A lot.
Sam: We laugh a lot, and I think laughing is really important.
Reid: I'm gonna be in your improv class tonight. I don't think there is a low point for you.

He knew she saw the bright side, only and always, so he skipped over that question.

Sam: Hehehe. Thanks, Reid.

She knew her positivity was a gift and demurred as she received the compliment.

Reid: So, what do improv and teaching preschoolers have in common?

Sam: Whoaoa, that's a great question. You never ... Know ... What's... going to happen! That's what I would say.

True that. Which is why she is so good at both!

Reid: So, Samantha, the LAST question is: *Reid dragged it out with a suspenseful flourish, mimicking Sam's last response.* What ... are your dreams ... for the ... future?

Sam: Ha! I would say, now that this class is starting to be established with improv, I want to start putting on plays with kids with special needs.

Reid: You do?!

Sam: Yup, I think that we could put on a play together.

Reid: I know a play we can do for kids with SPECIAL NEEDS!

He used the term as if it applied to someone else, matching her emphasis. He and Sam were in cahoots.

Sam: What play?

Reid: Let's do the *Singin' in Rain*.

Sam: YES! That would be awesome. I would love that. Maybe we could write a version together. Does that sound good?

Reid: Okay. I wouldn't be a conductor. I'd be ... How 'bout I be Cosmo Brown or Don Lockwood. You can be Dora Bailey.

She's the commentator who announces the celebrities as they step out of their limos onto the red carpet.

Sam: Thank you!

Any conversation with Sam is interspersed with belly laughs and hysterics, as well as whispers and dramatic pauses. She is able to both rile Reid up and regulate him down to a stage whisper. The brainstorming continued in earnest.

Sam: We need to have auditions. This is great!
Reid: I have some people I want to invite, and maybe they can be in it. How 'bout Luke Shortall? He'd like to be in it.
Sam: Ohhh ... He sounds like a winner. Luke! Let's get him in here!
Reid: Jacob Brown and Arricka, she could be in it. She could be Lina Lamont or Kathy Selden.

He was on his feet now, excited.

Sam: You're my casting director; this is wonderful.

I had more material than I could possibly use for the final seven-minute product. Editing this was going to be painful for me. I knew it would be hard to delete any evidence of the pure joy they stirred to the surface when they were together. Class was about to start though, so I gave the director's cue to wrap. Smiling ear to ear and chuckling under my breath, I walked out to the lobby. Reid stayed for more.

We can't get enough of Samantha Ginn. On the last night of Monday Night Live! in the spring of 2016, Sam told me she was leaving her preschool job in a leap of faith to pursue other passions. *What?!* Incredulous, I asked, "Do you know I'm hiring for Reid's adult program?" My heart leaped. We gasped in unison, "Let's talk. Call me tomorrow." Talk about timing.

In short order, Samantha began as Reid's acting coach three mornings a week. That's when the fun really began. Together they wrote song parodies, an open mic monologue, and comedy bits they posted on YouTube. They took a Masterclass with Steve Martin online. Reid learned more about screenwriting and movie making and collaborated with students from Joey Travolta's Inclusion Films program to create a short, social story film on problem solving. Sam was also Reid's co-star doing *Purple Party* assemblies at pre-schools every Friday all over San Diego County.

Once Reid escaped the confines of school, we were free to choose what we knew worked. And humor was part of it. I had always told babysitters and tutors to use humor with Reid. It worked to soften resistance when he was stuck. Laughter is contagious in the best way because it enlists cooperation and joint attention. Through God's immense grace, a comedic actress was available at exact moment we needed her. We find these gifted individuals one at a time and trust the organic process of collaboration in community. Each person introduces us to another who builds on what we learned from the last one.

Sam with her inimitable generosity introduced us to her community of actors and performers at multiple theaters in San Diego. She organized an internship for Reid at New Village Arts where he helps backstage and ushers. She also challenged him to ride the commuter train by himself to get there. As they hung out together, Reid was in the right place at the right time, and doors opened for him to write a song about the theater. He sang it at their fundraising gala with Paul Eddy, another local actor who played Buddy Holly in *The Buddy Holly Story* that season. He and Reid became "best bros" as fast as you can say "Peggy Sue."

As Reid and his new buddy, Paul, hung out practicing music and eating at Rubio's Coastal Grill, they amassed a number of new original songs. These ran the gamut from one about "Carlsbad" where the theater is located to another about "Mexican Coke." A year later, they released a CD of original songs, *Best Bros: Friday Sessions Vol. 1.* My personal favorite is song they wrote about Sam. At the release party, Reid pulled Sam up on stage and debuted the song as a surprise tribute to her. The song is a parody of "A Boy Named Sue," the Shel Silverstein poem that Johnny Cash set to music. Go ahead; steal this idea.

"A Girl Named Sam" by Reid Moriarty and Paul Eddy

Well, before I met her and learned comedy
I was sitting at home watching the TV
Just this little ole me in my own jam
Then she came into my life and I was off the grid
Lots of plays we surely did
Have you ever heard about a girl, a girl named Sam?

Well she taught me improv and some jokes
And it got a lot of laughs from a-lots of folks
She makes me laugh, she's quite a ham
We take the Coaster to New Village Arts
She hosted BRAM in the Park
Have you ever heard about a girl, a girl named Sam?

Well, as an actor, she's no stranger to the stage
She sure can bring words off the page
Playing a superhero, she makes the villains scram
Now she's a director with knowledge and skills
Both comedy and drama, she tops the bill
Have you ever heard about a girl, a girl named Sam?

Well, I'm so happy to have her on my team
She has helped me live my dreams
Making the Purple Party video with my fam
Sam is awesome; she loves to teach
We go to the library, shopping, and the beach!
Have you ever heard about a girl, a girl named Sam?

I've had so much fun, I'm sad to see her go
But she'll be around; don't ya know?
So thankful for her, I really am
She's kind and joyful, the very best
At helping me soon leave the nest
I hope the next girl I work with will be Carrie or
Lindsey or Mary or anything but Sam?

Our lives have been enriched enormously by this acting coach who loves to laugh and appreciates a good pun. Sam will always hold a special place in our hearts for launching Reid's adult program with me and legitimizing both his talent for comedy and pursuit of vocation as an entertainer. If it's baby steps all the way, Sam helped us across a pond of stepping-stones right at the trailhead.

"You grow up the day you have your first real laugh at yourself." —Ethel Barrymore, actress[36]

36 Ethel Barrymore Quotes. BrainyQuote.com. https://www.brainyquote.com/quotes/ethel_barrymore_100493, accessed October 9, 2018.

How Can I Build a Better Adult
Program for My Son or Daughter?

1. Order the Transition Kit from the Autism Speaks website (autismspeaks.org).
2. Be persistent with your government agency caseworker to identify and improve best practices and programs.
3. Share this book with your caseworker and parent group.
4. Team up with like-minded parents to create an inclusive community.
5. Make one improvement a month toward your ultimate wish list.
6. Follow programs and people that inspire you on Instagram or Facebook.
7. Ask for Life Planning as a service from your county disability services.
8. Connect with neurotypical mentors in the community who share a special interest.
9. Innovate and iterate. Repeat until you find the right balance that works.
10. Don't take "no" for an answer.

MONDAY NIGHT LIVE!
Carlsbad, CA
NewVillageArts.org

Samantha Ginn and Aleta Barthell are the masterminds behind a new program in San Diego. Monday Night Live! is an acting program for teens and young adults with special needs. Co-produced by Kids Act, a local youth acting program, and New Village Arts (NVA) community theater, MNL! becomes inclusive when neurotypical graduates from Kids Act and company members from NVA get involved. Through a six-week evening class, aspiring actors acquire skills in stand-up, scene work, choreography, and music based on material that interests them. Of course, they meet on Monday and end with a comedy sketch show: *Monday Night Live!*

Additionally for three weeks in the summer, MNL! pairs special needs students with neurotypical peers to create a one-act play on a professional stage before a public audience. The first year they did *The Little Prince*. This year, they are doing an original musical titled *Secret Superheroes!* Everything they do is exclamatory. No exaggeration.

A few years ago, another mom and I enrolled our sons in the Kids Act Improv camp with a shared aide. Sam was the teacher, and both boys loved it. Aware of Sam's passion and Aleta's outstanding work with typical children, we requested an inclusive class that would serve more young adults with special needs. Would Sam teach it if we came up with five participants? We knew we could do that in a matter of one email because the demand is great for quality programs with a social component. In addition to a theater degree and acting experience, Sam has a million tools in her back pocket from real improv exercises like Zip, Zap, Zop, and Taxi to games she invented specifically to address personal goals.

In her other back pocket, she has a number of teaching interventions she learned in special education classrooms. Let's just say when Sam dressed up as Miss Frizzle from *The Magic School Bus* last Halloween, she was already in character.

Taking our challenge as if her ship had come in, Sam teamed up with Aleta of Kids Act to offer the new class. NVA stepped forward to host and run enrollment through their box office. That improv class morphed into MNL! to develop endurance and story from students' creations. They built the program— recruiting the typical peers—and we came with the five young adults with special needs.

Reid was twenty-one at the time, and the program was a milestone success. No one came to ask me questions in the lobby or texted me with questions or for clarifications or suggestions of how to engage Reid like they had from school. Sam is gifted, and her genius zone is the intersection of acting and autism. There is a lesson here: no matter how wonderful a program is in concept or mission, it is individual people who make it or break it. A program can have a fabulous concept, but if the instructor doesn't click with your kiddo, forget about it. Chemistry is part of the equation.

Everyone loved Monday Night Live! Parents, students, and actors from the theater company converged on Monday nights when theaters are "dark" and actors available. That first summer, they embarked on a production of *The Little Prince* to cement the idea of performing a story. Aleta adapted the script to make each student shine and have a peer nearby for support. In her masterful adaptation, each of St. Exupery's planets had an assistant. Reid was the oldest and tallest of the cast and made a convincing pilot. A teen with tousled, sandy hair (and ASD) played the prince. Afterward, he told his mom, "This is what I want to do with my life. I want to be an actor." He is serious about it, as well he should be; he studied the role, memorized all his lines, took notes from a demanding (albeit funny) director, made all his marks, and brought the audience to their feet. In every other program he has been in, this same young man has severe behaviors and requires one-on-one support. Not here.

To prepare for this summer's *Secret Superheroes!* musical, Sam gave the Monday night class a little homework: think about what your superpower is and come dressed as that the next week. To prime the pump, Sam shared that her superpower is making people laugh. Agreed. Aleta then took the students' contributions and wove them into a script in which the students are fully vested. Her superpower is as a dramaturge.

If this is starting to sound like the Miracle Project, it's because the idea is catching. Inclusive performing arts programs are popping up all over the country from the Lincoln Center's Big Umbrella to the Ohio State University's Shakespeare project and from the Musical Theater Project in Columbus, Ohio, to the National Comedy Theater in San Diego. Do you need a program like this in your community? Take heart that the San Diego program started small and is growing to meet the demand to include more people from the community—including interactive audience members and funding sources.

Perhaps in your neighborhood, you can start by hosting a "sensory-friendly concert" to see who comes. Gaining popularity, sensory-friendly performances guarantee a non-judgmental atmosphere where everyone feels welcome. Modifications are made to lighting, loud noises, and other stimuli. Some include pre-visit materials and visuals. As attendance grows, a touring performance or satellite program by one of these groups could be a next step.

A distinction I appreciate about MNL! is their collaboration with New Village Arts. Having a home base in a community theater gives MNL! a legitimacy that eludes other special-needs programs. Rather than a preschool room or church basement locale, MNL! takes place in the same lobby and stage where patrons subscribe to *The Buddy Holly Story* and *Avenue Q.* Professionalism in the location as well as the production elevates the process for these talented young adults. It values them and takes them seriously as they pursue a craft. Legitimate choreographers, musicians, lighting techs, teaching artists, and a stage manager from the existing theater community raise the bar on the personal best for all the participants. People with disabilities are not "less than." It's a collaboration of shared passion where everyone thrives.

Our young adults deserve a lifetime of actual learning. Many programs dumb down the content for adults with disabilities. I've witnessed a roomful of thirty year olds playing kindergarten spelling games in exchange for treats from a treasure box. That's insulting. At MNL! participants learn legitimate acting techniques that are transferable to real life and are taught with dignity and age-appropriate expectations that stretch their horizons. Sam holds the bar high and cares enough to teach all of her students real terminology like "cheating out" to face the audience. Reid told me that today they are "going to run the whole show, start and stop." Yesterday, they did "scene work," and he will be "off book" by "tech week." Sam doesn't dilute the curriculum; it's full octane. By including her students in the theater world, Sam invites them to leave a watered down subculture and be included. Because she believes they can, they do.

Everyone benefits from the collaboration. Even when they are home from college, peer actors return session after session to be involved. Some are graduates of a local Catholic school doing community service; others have aged out of the Kids Act curriculum but carry the culture with them and want to give back. A

San Diego Union-Tribune photographer shot the *Little Prince* play. Completely flustered, he couldn't tell the students from the mentors. *That* is successful inclusion.

As the students gain skills in their area of preferred interest, they take on more responsibility. The costume intern (who has Asperger's) for this year's summer musical had acted in *The Little Prince*. Other MNL! participants composed original music for *Secret Superheroes!* Reid has become a leader, shadowing Sam closely as he does. He's known as an encourager. In fact, one of the actor-mentors told Sam, "I've learned how to be a better comedic actor with timing like Reid has. He sticks the joke *every* time." They are all learning from each other and finding their niche.

Mostly moms and a few dads stick around within earshot in the theater lobby during class. One student took multiple bathroom breaks that his mom supervised. A few listened for sounds of discontent in case it was their young adult. Sam or one of her assistants would pop their head out to ease our minds, "It's all good." In the early days, one mom instigated a modified pub crawl and introduced us to the hot spots—restaurants and craft breweries—within walking distance of the theater. We began to use the hour and a half to unwind. There was also heated discussion and strategizing on how to revamp the district's adult transition program. "Moms Helping Moms" is our closed-caption subtitle as we sink into the two oversized leather sofas waiting for us Monday nights. The therapy is included in the class fee.

Monday Night Live! continues to be in high demand in its third year. And each session ends with a showcase of unscripted comedy where you never know what's going to happen that is the best adventure of trust ever. Sam and her team are uniquely able to draw actors out. Students you didn't know could speak are on stage contributing to a Taxi game. Their suggestions may be muffled but are audible to the helper next to them who is tuned-in to their language and quirks. Anyone of the helping peers could steal the show with a monologue or tap routine, but instead they choose humility. They back off, step back, and stoop down in order to let someone else have their moment. It's a beautiful thing to watch—enough to bring grandparents, teachers, and friends to tears.

SINGIN' IN THE RAIN[37]

When Allie and Reid were in grade school, we hosted movie nights in our backyard. Jim borrowed a projector, and we showed a Netflix DVD on a flat queen-size sheet thumbtacked to the pergola over our patio. The grown-ups sat on quilts and blankets in our yard facing the back of the house. The kids climbed or perched on the play structure. These nights were a creative way to socialize with Reid. In those days, we had the established family ritual of Friday Night Classic Movie Night. Showing a movie kept Reid in the room—or yard—with us. We just added new faces to Reid's existing routine.

Our movie choices didn't always hold the interest of the invited guests. I recall the time we showed *Swiss Family Robinson*. The younger natives got restless during the second half before the pirates landed on the beach. Attention spans were longer in 1960. It was a novel experience for me to have the most attentive child in the room. Reid knew these classics backwards and forwards, often rewinding the VHS tapes to study them through the snowy static. He had the lines memorized and mouthed them in unison with the actors. Half the crowd watched the movie, half watched Reid.

Not many had seen *Singin' in the Rain* either, but we are suckers for musicals! Cosmo (Donald O'Connor) and Don (Gene Kelly) are hoofers looking for work in Hollywood in the late 1920s when silent films were being replaced by "talkies." Lina Lamont (Jean Hagen) has a raspy voice, like chalk on a chalkboard, and no couth. She didn't make the transition from silent to "talkies" so well. In the end, Kathy Selden (Debbie Reynolds) sings for her, hidden behind a curtain. Don and Kathy fall in love after a few ups and downs. It's hard to capture the comedy of this film in print because

---

37 *Singin' in the Rain.* Directed by Stanley Donen and Gene Kelly. Culver City, CA: Metro Goldwyn Mayer. 1952.

so much of it comes from Cosmo's physicality and gestures. So rent it please. It will lower your blood pressure and work your abs.

Cosmo was Reid's spirit animal. In the storyline, Cosmo is overlooked for the more debonair Don. Cosmo is a classic side-kick, just as good a dancer but not as suave with the ladies. He provides comic relief and helps the hero achieve his goal. Reid shared Cosmo's modus operandi. Behind the sheet, his little wispy silhouette resembled Peter Pan searching for his shadow. He leaped with Gene Kelly, somersaulted with Donald O'Connor over the back of a sofa, and bowed with Debbie Reynolds.

Reid played Cosmo in his special day class at the end of the corridor in his elementary school too. He jumped on a mini-trampoline keeping the teachers and aides in stitches during recess. He wore underwear on his head and hammed it up for attention. He challenged the best behavior specialists, who are rarely up for a joke. I was amazed how he remained their favorite while simultaneously pushing all their buttons and putting their protocols to the test.

At the beginning of the movie, Kathy boasts about being a stage actress, not a mere film star. Equally arrogant, Don reads his own press and treats the world like his red carpet. Their pride shows like spinach in their teeth. Kathy's cover is blown when Don sees her jumping out of a cake with a spray of confetti for a floor show. Turns out they're both building their chops, waiting for a break, and working wherever they can.

Kathy's chutzpah takes Don by surprise. She hurls a meringue pie at Lina's face. He can't get Kathy off his mind, nor can he find her. As he hangs out on the Monumental Pictures lot, Cosmo tries to cheer him up with the immortal words of "Make 'Em Laugh."

Cosmo is all slapstick. He hops onto a piano bench, banging out the notes with his elbows and feet, then jumps off the lid of the upright. After spoofing with a fabric mannequin and flipping over a davenport, he finishes the number with a leap into the sunset, ripping a painted canvas in two. Music and laughter are linked in the limbic system of our brains. I think they're also inexplicably linked to our heartstrings. Cosmo can laugh at himself, and he embraces the role of humble jester when his friends need a mood adjustment.

By the end of the movie, Don sprouts a new sprig of humility after *The Dueling Cavalier*, his first talkie, flops. Everyone is laughing at him. But the humiliation causes him to realize that his love for Kathy is more important than his own fame. A true hero, he finds an escape route from the pride that binds him by doing something for someone else.

WRAPPING UP CHAPTER 6

Laughing is good for our health, and comedy is an effective coping strategy. According to Stephen Colbert, "You cannot laugh and be afraid at the same time, and the devil cannot stand mockery."[38]

Humor has helped me through current political events as well as personal challenges. Our marriage is alive and well after thirty-two years, which I attribute to our sense of humor and shared faith. Hopefully this chapter has made you aware of times in your day when humor helps. Some parents worry about teaching boys not to cry; I'd worry if they can't laugh.

We have embraced Reid's mistakes and misfires in making *Talk Time* as comic relief and a service to the listener. We all need to laugh more, whether we have the hiccups or not. And when other people laugh, join them. It's a great opportunity to connect and

---

38 CBS News. "Stephen Colbert's poignant sign-off to the 2016 presidential election." CBSNews. Com. https://www.cbsnews.com/news/the-late-show-stephen-colberts-poignant-sign-off-to-the-2016-presidential-election/ (accessed May, 2018).

improve your quality of life. Controlling, curbing, or explaining emotions isn't your job. Trust me, it doesn't pay well. It doesn't even need to be done.

Imagine Reid's delight when he traded a teacher who thought laughing was inappropriate to one who thinks people need to laugh more. Reid had met his match. Like dueling banjos, he and Sam spar with each other, making improvisation look like a contact sport. Humor is such an effective way to open pathways for new learning and restore a beginner brain that is nimble and as pliable wet clay. We are more receptive to teachers, parents, and therapists when we are relaxed than when our blood pressure approaches a boiling point. Creativity and learning happen when we are relaxed and fluid. Comedy makes a great foundation for any curriculum and any relationship. The humble jester knew what he was doing as he taught the king.

Improvisation is the best way I have found to loosen up and grow in humility. Amy Lisewski, founder of Finest City Improv in San Diego, wrote *Relax, We're All Just Making This Stuff Up!: Using the Tools of Improvisation to Cultivate More Courage and Joy in Your Life*. She explains, "It is when we are knocked down that we learn the most about standing up. We stop trying to be perfect."[39] Knowing you can't make a mistake in improv, sets you free to go for it.

The marriage of Sam's passion for theater and special education gave birth to Monday Night Live! as well as a number of other new opportunities in Reid's life. Chicago has Second City; San Diego has MNL! where students can join something bigger than themselves. They can grow with teaching artists and fellow actors who

39 Lisewski, Amy. *Relax, We're All Just Making This Stuff Up!: Using the Tools of Improvisation to Cultivate More Courage and Joy in Your Life.* Finest City Improv, 2016.

humbly act, sing, and dance alongside them on a legitimate stage. They all grow in their craft, especially as they step out of the limelight to let others to have their moment. They learn as Cosmo in *Singin' in the Rain* did, that being a sidekick is a calling all its own. Supporting the hero in achieving his goal makes the sidekick a hero of another kind. Doing something for someone else is the escape route from the pride and need for prestige that isolate us.

People make or break a program, so if there isn't one in your town, look for people who share your vision and have a passionate heart, humble attitude, and good sense of humor to start one with you. They may be other moms or single professionals in whatever area of specialty, be it improv or baseball. All adults deserve a lifetime of genuine learning surrounded by people who believe in their potential.

7

Learn from Experience

The deadline for finishing my first book *One-Track Mind,* was November 2016 in time for the American Music Therapy Association conference where Angela, Reid, and I would speak. Allie would also be attending as a student member with her friends from Berklee. Worlds were colliding. It was a motivating deadline; I wanted to sell copies hot-off-the-press. The conference was in Kansas City the week before Thanksgiving. Our entire extended families on both sides are in Cleveland, which is much closer to Kansas City than San Diego. My ambitious brainstorm was to fly to Kansas City, rent a car, and make a road trip/book tour interviewing people across the Midwest on our way home to grandmother's house in Cuyahoga County.

My mom decided to join Reid and me for the first leg of the drive. Her decision was partly because the trip sounding enjoyable and partly because she figured I would need help. I mapped our route and researched notable people in the cities along the way: St. Louis, Nashville, Bloomington, and Indianapolis. (Okay, so Nashville was a detour.)

We were stoked! And a little nervous about how it would go. Flying with Reid is always better with a two-to-one ratio. If he becomes agitated or his maladaptive behaviors began to escalate, one of us (usually me) can attend to him while the other runs interference with the general public of concerned bystanders. Jim is good at that. Flying alone with Reid gave me pause for sure, but I was determined not to let a little trepidation cramp my style.

We modified what we could and prayed over the rest. On the direct flight to Kansas City, I would only have one seatmate to contend with as we sat about four rows from the front on Southwest. All was uneventful until after the drink service. Reid was bored; who wasn't? He began to rock back and forth playing a movie in his head, which he does a lot, sometimes subvocalizing the script under his breath, other times just silently. At home, this is no big deal. We can ask him to "pause it" when it's time to go somewhere or do something. Most of the time, he relegates the activity to his free time, so it's not an issue.

On a plane, you can imagine how this behavior violates unwritten social norms and disrupts the passengers around us. I was mindful of this, even if Reid wasn't. We were three abreast on the left side of the plane. He likes to sit cross-legged—on piano benches and on planes. It's almost a signature stance, like his checkerboard Vans. I had the middle seat, so his knees bumped up against my thigh, and Reid was by the window. Moms always take the middle seat, right? I have a friend who used to say, "I'm a mom; I have no personal space."

"Reid, easy. Hold up." I whispered to him as the rocking continued. Silence. "Don't bang the seat."

Reid continued developing his core muscles like an incessant human pendulum reaching seventy beats a minute. The light from the open window flashed as he obstructed it then exposed the sunbeam. I glanced at the man next to me checking for nonverbal signs of annoyance. He was working on a laptop, a business traveler no doubt.

"Reid, do you want an apple?" More silence. Shaking his head for no. "Let's do a word search." I offered him items from my bag to divert and distract, hoping to change the stimulatory tide ever so subtly. Stimming, or self-stimulatory behavior, is an ASD trait that involves repetitive behavior that is soothing to the individual. It might be rocking, twirling hair, humming, or spinning objects. Reid was in the zone, bracing his hands on his knees now, shifting the rocking motion into full throttle.

"Do you want to listen to music with these earbuds?" Silence. "Don't rock so hard. We don't want to bother the people around us." I was doing all the talking.

The rocking continued. I wondered when they would come around to collect the trash or offer refills. Anything to interrupt this cycle. As I took a shallow breath and exhaled strain, the middle-aged man next to me offered, "Don't worry about me. Believe me, there's nothing he can do that will bother me."

"Oh, that's... Thank you. I appreciate that."

"Seriously, my wife can't sit still and fidgets all the time. I am totally used to it."

"Ha, really?" My shoulders dropped, and I felt the back of the seat catch my full weight.

"That's funny. You're sweet."

We continued to chitchat giving Reid space to do his rhythmic thing. The man was flying home to Kansas City. His daughter was a teacher and had some students with autism in her classroom. I told him a bit about Reid's podcast and that we were headed to the conference.

"My daughter might like to know about that," he pulled up the website on his computer and sent the link off to his daughter. He also pulled up my book on Amazon and Reid's website. I told him about our appointments with Chris Duh, head designer at the

Hallmark headquarters, and that we had reached out to the Royals team mascot, Sluggerrr. The Royals had just won the World Series.

"It was last minute, and I haven't heard back. But we'll see," I said.

"You know, my realtor lives next door to Sluggerrr," he offered.

"Really? You're kidding me."

"No, he does, and we're in the midst of selling and moving across town. So I'm actually talking to him a lot lately. Want me to ask him to help somehow?"

"Aw, that'd be so nice. Maybe he could lean over his back fence. Yes, if you're willing that'd be great," I was relaxed now and joking.

"Let's see. How should we do this?" We strategized and came up with a plan, forwarding emails and swapping phone numbers.

"Perfect. I really appreciate it." I was tickled by his kindness and humility. He had taken an awkward situation and made it more than comfortable.

"Well, we'll just see what happens. You never know. Wouldn't it be cool if it worked out?"

"Totally cool. I better start working on the questions."

We were having fun now visualizing possible outcomes. We clicked away on our devices implementing the grand scheme and enjoying each other's company. We'd become friends instead of enemies. A man who might have been disgruntled, or demanded a new seat assignment, was now texting his realtor and wanting me to keep him posted. It wasn't about him. He was deferential and chose to prioritize Reid (and me) over his own comfort on the plane.

A few texts and some time later, I was in the hotel room on the phone with Brad Collins, a gymnast actor who plays Sluggerrr.

"Could you be at the Life Time Fitness in Overland Park Saturday at 10 a.m.?" He clearly worked on weekends.

"Yes," I would figure out where it was later.

TRACKING THE KING OF THE JUNGLE AT A FITNESS CENTER: BRAD COLLINS AS SLUGGERRR

Sluggerrr had an appearance in the suburbs, and Reid could do the interview afterward. I couldn't believe this was happening. Giddy, I texted Mr. Aisle-seat to thank him profusely. He was excited too. "Glad I could help. Let me know how it goes," he texted back. Aren't people amazing?

Believing that half of success is showing up, we used our handy-dandy GPS to find the fitness center. They were expecting us with a giveaway drawstring pack for Reid. It was a swishy fitness club with a salon, coffee shop, and beautiful childcare rooms. Reid set about on a self-guided tour of each one until he found the uniformed Royals player with the giant yellow-crowned head and upturned tail towering over the preschoolers. Reid patted him on the back and retreated to wait his turn.

We settled into an empty membership sales office and waited behind a closed door for Sluggerrr to change out of costume. The door had one sidelight, so we watched people pass wondering which one was Brad Collins. "That's not him," Reid would say as people came and went from their workouts. Then, breathless and perspiring, a boyish thirty year old with a tall Gatorade in his hand entered. His ginger hair matched Reid's if you add a trim beard and mustache.

Reid: That's your grand entrance! So, here we are. This is Brad Collins.

Brad: That's right.

Reid: He's part of the Kansas City Royals mascot. I'm here to ask him a couple questions. Hey Brad, how did a seven-foot lion get to Kansas City?

Brad: Well, if my memory serves me correctly, in 1996, Sluggerrr became the official mascot. He is a lion because he is the king of baseball. So, the king and Sluggerrr and lion all kinda fit with the Royals theme quite well.

I would find it easier to be humble with my face hidden, I think. I wouldn't be accountable as myself, so maybe the pride would subside. In Brad's case though, the costume seemed to imbue the man with a personality that was not his own. He had left the King of the Jungle's lion-sized ego in the locker room and was just a regular guy sipping a Gatorade who had young kids waiting for him at home. Reid asked about Sluggerrr's high point of the World Series parade, and how he got so many followers on social media. He hadn't had a low point in two years.

Reid: How would you describe what a mascot does?

Brad: What do you think a mascot does?

Reid: I know what he does. He cheers people on and gets the crowd going!

Brad: That's exactly right. We help Sluggerrr get the fans going. We serve as a conductor during the game to get the crowd pumped. It helps build fans for the next generation, and, especially, if parents have little kids, about the third or fourth inning the kids can't sit still. They go on a mission to find Sluggerrr to entertain the kids.

Reid: Alright. I think he's tame or wild.

Brad: He's more of a tamed lion. He used to be a little bit wilder, but these past couple years he's really become more of a family man and straightened out his priorities a little bit. He has gone to mascot camp before, and ya' know, learned some new dance moves, learned new ways to do improv comedy in the crowds is the bottom line.

All roads lead to improv.

Reid: How many parties does Sluggerrr get invited to a year?

Brad: Whew, we do probably close to eighty or ninety kids' birthday parties a year. So, we do about four to five hundred appearances a year, plus games. We are a very busy mascot program.

Reid: Alright!

Reid asked everyone in Kansas City what their favorite barbecue place was. We got a variable ranking of the top five places and an education on the different styles of sauce and accompaniments. Sluggerrr, of course, preferred zebra to pulled pork or burnt ends.

Reid: Alright, that's the interview with Brad Collins. Is there anything you'd like to ask me?

Brad: Yea. What brings you guys to Kansas City?

Reid: Well, what brings us to Kansas City is doing conferences. I just did one on Thursday. Can you guess what songs I sang? *Reid began a lengthy monologue describing the whole workshop including the songs he sang and Angela's songwriting principles.* Oh, I can tell you a secret: I've been interviewing people from around the world. Do you know Kim Faure and Brittany?

Brad: What do they do?

The monologue turned into a short advertisement for the podcast—this was a first for Reid to promote himself—with a trailer for his *Purple Party* CD. He rattled off the color songs and told Brad about the bonus track. Brad listened intently.

Brad: You're quite the pitchman. Well, thanks for having me, Reid.

Reid: You're welcome.

Maybe with a little more life experience, Reid will develop some humility too.

Sluggerrr is one guest who literally removed his mask to reveal his authentic self. Underneath, he wore humility from his experiences as a versatile performer who could rile up crowds of fans just as easily as winning over new ones. All in just fifteen minutes. Brad left with a CD for his girls who are big *Sesame Street* fans.

RENTAL CARS AND RADIO STATIONS: BILL CODY OF WSM-RADIO

After the conference, we drove about four hours a day to each new town. Reid loves a schedule and follows it to a tee. He also enjoys riding in a car, so this travel mode was working for us despite the suitcases, strange hotel beds, different bath products, and other uncontrolled stimuli. We stayed at one Sheraton and two refurbished train stations and consumed mashed potatoes and French fries at one too many Cracker Barrel restaurants.

The shipping boxes of books rode in the backseat with Reid. Every morning we rearranged making room for our luggage. Reid was practicing flexibility on the road and independence in the hotel lobby business centers. Halfway through the fourteen-day trek, it was getting monotonous for me. I was beginning to miss my own coffeepot and pillow. As we piled back in the dew-covered red Mazda rental car in view of the freeway exit ramp, Reid buckled up and said, "Mom, I just love road trips!"

"Me too, buddy. I do too."

With the itinerary in hand, Reid knew what he had to do. It's Tuesday, this is St. Louis. Where's the Arch? Like a rock star with a set list that stays the same and a crowd of fans that switches, Reid nailed each appearance. We met Ranger Rich Fefferman at the Gateway Arch and learned that his boys are on the spectrum. Reid rode up to the top of the Arch in a space capsule the size of a phone booth. I never thought I'd see the day. Lots of new experiences were expanding his horizons.

One rainy day, we were the only passengers on a guided trolley tour of St. Louis. We found the only Mexican restaurant in the historic Soulard district. Reid marched into the Anheuser-Busch visitor center to find general manager Jeff Knapper. We toured the Clydesdales barn asked about the pets he had as a kid.

What Reid was learning on this trip was how to be a professional. The show must go on, when you're thrilled and when you're not. You gotta get up, put on your pants, and do what you said you'd do. Life on tour is not always glamorous. But Reid was gaining a sense of responsibility and internal motivation as we clocked all those miles.

After another sleep and four more hours of driving, we arrived in Nashville. I navigated the 155 beltway to the McGavock Pike exit. WSM-Radio, the famed country music station, had their offices in a single story manor house right off the freeway at the entrance gate to the Opryland Resort. A custom wrapped vehicle with the call letters let us know we were in the right place. We hit the buzzer on an intercom in the breezeway, then waited for Bill Cody to join us after his live broadcast from the Opryland.

Bill Cody walks like a cowboy with an appointment. This Nashville deejay and host at the Grand Ole' Opry has been on the air for forty-five years. His friendly face is on billboards, busses, and a banner at the Country Music Hall of Fame where he narrates the audio tour. In Nashville, he's the man! And he loves to laugh.

Bill has short, cropped hair that flips up in a cowlick at the front and center just like Reid's. We caught him slightly off guard by being a few minutes early. He wasn't sure where to do this thing. Reid followed him as he put his papers down, then into a conference room before he thought of a better idea. "Want to do it in the studio?" He was magnanimous and bonded with Reid quickly. Reid followed him down a hallway like they were running a three-legged race. Bill and Reid settled into chairs in the WSM Radio recording studio behind a swivel boom mic with the cage and all the bells and whistles. An engineer sat at the mixing board. I sat behind them on a leather couch. My mom watched from the doorway. Bill opened his can of sparkling water.

Phfew!! Water sprayed everywhere. *Oh no!* I thought. Reid didn't like unexpected occurrences like this. When splashed accidentally, I had seen him jump in a fountain or run his arm under a faucet on purpose, as if to cancel out the involuntary surprise of the splash. I expected some reaction, but no, he was fine, en pointe in fact. This was Bill's deal, and it wasn't going to throw Reid off his game. Accidents happen I guess to all of us, even this pro.

Bill: Whoop-whoop, its okay, just water. Hang on.
Reid: Hang on.

Reid repeated his caution. And they were rolling.

Bill: Reid, what's going' on?

It was as if they had they were old chums.

Reid: Hi, Bill Cody.
Bill: How you doin' man?
Reid: You were on the air.
Bill: That's what I do, man!
Reid: We're here at WSM Radio in Nashville. We're here to interview Bill
    Cody, the host of Coffee, Country, and Cody.
Bill: Say that again. Say that part again. Say it just like that.

Bill began with a challenge that raised the bar of expectation for

Reid. Bill had listened to the links I sent him and referenced a few particulars from Reid's interview with Keb' Mo'.

Reid: Okay. "We're here at WSM Radio in Nashville. We're here to interview Bill Cody, the host of Coffee, Country, and Cody."

He repeated himself with more feeling and panache.

Bill: YES! It's just like I'm on the air when I hear that.

How generous he was with his praise and affirmation of a young upstart like Reid.

Reid: So, Bill Cody, what's your usual coffee order?
Bill: Seattle's Best organic number four.
Reid: Alright.
Bill: Yeah.
Reid: What do you think is the secret to making country music?

Reid whispered this in a leading way.

Bill: Boy, if you had the answer to that, I would take you down on Music
   Row, and we would own this town. Reid would own Nashville if you
   had the answer to that!
We all stifled a laugh, except Bill who let his out.

Reid: Of course!
Bill: I think to making great country music it's looking for that ... you hear
   a little something. You know, as a trained ear, you hear a little something, and you go, "hmhmm that's unique, that's different, nobody else
   is doing that." So that you hear them on the radio, and you go, "nobody

sounds like ..." that person from that point on, from the first time you hear them, and then from then on, you know EXACTLY who that is.

Reid: *squealing in delight* Alright!

Bill rested his head on his hand to show how intent he was on listening to Reid. He showed the humility of a man who is more interested in what his grandkid wants to talk about than, let's say, what's on the radio. He told Reid about his first visit to a radio station with his dad when he was twelve. He shared an embarrassing low point of starting his first LP on high speed so it sounded like the Chipmunks. And that he wanted to be a cowboy.

Reid: So, Bill, I'm a big George Jones fan. Can you tell me a story about him?

Bill: Oh, I could tell you a lot of stories about him.

He told us one about when he had been shooting a Christmas special at George Jones' house, Possum Holler. Bill's nose was running, his hands were blue, and he was freezing his face off. Of the whole crew and cast filming a series of holiday shows, George invited Bill inside to warm up and change clothes between takes.

Bill: I got, like, red carpet preferential treatment from the Possum himself.

Reid: Really amazing! What song is the most often requested, Bill?

Bill: You're gonna like this answer. Our number-one song in our ninety-year history was your buddy, George Jones, singing, "He Stopped Loving Her Today."

Reid: Of course! Do you think the TV show *Nashville* is a realistic portrayal of the music business?

Bill and Reid alternated all manner of laughs here for a few seconds.

Reid echoed a perfect impersonation of his tone and timbre on each outburst. We had hit Cody's funny bone.

Bill: That's a great question, Reid. Yes! That's right. What you see on ABC
TV, that's exactly how we all act in Nashville.
Reid: Of course!
Bill: Which couldn't be further from the truth. But yet, you know what,
Reid? They must've gotten the idea somewhere. Something's going
on while I'm asleep in this town. There's behavior going on... that
shouldn't be going on. That's how they know to write it for television.
Reid: I never watch *Nashville*, but I like to watch *Sesame Street*.
Bill: Do ya'? I love *Sesame Street*. And you know what they need on that
ABC TV show *Nashville*? Those people need to watch more *Sesame
Street* and quit doing the things that they do that they know better.
Reid: Of course!

Reid asked this man with the rich mahogany voice what his top-five country songs would be if he was making a road trip playlist.

Bill: Mercy, mercy, mercy. These are the questions I ask people and they
go, "Oh man, why did you ask me that? I'm gonna make somebody
mad if you leave them out." And now, I know how they feel.

Bill laughed heartily, and Reid copied his laugh again down to the slightest intonation and cadence. It was hilarious. I sat within arms' reach of Reid stifling my own guffaws. Bill shared a few of his choices with us nonetheless: Bob Wills and the Texas Playboys. Leroy Parnell. Kelly Willis and Bruce Robison's duet project *Americana*. Michael Martin Murphy. Corb Lund and the Hurtin' Albertans. It was our primer in country music that livened up the rest of our road trip.

Reid was adlibbing now, having finished the list of written

questions. As a result of making the podcast, Reid has improved his spontaneous language and conversation skills. This interview was a case in point. Unlike rhetorical questions a speech therapist asked about today's weather or comprehension of a story, this was the real Bill Cody answering exactly what Reid wanted to know. Bill had genuine interest that Reid reciprocated.

Reid: Do you love Dolly Parton?

Bill: Yes and you know what, Reid?

Reid: What?

Bill: She. Loves. Me!

Reid: She loves you?

Bill: Yes, she does, you ask her. Have you interviewed her yet?

Reid: Nooo ...?

Bill: When you get a chance to interview Dolly Parton, ask her if she loves Bill Cody.

Reid: Alright. I'll think about it. I'll consider it.

In Reid's mind where reality and fantasy blur, Dolly may have been around the corner in a waiting room. He didn't have those questions printed out. He doesn't do anything without thinking about it first. Bill belly laughed.

Reid: That's really funny, Bill.

Bill: Can't get enough a' her. She is so special. And if you meet her, you'll say the same thing, buddy!

This interview was one that went over the promised twenty minutes. But Bill seemed to be enjoying it so much, as were my mom and I. On our way out of the building, I checked my watch. It had been nearly an hour.

Reid was expanding his horizons as people invested in his life through conversation and personal storytelling. The next day, we went to the George Jones Museum because now we had a hook. We didn't stay long, but the experience of finding it on the map, buzzing through each exhibit room, and taking a photo in front set a new precedent. In the long run, life experience yields humility like it had for Bill Cody, who has no doubt seen it all and still made time for us.

> *"Travel is fatal to prejudice, bigotry, and narrow-mindedness, and many of our people need it sorely on these accounts."* —Mark Twain[40]

---

40 Twain, Mark. *The Innocents Abroad.* T. W. Press, 2013.

SPROUT FILM AND TRAVEL PROGRAMS
New York City
GoSprout.org

I realize not everybody can drive across the country with his or her own tour guide. I happen to enjoy living much of my life as a Reid-centric adventure. It works for our family. An amazing program called Sprout Travel offers another option. I love their tagline: making the invisible visible. Their programs are not just about getting otherwise housebound individuals out and about; they are also about them being seen. Which begs a profound question: Who benefits more? The traveler or those who see them out and about?

Founded in 1979 by Anthony Di Salvo, Sprout is a nonprofit dedicated to bringing innovative travel and film programs to people with intellectual and developmental disabilities. Di Salvo worked for Hostelling International around the time Geraldo Rivera was exposing the horrific conditions at Willowbrook State School on Staten Island. Against that backdrop, Di Salvo began to meet individuals with disabilities who were staying at his hostel. In a remarkably humble move, he befriended them and took the initiative to organize day trips around the region with them. Over time, these developed into a brochure of trips to the Catskills, Atlantic City, the Bahamas, Hawaii, and the Beatles' Liverpool. The trips are in great demand from respite agencies, group homes, family support programs, and state-funded departments of developmental services. Groups have eleven travelers on average with three leaders. Many are custom designed for the needs of the participants.

Over time, Di Salvo's contagious passion for film impacted the educational travel experiences. He offered a Make-a-Movie trip on which the travelers created films with NYC actors, writers, and directors who came along on a weeklong adventure. At first, the finished movies were screened in the Sprout office. But as a body of work accrued, they hosted a Sprout Film Festival at The Metropolitan Museum of Art. The festival gained attention and attendance, and people began submitting related films from all over the world. Now, Sprout offers touring film festivals throughout the year in thirty-five cities across the United States, and they will customize a selection of films for your gathering. Di Salvo curates them, many as fundraisers, to give local nonprofits, colleges, and organizations an alternative to flying to NYC. Check their website for a film festival near you.[41]

Sproutflix, Sprout's film division, now includes more than 250 titles, making them the only distributor of films that exclusively feature people with intellectual and developmental disabilities. Their one caveat is that they do not accept films in which actors portray disabilities they do not have. Di Salvo's favorite is *One Question,* a short film he directed in 2012 in which thirty-five people with intellectual and developmental disabilities answer the same one question: If you could change one thing about yourself, what would you change?

Director of operations, Scott Randall, says his favorite aspect of Sprout is seeing awareness grow in communities. He has witnessed people with no exposure to disability get involved as an obligation for a class project, then leave emotionally affected, more aware, and return again as a trip leader. Hotels want to know when Sprout groups are coming back, and passersby at restaurants pick up the tab for Sprout groups to show their appreciation and acknowledge them. The invisible *are* being made visible when they share a karaoke floor in Orlando or sample mochi with surfers on Waikiki.

---

41 Sproutflix.org.

Randall receives gratifying thank you calls from guardians and case managers who describe how a timid, reluctant traveler blossomed and returned a changed man or woman. Of their entire database, Randall's favorite film is *The Social Club,* the result of a Make-A-Movie trip in 1998.

Like travel, films can inspire, entertain, and affect social change. Hopefully, you've been impacted by a few films described in this book. Sprout has films on many intriguing topics including autism, Down syndrome, employment, family, independence, and art. I think these films should be required viewing for ability awareness in high schools and colleges. Watching lead actors and subjects of documentaries who have disabilities exposes the general public to the important issues they face and moves these people from the margins into the limelight. The more we see people of different colors, genders, nationalities, and abilities, the more "art can imitate life" as Henry James the great novelist first suggested. If we live in a bubble, whether due to color, creed, or ability, we create the equivalent of white bread for art.

Imagine how empowering it would be to grow up with a disability and watch a family that looks like yours on screen. Representation is a powerful precursor to social change and supporting human rights. The way people with disabilities are portrayed in the media determines whether they will continue to be marginalized or not.

One of the Sproutflix titles I enjoy is *How's Your News?* In 2012, *The New York Times* called *How's Your News? On the Campaign Trail* installment "the highlight of tonight's election programming."[42]

---

42 Daily Mail. "Laughing all the way to election! Disabled reporters' hilarious and touching interviews with Republican big guns on campaign trail."DailyMail.co.uk. https://www.dailymail.co.uk/news/article-2220585/So-Hows-YOUR-News-Developmentally-disabled-adults-interview-politicians-campaign-trail-hilarious-touching-video.html (accessed March, 2018).

The team of reporters with mental and physical disabilities are sometimes articulate, other times unintelligible, and often hilarious in humbling politicians like no one else can. Even when you aren't sure what the reporters asked, their interactions with convention attendees like Hillary Clinton and John McCain provide unique insights. Experts figure that ninety-three percent of communication is nonverbal, right? Watching the body language of the politicians is as informative as the unorthodox line of questioning.

I love watching people take the trip from shock to surprise when these newscasters approach them. Most of them progress to comprehension, and then to participation. The interviews are a slow-motion illustration of how we move from thinking only about ourselves to noticing, engaging, and even appreciating someone else. As our pastor, Mark Foreman, has said, "We really learn to love when we notice there is someone else in the room." These very visible people "in the room" change the playing field. It's impossible to ignore a man who has to be lifted in and out of a wheelchair or a reporter who drools. The responses of those interviewed move from predictable sound-bites of rhetoric to meaningful interchanges that reveal personhood on both sides of the mic.

As you might imagine, the Sprout travel program leaders have a strong sense of personhood. They have enough humility to disregard the awkwardness, stares, and potential incidents they may encounter in favor of giving their friends meaningful experiences and a chance to influence others. Lawyers, engineers, teachers, and college students alike are drawn to these direct experiences where they can see the impact of their investment in others. Motivated by this sense of fulfillment, Sprout trip leaders have a compassionate heart for humanity. With an average age of twenty-two, these young volunteers hail from all over the world including Brazil, Denmark, Greece, and Argentina. Many learn about Sprout through word of mouth and volunteer their time as part of three-week work camps that provide a cultural exchange. Some leaders return multiple years at their own expense. They fly to New York City and use their own vacation time to create a travel experience for adults they've never met. After two days of training on logistics, developmental disabilities, possible scenarios, and driving a fifteen-passenger van in Manhattan, they embark together on an adventure of a lifetime.

Cody Blakley, the director of leadership at Sprout, told me his favorite part of being a leader is the autonomy they have to add activities to the itinerary at their own discretion like finding local music festivals. That independence and freedom attracted him and is equally valuable to the differently-abled travelers as a departure

Ten Ways to Meet Friends with Different Abilities

1. Take cookies or a meal to group home near you.
2. Share your passion or skill with adults served by an agency providing supported living.
3. Be a Miracle League baseball buddy or Special Olympics coach in your favorite sport.
4. Volunteer with Sprout Travel or at Camp Pavlika, Young Life, or Adams Camp.
5. Join a Best Buddies chapter.
6. Attend a Down Syndrome, Autism Speaks, or Williams Syndrome Walk.
7. Offer to help someone maneuvering in or out of an accessible parking spot.
8. Build a Buddy Bench for your local park or school.
9. Employ someone with different abilities at your business.
10. Introduce yourself and show an interest in someone you see regularly.

from their supported living environments. It's no wonder the goodbyes at the end of trips are often tearful. Cody sums up the crux of Sprout in the words of Bill Wilson, founder of Alcoholics Anonymous: "To the world, you may be one person, but to one person you may be the world."[43] His Blakley's favorite movie in the catalog is *For the Love of Dogs* about a boy with Asperger's syndrome whose passion for dogs expanded his world.

There's no question travel is educational. I imagine Sprout travelers come home changed, stretched, better able to problem solve, and standing a couple inches taller. Reid came home after our road trip saying he wants to go to China. (I blame Big Bird and Mulan.)

---

43 Goodreads. "Bill Wilson Quotes." Goodreads.com. https://www.goodreads.com/author/quotes/28223.Bill_Wilson (accessed July, 2018).

LOST IN AMERICA[44]

As you know if you're a *Talk Time* subscriber, Reid's favorite movie of all time alternates between *Mary Poppins* and *The Jungle Book*. Allie's is *National Velvet*. Jim's is *Sprout*, an artful surf film by Thomas Campbell with a soundtrack by Brushfire Records' artists. Mine is *Lost in America*.

A quirky Albert Brooks' comedy, he plays an advertising executive who convinces his wife to drop out of society when he is passed over for a promotion. They sell everything, buy a deluxe RV complete with a toaster oven and browning element, and drive east. I laugh out loud even now recalling the premise, Brooks' delivery of lines, and the outcome.

It took me a while to understand why I liked this movie so much—it appeals to the outlaw and explorer in me. And like David Howard (Albert Brooks), I would rather leave town than deal with injustice and a broken system. He knows he deserves the promotion to a partner in the firm. He's already ordered a new Mercedes with Corinthian leather when Phil Shibbano, "the under-qualified sonnofabitch," gets it. Instead of a promotion, they offer David a transfer to New York to work on a new account.

So he's outta there. Screw the establishment. That just resonates with me. After a farewell send-off, David and Linda stop in Las Vegas to get remarried and proceed to "touch Indians" and find themselves. This doesn't go as planned. To David's great surprise, Linda gambles away their entire "nest egg." Though he pitches idea after idea to the casino owner to get his money back, they are now so broke they do not have enough money to fill the tank of their conspicuous, gas-guzzling vehicle. That's humbling.

Two scenes speak to me. In one, David and Linda are pulled

---

44 *Lost in America.* Directed by Albert Brooks. Burbank: Warner Bros., 1985.

over by a motorcycle cop for speeding. Desperate, David talks his way out of a ticket by bonding with the officer over a movie. David based his life on *Easy Rider*, and it turns out, so had the highway patrolman. This quick bond melts the officer's pride, and he decides not to display his full authority. Instead, he tears up the ticket.

I had a similar exchange with an officer recently when I rolled through a red light. I think it was Reid rocking out to the blaring radio of my Volkswagen Beetle that softened him.

"Where are you headed?" He asked after the license and registration bit.

"Band practice at the Boys and Girls Club." We were already late, so I kept it brief.

The officer peered in wondering why the full-grown male in the passenger seat wasn't acknowledging him. Fearing a horror story of police violence like I see scrolling on my Facebook feed, I quickly explained using the label I loathe. "He's got autism." The officer went back to his cruiser with it's high beams in my rearview mirror.

The officer returned gentler, "Alright, I don't need to ruin your holiday. (It was two weeks before Christmas.) Just slow down and pay attention. Have fun at choir."

I showed humility then and didn't correct him. *Choir is Sunday. Tonight is band. Close enough,* I thought to myself. Receiving his grace was more important than accuracy.

Another scene from *Lost in America* showcases humility. In the middle of Arizona, after Linda squanders the "nest egg" that was to last the rest of their lives, she and David find jobs. The best they can land are as an assistant fry cook at der Wienerschnitzel and a school crossing guard. Linda's boss, Skippy, is "real impressed" with her suggestion to thaw the fries before cooking them. It takes all of David's self-control not to level the schoolchildren with his handheld "STOP" sign when they taunt and bully him. David and Linda are humbled, if not humiliated, by their new reality. Skippy's visit to the RV park to see their "home" underscores their plight. They need to drastically reconsider and regroup.

As Skippy leaves, David and Linda realize they have hit rock bottom. They have a tête-à-tête that night, hesitant to share the same idea with each other. Eventually, they're both out with if: they haul ass to New York City and he gets his old job back. They can't agree fast enough. The experiences have shown them what really matters—they still have each other. Tearing it from the hookups, Howard guns the RV east and prepares to grovel.

If pride comes before the fall, maybe it's the falling that teaches humility. David falls dramatically from pride. He starts out feeling entitled to the position of firm partner. Three weeks later, he is begging for his old job back at any salary. Along the way, he's learned that loving—and forgiving—his wife is a greater accomplishment. His priorities change as a result of experience (and travel). A little time on the road is good for all of us.

WRAPPING UP CHAPTER 7

The longer I live, the less I need to hide my imperfections. The more I travel, the farther I move from the center of the universe. The more I experience of life, the less I need to control and the more willing I am to loosen the reins. Letting go, I enter a whole new speed that allows me to connect to something bigger than myself. It's as if loosening my grip of control lets in more possibility. Humility breaks the ice, cracks the veneer, reveals our humanity, and in fact makes us greater.

Taking Reid on a two-week road trip was daunting when we started, but staying home isn't a cakewalk either. I wanted Reid to grow from travel experiences like his sister had. As we began to be vulnerable and honest with fellow travelers, we made unexpected friends who opened unexpected doors. Like peanuts from a stewardess, an interview with Sluggerrr the mascot of the Kansas City Royals fell in our laps. Removing his mask as king of the jungle, Brad Collins shared with us how he has been tamed by life experiences. Behind the mask is a family man who doesn't need a stadium-sized audience to be fulfilled.

Reid grew in responsibility and internal motivation as we found common ground and mutual interests with total strangers in Kansas City, St. Louis, Nashville, and Bloomington. He met a radioman that wanted to be a cowboy. Bill Cody, the ultimate host on air and off, welcomed us into his world and showed Reid another slice of life in Nashville.

Travel expanded our knowledge of barbecue options, country music, and regional dialects. And maybe we spread a little autism awareness to others. As people met Reid and heard about his interests, their awareness turned from general to specific, statistics to realities. As Sprout does through travel programs and films, we were making the invisible visible. Reid moved from the margins into the limelight, much like Sprout leaders take groups of individuals with diverse needs to new places to see and be seen. Awareness, acceptance, and belonging are a sequence in which one builds on the one before. Sprout is moving the needle toward a more inclusive world one traveler, one group, one destination, and one film at a time.

Linda and David in *Lost in America* face many obstacles when they leave their home and jobs. They have to humble themselves more than they imagined. Even though they make mistakes and fail, they learned to draw from a deep well of ability and rise to the occasion. Can you recall a travel experience when you were humbled by a challenge? In hindsight, are you glad you went? What

Interacting with Police

Dennis Debbaudt is the father of a young man with autism and a professional investigator who has developed law enforcement training materials to keep individuals like his son safe. His videos, presentations, and downloadable resources set the standard on how first responders interact with people on the spectrum. They also train those with ASD on emergency preparedness and interacting with the criminal justice system. His website is www. autismriskmanagement.com.

Law enforcement departments are training their officers to understand more about autism interventions to avert unfortunate episodes, especially those that could result in death when officers misinterpret a situation. Of course as supportive neighbors, you aren't ultimately responsible to keep the peace or enforce laws, but Debbaudt's information is helpful background for citizens too.

new experience could expand your horizons? Is there someone you can take with you to force new growth in you both? Stepping out will expose you, humble you, and stretch you into a place of belonging in the greater world.

8

Be a Hero

My heroes are real people who do ordinary things in extraordinary ways on a consistent basis. They don't do it for glory or to get credit. They step in just when you need help to salvage a moment or save the day. They see opportunities to make a difference and grab them. They've got your back when you're tired or about to break. They hold things together.

I've met many heroes who work with children who have special needs. These heroes never give up. They believe in people and possibilities by faith, not by sight. Heroes fortify the air we breathe and strengthen everyone in their orbit. We watch and follow them and are compelled to emulate their attitude and actions.

Jim and I were hooked on the ABC series *Nashville* until Rayna died. We loved the psychological drama and glimpse into the music industry. The Bluebird Café is a veritable character on the show, and possibly the best thing about it. This tiny music venue is legendary, despite its inauspicious locale in a Green Hills strip mall. Taylor Swift was discovered there as was Garth Brooks and Kathy Mattea. Many careers have been nurtured there. Although she has sold the Bluebird Café, one woman remains its unsung hero: Amy Kurland. An interview with her would complete our *Talk Time* tour of musical highlights Nashville.

QUEEN OF HER CAFÉ WHERE MUSIC IS KING: AMY KURLAND OF THE BLUEBIRD CAFÉ

My mom, Reid, and I arrived mid-morning which is a quiet time at the Bluebird, before the usual lines or tour buses. Walking up a concrete ramp, we entered through the front door under the iconic blue awning. Reid let out his first impression, "Whoaaa, look at that." He slid into a banquette to study rows of framed and signed portraits and CD covers filling one wall. In short order, Amy Kurland came in the back door, through the kitchen I presume. She was a short woman of about sixty, wearing glasses and with her hair pulled back.

We shuffled around deciding where to sit. All the tables were available, unlike what we would find that evening if I could convince Reid to return for the "In the Round" show. Amy reminded me of a cross between singer Carole King and Alice Waters, the activist chef who owns Chez Panisse. She approached Reid with genuine and attentive interest.

Reid: We're here to interview Amy Kirkland. *Oops, he subbed in a familiar name for this new one.* So, Amy, I know the Bluebird Café is like the main character in the TV show *Nashville*. Do you think it is portrayed realistically?

Amy: I like the way it's portrayed in the TV show, and I'll tell you why. Everything else that happens in that show has got greed and lust and all of the seven deadly sins in it. But when you get to the Bluebird, it's always the place where everything is good and done for the right reasons. So I like that about it.

Reid: Alright. How did you pick the location originally?

Amy: I grew up in this neighborhood, and I was looking for a place. I went by and it said, "For Rent" in the window.

She opened the Bluebird as a restaurant initially. As legend has it, the guitar player she was dating convinced her to put in a stage where musicians could play at night.

Reid: Alright. Way back in 1982, did you ever imagine how legendary it would become?
Amy: Absolutely not. I think it's totally an accident and the grace of God.

Her humility started to show. She didn't take credit for the food or the music or success.

Reid: What makes the Bluebird unique?
Amy: It's small. People really listen here. It's very intimate. And it's all about the songwriters.

She knew their brand and identity before that was even a term.

Reid: What do you appreciate most about songwriters, Amy?
Amy: I appreciate that they can take my experience or anybody's experience and just cut right to the heart of it—the most emotional part of it—but make it general enough so that everyone can feel what I feel.

She is well known for supporting songwriters. She wasn't one herself, though her dad had been a session musician and arranger.

Reid: How did you develop such a good ear?

Reid was trying to get at her superpower.

Amy: *She chuckled at the thought.* My mother raised me to listen to Broadway musical shows. So I listened to *Oklahoma* and *Kiss Me Kate*, that sort of thing.

Reid: I have a favorite musical, *Chitty Chitty Bang Bang* with Dick Van
    Dyke, Sally Ann Howes.
Amy: Oh, I love that one! Yes. The songs in there are a lot like country
    music because the lyrics tell a story. In rock and roll music, the lyrics
    tell an emotion. But in country music, they tell a story.
Reid: Alright. What audition advice would you give a young songwriter?
Amy: Well, I guess there's two kinds of advice. One is about the kind of
    song they write. They need to write something that is real and mean-
    ingful ... and not about trying to get a hit or get on the radio. It has to
    mean something to them. And then, when they get here, they should
    not come in wearing a big cowboy hat and a lot of sequins.

She must have given this advice to a thousand aspiring musicians.

Reid: Alright.
Amy: And ... they should remember their lyrics!
Reid: What should they wear, Amy?
Amy: Blue jeans, tee shirt, and a baseball cap ... or whatever they're com-
    fortable in.

Easy enough. Fancy did not impress this woman as much as authentic. Amy confessed that she was always nervous on stage. Reid
asked her about a funny audition story. The only one she could
remember—or wanted to share—was of a guy whose middle finger
was wrapped up in a big white bandage. He seemed to be flipping
off the whole audience, "Bless his heart."

Reid: I know they call you the "First Lady of Nashville." What's your high
    point of living here?

She demurred at this question. So many good things had happened to her. Nashville was home. She didn't brag, but I reckon the title was given to her as a result of her extensive effort and investment in the common good.

Reid: Do you have a low point?

Amy: Oh, goodness, the first five years I was in business were terrifying to me. And I was going broke. I don't know if I could pinpoint a particular day, although some mornings when the cook didn't show up and I thought, "How am I gonna run a restaurant?" Those were some bad days.

A hero not only protects and defends others but also displays courage in the face of obstacles. Amy had done both for the community, not for her own fame or honor. The Bluebird was a community watering hole and a songwriter's safe place long before the tour buses started pulling up and it was a tourist attraction.

Reid: Alright. How did you train audiences to be respectful?

Amy: That's a wonderful question. To be honest with you, the audiences trained themselves. And then, they trained each other. I'd come in, and there'd be a show going on, and nobody would make any noise. Then somebody would talk, and the audience would turn around and go, 'Shhhhhh,' to them.

We did not make it back for a show that night. Truth be told, I didn't want to get "shhhhushed" if Reid started singing along. No regrets though; this spoken word podcast was a song in itself.

Reid covered favorite movies. Amy is partial to Audrey Hepburn oldies, but when Reid listed his classics adding *The Wizard of Oz*, she had to rethink her answer.

Amy: Let's just change mine to *The Wizard of Oz* too. Some great, great
    songs in there.
Reid: So, is there anything you like to ask me?
Amy: Oh, I want to know everything.

She was serious. Her superpower isn't her ear for music after all. It is her hospitality and desire to help people thrive. She is the perpetual booster, the one in your corner, a behind-the-scenes encourager who is more concerned that you look—or sound—good than what you thought of her. Since leaving the daily operations at the Bluebird, Amy has committed her time to helping the people of Nashville. Having known so many musicians struggling with addiction, she champions recovery causes.

The modus operandi of a hero is humility. They slip in unannounced and do significant work to pave the way for others.

> *"Heroes are people who rise to the occasion
> and slip quietly away."* —Tom Brokaw[45]

---

45 The Seattle Times. "Plains-born Tom Brokaw signing off." Old.SeattleTimes.com. http://old.seattletimes.com/html/television/2002103460_brokaw29.html (accessed August, 2018).

NONPAREIL INSTITUTE
Plano, Houston, and Austin, Texas and Orlando, Florida
NPItx.org

The word "nonpareil" has a French origin and means "no parallel." It is both a noun and adjective, and Webster's defines nonpareil as an unrivaled or matchless thing. Synonyms include peak of perfection, finest, crème de la crème, incomparable, unrivaled, and peerless. NonPareil is an apt name for this program.

NonPareil Institute offers adults with autism post-secondary educational training in digital technology as well as the soft skills required to succeed in the workplace. Their students have an unparalleled competitive advantage once it is nurtured. Two fathers, Dan Selec and Gary Moore, shared my quandary: "What happens when my child grows up?" So in 2000, they founded nonPareil in Plano, Texas, and it now serves more than two hundred adults at training sites in Plano and Houston. The Institute is currently expanding to Orlando, Florida and Austin, Texas. Their crewmembers, as students are called, build market-competitive products while gaining skills to become more independent, self-sufficient, and contributing members of the community.

As heroes do, the founders Dan and Gary recognized their sons' natural inclination for technology and helped them harness this potential like a superpower. Mindful that their sons would need technical training to pursue their passion, as much as Julia Child needed training to become a chef, Dan and Gary designed a flexible, self-paced training program that is "gamified." Crewmembers complete "quests" to attain their personal goals. The focus at nonPareil is on the relative strengths of those with autism instead of on their weaknesses. Students gain an entirely new mode of communication and potential for productivity.

All of the technical training at the nonPareil is focused on bringing digital products to life. As a result, learning is meaningful and motivating. Through one-on-one and small group courses, crewmembers learn industry skills including 3D modeling, programming, digital arts, video game design, animation, workplace readiness skills, time management, teamwork, and project management. The Institute also offers core classes in communication and professionalism in a supportive and accommodating community of like-minded individuals. "All for One and One for All" is their collective motto that expresses the sense of belonging we all crave.

Each campus also has a robust social calendar of clubs and events born of crewmember interests. In these clubs and events, crewmembers practice compromise, responsibility, accountability, and leadership. The Institute's "Programming Hope" video online captures the camaraderie that is inevitable when people with the same passion unite. Like a convention of young programmers, a scene at Comiccon, or name-your-special-interest gathering, nonPareil Institute is irresistible to young adults who want to work at what they love.

Mark Theurer is the director of operations at the Plano nonPareil site. Having been a Dungeons & Dragons gaming nerd as a teen, he appreciates how the culture at nonPareil moves so many students from the fringe to the norm. When Theurer's son became a crewmember, Theurer was right at home facilitating board games and elaborate imaginative social games with other parent volunteers. Eventually, he joined the staff at nonPareil. Theurer has watched his son's initial interest in anime expand dramatically. After five years at the Institute, his son has blossomed as an artist and taken on new responsibilities as an associate instructor, sharing his subject matter expertise with crewmembers. Six other crewmembers have become full-time employees. Theurer's high point is partnering with other parents to help their sons and daughters find fulfilling adult lives. He enjoys welcoming crewmembers to nonPareil with the message that, "It's okay to be you."

In addition to training, nonPareil provides meaningful

employment for adults with autism. To date, nonPareil has provided more than 120,000 hours of paid employment. They connect with large and small companies that outsource technology-related work, so inclusive teams can work side-by-side to provide software and app development in the marketplace. NonPareil crew have published more than ten games and apps that are commercially available on iTunes, Android, and Steam as well as several books and comics that are available through Amazon.

From the beginning, the founders of nonPareil planned to take the program across the country. Their computer-focused training is designed to be duplicated efficiently in other locations. Plans to expand in Connecticut and Fort Worth are in the works.

Ways to Amplify Your Child's Special Interest

1. Study your child
2. Notice what others notice
3. Embrace differences
4. Look for the affinity
5. Teach to the strength
6. Experiment to find a niche
7. Adapt as age appropriate
8. Play to the strength
9. Cultivate mentors
10. Generalize every skill everywhere
11. Never mind the box
12. Define success

See the expanded version of this list in my first book, *One-Track Mind: 15 Ways to Amplify Your Child's Special Interest*. JAM Ink, 2015.

JULIE & JULIA[46]

As a foodie and a blogger, I devoured Julie Powell's book *Julie and Julia: My Year of Cooking Dangerously*. I had already read Julia Child's *My Life in France* and *France is Feast*. When the movie came out, I was first in line. After it released on DVD, Reid and I made a study of Julia, pulling up episodes of *The French Chef* on YouTube and enjoying her accidental hilarity and signature quirks. At the time, Reid was practicing independent cooking skills. I filmed him juicing lemons and doing Julia impersonations of her catchphrases like "butt-h-er" and "Bon Appétit!"

From the moment Julia Child set foot on French soil in the movie, I wanted to be her. She is on an adventure with her husband, has free time in Paris, and pursues a delicious passion. I relate to her largeness; we both have shoebox-sized feet, frizzy hair, and the inability to get pregnant.

But as accomplished as both Julie Powell and Julia Child were, it is their husbands who were the heroes. Paul Child (Stanley Tucci) makes me cry. He is all in for Julia (Meryl Streep); he supports her interests, believes in her, and loves her wholeheartedly. He happily eats the mountain of onions she has to chop to practice for *l'ecole*. He lugs home a giant mortar and pestle as a gift for her. When Julia's manuscript is rejected, he's madder at Houghton-Mifflin than she is. Ultimately when they come back to the States, he resigns from his own career to help her prosper her burgeoning television work. Although he toasts her as the "butter to his bread," I think the relationship works both ways. He is the vital piece, the helpmate, and the reason for her success. After all, she wouldn't have even been in France if it weren't for Paul.

Their storied first meal in Rouen was sole meunière. After the waiter debones the fish tableside, Julia breathes in the "butt-h-er"

---

46 *Julie & Julia*. Directed by Nora Ephron. Columbia Pictures, 2009.

and exhales orgasmic groans of pleasure with every morsel. She offers Paul a bite, and they are speechless together. As the next course arrives, they brainstorm what Julia will do during Paul's assignment at the embassy.

They joke about hat making and recreational activities the other expatriate spouses are doing. Then Paul presses Julia for what makes her truly happy. Patient and cultured, Paul helps Julia discern her true passion. Half joking, she says she does love to eat. The scene reveals her passion for cooking and methodology in dissection and translating French processes for American cooks.

Heroes invest in others. They listen closely and care. They invest brainpower and give honest, helpful guidance. Heroes also stick around until a solution is found and until the mission is accomplished. Paul Child does all this for Julia.

Eric Powell (Chris Messina) is also supportive when his wife, Julie (Amy Adams), decides to cook her way through Julia Child's *Mastering the Art of French Cooking* and blog about it. He ingests copious amounts of butter, emboldens Julie to be a lobstah' killah' (using the Maine pronunciation), and washes all the pots and pans she dirties in the tiny kitchen of their Queens walk-up. It's fun for the first month but eventually becomes self-sacrifice.

The scene I love with Eric is when he indulges Julie with a set of pearls to complete her fantasy of becoming Julia. Julia Child wore a string as consistently as Barbara Bush did. The Powell's closest friends are over to celebrate Julie's thirtieth birthday. Dressed as characters in Julia Child's inner circle, they recreate one of the Child's storied dinners. Eric presents Julie with the fake pearls after devouring a meal of lobster, braised cucumber, and chocolate cake.

Chris Messina, the actor who plays Eric, was interviewed about the movie. "It is really about finding your own voice, enjoying the sound of it, and singing loud. In that way, it is a story of possibility."[47]

Doesn't everyone deserve the same? We all need a champion like the one Chris played. His constant vote is one of confidence. I have a husband who is for me in action and deed. Like Eric Powell for Julie and Paul Child for Julia, Jim Moriarty believed in me before I believed in myself. We can be heroes to people with disabilities by helping them define their passion and pursue it. Believing in someone before they know what they can accomplish is life changing.

WRAPPING UP CHAPTER 8

The world contains many unsung heroes like Amy Kurland and Paul Child. Amy Kurland claims that the success of the Bluebird Café was an unexpected accident, but she has made it a place of hope, honesty, and encouragement for songwriters and musicians. Her life is not about herself, but about others. She made a place—literally a stage—where people could share their voice, find an audience, and practice their calling. A true hero, Amy protects and defends others, displays courage in the face of obstacles, and preserves the common good.

The founders of the nonPareil Institute, Dan Selec and Gary Moore, are heroes for recognizing the natural inclination for technology in their sons and harnessing that passion as a marketable skill. They created customized training and a place where students can interact, socialize, and pursue employment with the assistance they need to be successful. That's heroic.

Once her passion was identified, Julia Child needed training. She threw herself into mastering the art of French cooking for nearly ten years. Supporting her was Paul Child, her heroic

---

47 Tribute. "Chris Messina Interview 2009." Tribute.ca. https://www.tribute.ca/interviews/chris-messina-julie-julia/star/35276/ (accessed July, 2018).

husband, who invested in her career as much as or maybe more than he did in his own. He believed in her before she believed in herself. In the movie *Julie & Julia*, Eric Powell also plays a vital role in his wife's zealous ambition. Both husbands humble their egos to conspire, console, and congratulate. As true heroes, they sacrifice for their wives.

Do you know someone who has a gift they don't see in themselves? How can you help them identify their passion, find relevant training, and stay the course to completion? Maybe you can be a hero to them.

KINDNESS

When I tell the story of how Jim and I fell in love, it includes a treacherous drive home in a blizzard after work. We were seniors in high school bussing tables at a restaurant. I gave him a ride home in my mom's Volkswagen Rabbit after midnight through the snow belt that runs along the edge of Lake Erie. As we inched down a steep hill on South Woodland Road, we passed a car in the ditch. *Yikes*.

At the bottom of the icy hill after we escaped the danger of skidding ourselves, I exhaled. We were silent until Jim said, "There's a phone booth at the polo field. Pull over, and I'll call to get them help." This was decades before cell phones. Phone booths dotted the landscape, and you knew where they were in your neighborhood.

"Let's just call from your house, if we make it there," I replied. We had two miles more to go on a sloped brick road. "I don't want to pull off the plowed road," I reasoned. "What if *we* get stuck in a snowbank?"

"We need to call them help. They might freeze out here," he insisted. "You have to stop."

"Alright."

I pulled off the road, and Jim phoned the local police. It was a small thing, but I took note of his kindness. This guy did the right thing even when he had nothing to gain. He took the responsibility and the time. He was kind. It's an attractive trait more people need—then and now.

Twenty years later, Jim made a vow to give money to every

homeless person he sees—at home, on off-ramps, in cities, and when he travels. He is consistent about this, and if you debate it he insists, "If they spend it on booze, that's between them and God. It's on me to share. So that's what I'm gonna do." Jim once gave a pricey tweed sports coat to a homeless man in New York City because he looked cold. People like to talk about random acts of kindness, but these aren't random. They're intentional, predictable, and consistent.

We tend to live egocentric lives that can speed by quickly. And when we are busy revering efficiency and power, we may find that we barely have time to show kindness. Being consumed with getting ahead leaves no time for the few minutes that showing a little tenderness requires. We are lost in our own worlds, social media walls, and distracted minds. We can begin to treat others as competitors in a race in which we are all vying for the same prizes—the finite supply of love, money, or fame. Or worse, we might perceive others as being in our way, which can breed selfishness, indifference, or hatred—the opposites of kindness.

What's even more concerning is that if we are not showing or experiencing kindness, we run the risk of becoming disconnected and depressed. Wise psychologists and recovery programs prescribe volunteering as an antidote to isolation, depression, and addiction. The intentional effort of caring for someone else lifts us out of the doldrums.

The results of a lack of kindness can be circular, just like refusing to take risks or to cultivate humility. As we eliminate these attributes from our daily lives, we can become fearful, prideful, and consumed with ourselves. The world then becomes a more fearful, prideful, unkind place without even a glimmer of the alternatives. Then we can't see the solutions—the examples of risk, humility, and kindness—that provide a way to save us. Our reality darkens exponentially. Like the displaced, boneless blobs in the movie *Wall-E*, we scoot around in "antigrav chairs" and forget what earth used to look like. As *Wall-E* director Andrew Stanton said, "love defeats programming" in this consumerist dystopia.[48]

SEEING KINDNESS IN *TALK TIME*

Meeting Reid in all his exuberance is like having Tigger bounce into your personal space. He can be a friendly steamroller who asks personal questions with a charming sort of brass, and his manner gives podcast guests pause. In a moment, they have to make a choice. They could offer a correction, take offense, or show him the door, but so far none have. Instead, each one has chosen kindness and responded with grace to Reid's mispronounced words, sticky hands, and awkward entrance. They've also shown me how much kindness matters.

These people make kindness more than a random act. Whether being kind is part of their brand or their personal background, it is intentional. They have rolled with Reid's missteps and given him tee shirts, hats, and credit when it wasn't due. Reid is learning kindness by mirroring and matching the tone of their voices, sending them thank you notes, and listening to them on repeat on SoundCloud.

My experience is that people with disabilities lift us out of apathy without trying or realizing they are. Engaging with them requires some risk. But their inabilities spark kindness. Steering clear of "inspiration porn" here, I don't mean that we should objectify them based on their disability. We dare not exploit them to become better people ourselves. It's just that their needs are an invitation to

---

48 Voice of America. "Robot 'Wall-E' Holds Unexpected Message About Love in Animated Film." VOA News. https://www.voanews.com/a/a-13-2008-07-01-voa16/406790.html (accessed April, 2018).

live more intentionally in community. When we do, we all thrive. This synergy is mutually beneficial.

When people show kindness to Reid, they have nothing to gain. They do it out of pure motives rather than to get ahead. He doesn't always reciprocate. Neither diluted nor convoluted, kindness shown to individuals with a disability is like an essential oil, a concentrated fragrance because it is kindness for kindness' sake.

Having a child with special needs who is spirited, challenging, or just noticeable (you choose the euphemism) means you experience a lot of awkward, stressful moments in public. I've shared a few with you already. What I can also recount is a larger-than-average number of kind and generous acts. More than once, I've had a stranger pick up my tab at our favorite local Mexican joint. One time when we flew into London we were whisked to the front of a massive customs line by the mercy of an observant customs officer.

THE POWER OF UNEXPECTED KINDNESS

I remember a woman whose kindness brought tears to my eyes. I can still see her face. In the midst of a family reunion, we had stopped for lunch at a bustling clam-and-crab house on Cape Hatteras. If you've traveled with someone with ASD, you know that new places, extra people, and unusual sights and smells can be a recipe for a meltdown. Everything about being on vacation is overwhelming, even if the itinerary is carefully managed. The more people involved—picture a family reunion in four houses for Jim's five siblings and their offspring—the harder it becomes. Still, we were having some fun, and how else can you learn flexibility besides practice?

Wind was whipping across the inlet, tummies were growling, and the table was cramped. Reid was gonna blow, I could smell it like the salt in the air. Though he was twelve, he was wiggling like a toddler. His eyes darted around the room as he took in the clinking of silverware and smell of clams. He pushed away the kiddie menu and complimentary crayons. I was afraid he might go off like a siren and empty the place. Cousins and uncles at our table for six were carrying on in full voices. They were uninitiated in how fast a full-scale meltdown could result from so many new variables. I must have had those familiar beads of sweat at my hairline as I fished for a fidget in my purse or something familiar on the menu for Reid to eat besides the ubiquitous fries. This juggling act made me crave takeout over conversation.

As I was scrambling, soothing, and exhibiting signs of tension, I became aware of grandmother in her seventies across the room staring at me. She caught my gaze and mouthed, "He's doing great. Don't worry. You are just fine."

What? What did you say? My brow must have furrowed or my face recoiled while I tried to make out her pantomime. I expected people to complain, snicker, and judge. I was taken aback by her compassion. I returned a weak smile. *Okay, we're not ruining everyone else's meal.*

That's kindness, intentional thoughtfulness extended at just the right moment. A smile can get someone through an impossible day. A compliment can change the tide in your attitude toward life. Someone holding a door reminds us we're not alone. Graciousness breaks a tie in the war of good against evil and lets you know love is winning. It can reframe a memory for all time.

Being faced with the unexpected, or someone exhibiting unexpected behavior, reveals a person's true nature. You might catch a glimpse of annoyance or hatred. Other times compassion. I'm impressed by how many people I can recount who have been nicked by our infractions to reveal a cross section of solid, hardwood kindness through and through. Even some whose veneer is brusque have an inner layer that is forgiving, allowing, and accepting. What do you see under your own skin?

Kindness ricochets. When you are kind, people respond in kind. Now that Reid is older, those near and actual meltdowns are infrequent because people are showing him good will directly rather than vicariously through me. Like the times the grocery checkers let him scan his own items or extend grace as he elbows a bagger out of the way. He likes to do that himself too.

Reid now extends kindness to me quite often. He has learned it not through osmosis but through careful, calculated observation of those around him. Regulating kindness by requiring manners and politeness works moderately well. But I think Reid has learned kindness more from experience. Amazing teachers, mentors, and friends have modeled open-heartedness for him. If you haven't experienced kindness yourself, it might never occur to you that you can give it to someone else.

Reid and I were at Panera Bread last week when out of the blue he asked, "Mom, how is your soufflé?" It caught me off guard; it was so thoughtful. That's how I speak to him. He went on, "Do you want a bite of my cookie?"

Often, Reid gets nose to nose with his buddy, Paul, or me with a very direct, "I love you!" He means it. You can't drill that into someone with autism. They catch it by copying what's been shown to them, which is also the best motivator of all. If we show goodwill to children, they will likely repeat it as adults.

FOUR RESULTS OF SHOWING KINDNESS

In this last section, I will describe four results of kindness. First, I think kindness restores our faith in humanity. When we witness small gestures of goodness, we believe in each other anew. Often sheer kindness brings adults with disabilities to center stage, if only for one scene. When we as humble supporting actors take a risk and show concern, our attitude and action create connection that restores faith in humanity in others. It feels good to everyone to know someone cares.

Second, in this culture where time is money, giving our time away to be kind renders it priceless. Even if you're multitasking, just offering a smile changes the atmosphere. Kindness is that powerful. Elusive as a vapor, it spreads and refreshes the environment. As it accumulates people notice. Whether in homes, schools, in the media, or Congress, when we take the time to show kindness rather than minimize or belittle others, respect and decency become the new normal.

Third, kindness is an expression of grace that brings heaven down to earth. Kindness is a derivative of love. When we exercise kindness, we are practicing the law of heaven. We are enacting the promise of "no more tears, no more sorrow, and no more pain" here and now, instead of waiting until eternity to experience it (Rev. 21:4). I believe God has "placed eternity in our hearts," (Eccles. 3:11) meaning we all have a sense there is "something more" than this transient, fallen, broken world, which drives our instinctual craving to belong. Our hope for heaven drives us to a higher standard—aspiring to lives of kindness.

"What sunshine is to flowers, kindness
is to humanity." —Joseph Addison,
English playwright[49]

---

49 Joseph Addison Quotes. BrainyQuote.com. https://www.brainyquote.com/quotes/joseph_addison_121178 (accessed June, 2018).

Presume Competence

Presuming competence means assuming a person with disabilities has the capacity to think, learn, and understand—even if you don't see tangible evidence. It means assuming they can succeed with the right supports and systems. The idea known as "the least dangerous assumption" was formulated in 1984 by Anne Donnellan.[*] In the absence of any evidence one way or the other, which of two assumptions will do less harm to an individual should it prove to be wrong: the assumption that they are competent or incompetent? It is far safer to assume that an individual is competent.

Presuming competence is about giving someone a chance and helping them take that chance in any way you can. Scientific research has revealed that we have been underestimating the intelligence and capabilities of people on the spectrum by giving them tests that inherently stack the odds against them. For example, we wrongly link an inability to speak with an inability to think.

Specific actions that presume competence include the following:

- Find a way to help a person communicate, whether through speech, speech-generating devices, pictures, gestures, or sign language.
- Pay close attention to what they're trying to tell you. Behavior is communication, and it may very well be that the person is expressing something important in this way.
- Expose them to the things you would any other person.
- When describing a person, focus on her abilities and needs.
- Use age-appropriate vocabulary, topics, and inflection when talking to people. (Not baby talk or shouting.)
- Respect the person's privacy. *Never* talk about him as if he was not in the room.

[*] Ollibean. "Outing the Prejudice: Making the Least Dangerous Assumption." Ollibean.com. https://ollibean.com/outing-the-prejudice-making-the-least-dangerous-assumption/ (accessed May, 2018).

9

Restore Faith in Humanity

When kindness stands out as unusual in our day or our week, we realize how scarce it has become. Like a rare animal nearing extinction, one simple act of benevolence can surprise us when it crosses our path. Its very existence restores our faith in humanity. Goodwill convinces us we can survive anything. It makes me sing the immortal lyrics of *Mister Rogers' Neighborhood* theme song in my head. Kindness is comfort food for the spirit.

You know where you can find both affection and comfort food under one roof? Your nearest Trader Joe's store. A trip to this neighborhood grocery with free samples of amazing food from around the globe, engaging clerks, and a fun atmosphere lifts my spirit in more ways than one. Not only can I get a quart of Coffee Bean Blast ice cream, I can also stock up on creamed honey and gorgonzola gnocchi and browse wines with a knowledgeable French woman. I'd rather buy my Himalayan pink salt and lavender dryer sachets there than anywhere else. And where else can you enjoy karaoke while holiday shopping?

THE RADIO VOICE OF AN EXECUTIVE: DAN BANE OF TRADER JOE'S

Reid loves Trader Joe's as much as I do. The dozens of tortilla chip flavors have him hooked as well as the French sparkling lemonade in three flavors and their vintage radio ads. We knew their chief executive officer, Dan Bane, from his radio voice long before we ever invited him to be on Reid's podcast.

We were bold to email him. He replied, "Sounds like fun." He said he was out of the country (purveying new foods, no doubt) and would connect when he returned. He was true to his word. While travel, health, and scheduling stood in our way, nine months later we were driving to Trader Joe's corporate offices in Monrovia in the foothills of the San Gabriel mountains in Los Angeles County. Reid was learning delayed gratification.

What a man—the perfect blend of humility, hard work, compassion, and ethical wisdom. Seventy-one, he wore glasses and a blue and white, harpoon-patterned Hawaiian shirt. You might mistake him for a favorite coach, a regular vendor at the farmer's market, or an accountant on vacation. He is approachable, experienced, and helpful, maybe because of the nametag he wore as much as his gray hair. We followed him through a maze of cubicles that struck me as a cleaned-up spice market with low dividers to encourage barkers to negotiate. On the wall of the conference room hung a framed Hawaiian shirt that was six feet by six feet across, no kidding.

Dan Bane: See that shirt?

Reid: I like it!

Dan Bane: I wore that shirt at one of our annual meetings. I was trying to get everybody to think we're going to go BIG into produce so, I wore the biggest shirt I could find.

The nametag on the framed shirt read, "BIG KAHUNA."

Reid: It's so huge.

Dan Bane: *(aside to me)* That was actually a shirt ... I found a lady in Hawaii that made 'em. It was actually the size shirt that a guy wore who was a singer: Iz. *(to Reid)* Remember, Iz?

Reid: Israel Kamakawiwoʻole?

Reid knew who he was and could pronounce the last name of the "big Hawaiian man" who sang with a tiny ukulele.

Dan Bane: You're better than me. That was his size when he was alive.

Reid: Oh, my goodness. I'm here to interview you.

Dan Bane: I know!

He said it like he was ready to relax and enjoy this.

Reid: Are you ready?

Dan Bane: I think I'm ready. I've seen some of your stuff. It's pretty tough.

Reid: Alright, the first question is: How many Hawaiian shirts do you have?

Dan Bane: That's a good question. My closet is absolutely full of Hawaiian shirts. There are probably fifty, and I throw away ... I don't throw away. I give to Goodwill probably ten a year, 'cuz everybody buys me Hawaiian shirts for all birthdays and holidays. I get most of them through the company, cuz' the company gives everybody eight shirts a year. For everybody. And at the end of the day, I'm gonna give you a couple shirts.

Reid: Of course, Dan Bane! *Dan giggled in a cute way. Reid's missing politeness markers didn't offend him. Acts of kindness are not dependent on other people's manners or thanks.* I love nametags. Why do you think they work so well?

Dan Bane: I like nametags because .... All of us in the office have our nametags on. We wear 'em because we want the store people to

know that we're ready to come work in the store at any time. If they
need us, we're there.

Reid: They're so pretty.

Dan Bane: So, you wear nametags?

Reid: Yea, I always wear nametags. Jam Session has nametags, but maybe
I should wear a nametag when I work at Marshalls. What's one thing
you are carrying on from the founder, Joe Coloumbe's, legacy?

Dan Bane: Joe Coloumbe. *He helped with the pronunciation.* Well, Joe
started Trader Joe's back in the '50s, and he started it with Hawaiian
shirts. So I think that's real important for us because it gives us a sort
of signature. It lets people that work in the store know that when
they put on their Hawaiian shirt and the doors open up, it's sort of
like you're on stage ... you're working in a play and you happen to be
in character.

Reid asked Dan Bane who discovers the distinctive products, and
he explained how we had walked through the room of buyers. They
look all over the world for items they find on the internet to im-
port, package, and sell.

Reid: What are some of your favorite staples on your shelves at home?

Dan Bane: Well, one of our favorites is mandarin orange chicken. We always buy that. It's in the frozen section, and it's one of our customers'
favorite. I also love popsicles, so any of our frozen popsicles you'll
find covered in our freezer at home.

Reid: I love Caribbean.

Dan Bane: Yea, me too.

Reid: That's great! Where do you shop if you're in a town without a Trader
Joe's?

We had experienced this dilemma ourselves on the road trip.

Dan Bane: I keep driving ... until I get to a Trader Joe's.

Reid: You keep driving?

Dan Bane: We have 448 of them, and we're in forty states, so I can find one.

Reid: You can find one?

Dan Bane: I just keep driving, Reid. I just keep going.

Reid: Of course.

We learned that Dan Bane has no Vons card in keeping with Trader Joe's policy of giving you the lowest price every time you shop. He pays more for gas to uphold that principle. His first job as a kid was as a recreation supervisor at parks taking care of kids on break during summer. Clearly, he is a people person as well as being able to crunch numbers.

Reid: Do you like to cook or grocery shop with your family?

Dan Bane: I love to grocery shop 'cuz that's fun to do, and I like to watch customers when I grocery shop. I'm a horrible cook.

Reid: Alright, so tell me about the helmsperson.

Dan Bane: The helmsperson, how do you know about that?

Reid: I don't know about it.

We had an insider tip from someone at our location.

Dan Bane: Well, our helmsperson is supposed to be in charge of the customer's experience in the store. We think that's real important, so we have a specific job for everybody in every store. We have one helmsperson at a time to be in charge of what's going on for the customers.

Reid: I know Trader Joe's likes to create "WOW" moments for customers. Mine was when Kelsey made friends with me at my Encinitas store.

Dan Bane: Yeah, that's great. That's what we want to have happen!

On one of our frequent trips to Trader Joe's, Reid plopped himself on the floor in the chip aisle. There he opened a bag of Hawaiian Style Hickory Barbeque potato chips and decided to partake while I finished the shopping. That's when Kelsey befriended him. She must've been the helmsperson that day. They talked about his favorite beans, what was on the shelf behind him, and where his mom was. Their lively conversation made it easy for me to find Reid. Kelsey was a bubbly young woman who was considering a career in occupational therapy and paddled outrigger canoes in the ocean for sport. After that first encounter, we always picked Kelsey's check-out lane. I even tried to hire her as a babysitter. She had the gregarious temperament I look for in someone to hang out with Reid and make his time productive. Instead, we gave her a plug with her boss's boss's boss.

Reid: What's one of the unique qualities you look for when you're hiring an employee to work in your stores?

Dan Bane: What we want to do is hire people that have great personalities 'cuz we can teach 'em most everything else. But if they're not "people people" with good personalities—like yours—we wouldn't hire them. Like Kelsey.

Reid: Kelsey has a good personality.

Dan Bane: Mmhmmm.

Reid: You have a great radio voice. I love your Trader Joe's ads. Can you tell me a story about making them, Dan Bane?

Dan Bane: We make the radio ads at a studio over in Hollywood. It's always fun to go over there and you practice—like you probably practice—before we go over. But we always sort of mess up, and the mess-ups are the most funny parts. One time, when one of our guys was retiring—Ira who used to be on the radio—we made a whole reel of his mess-ups over the years. It was really funny.

Reid: That was really funny, Dan Bane. Do you have any tips for me doing radio work?

Dan Bane: I've listened to a lot of your stuff. I think you do really well. I can't give you any tips. Giving compliments is as kind as giving free samples of grilled carnitas with peach Bellini jam.

Reid: Thank you very much, Dan Bane. Alright, we have three more questions.

Dan Bane: I have a question though about radio.

Reid: Go ahead, Dan Bane.

Dan Bane: The voice that introduces your show—that is a great radio voice. Who is that?

Reid: Mark Spalding. Someday in the future, I want to interview him.

Spalding was a board member at Surfrider during Jim's tenure. He is a baritone who, much to everyone's dismay, never did radio. Dan Bane and Reid closed with the Trader Joe's outro together—the one that led us there.

Reid and Dan: "For the location of your neighborhood Trader Joe's, check us out at traderjoes.com. Thanks for listening."

Reid: Thank you very much!

Dan Bane: You had it memorized, that's great.

Two weeks later, a package arrived with a handwritten note from Dan Bane and a custom-embossed nametag for Reid. It said, "Reid Moriarty," with "Talk Time" below where you might expect to see "manager." The minutes Dan Bane took to schedule us and then follow up with a personal note and that nametag go down in our books as hallmarks of kindness.

Dan Bane also sent a handwritten note to the manager of the Encinitas store calling Kelsey out as an outstanding employee. That store manager told me in front of the red onions, "In all my years, I don't know anyone who has ever gotten a note from him." Dan Bane knew how to take the extra few minutes to show thoughtfulness. And he started a ripple effect that goes on and on.

Dan Bane restored my faith in humanity. He demonstrated that big business is still small business. He embodied the neighborhood store with a face of a real man who cares about his customers and wants to make their day with a "WOW" moment. It doesn't take a lot of time to make a huge impact. It took Dan Bane less than an hour to implement a generous idea that ran through his mind. Kindness requires an action of follow through that is like tossing the stone in a pond to start the ripple.

Why don't we perform these easy, kind actions more often? We can lead with friendliness, give a compliment, or lend a hand. Let's wake up the dormant ability we each have to restore faith in each other. We can get off our coccyx, as it were, and show that we're capable of great kindness.

> *"Wherever there is a human being, there is an opportunity for a kindness."* —Lucius Annaeus Seneca, Roman philosopher, 50AD

BITTY & BEAU'S COFFEE
Wilmington, North Carolina
BittyandBeausCoffee.com

Food is a common interest almost all of us share. Eating connects and nourishes us three times a day, or more if you snack like me. Food motivates and unifies us. A number of coffeehouses, restaurants, and food truck businesses have recently cropped up as training programs and employment opportunities for adults with disabilities. Remember, working is a primary way to belong in the community.

Perhaps the most publicized and developed establishment is Bitty & Beau's Coffee. This coffee shop has three locations in the southeast: Wilmington, North Carolina, Charleston, South Carolina, and Savannah, Georgia. Bitty and Beau are the youngest siblings in the Wright family. They have Down syndrome, and their parents founded the café in 2016 to make the world a better place for their children and others living with intellectual and developmental disabilities. Amy Wright, Bitty and Beau's mother, was given CNN's Hero of the Year award in 2017. I convulsed into tears watching her acceptance speech. Speaking to Bitty and Beau who were watching from home, she said, "I wouldn't change you for the world, but I'd change the world for you." A mother's passion and adrenaline will move heaven and earth.

Nineteen employees with intellectual and developmental disabilities ran the original five-hundred-square foot Beau's Coffee in Wilmington. Six months later, the shop was renamed because Beau's twelfth-birthday wish was to have his little sister's name put up in lights, too. They moved to a five-thousand-square-foot building that now serves as both a local coffee house and their company headquarters. They employ sixty people and have been featured on *The Today Show*, *Rachael Ray*, and *Good Morning America*.

Amy Wright sees value in people of all abilities. In this visible way, she is changing the way her neighbors perceive them too. Bitty & Beau's Coffee has created a culture where diversity is not just appreciated, it's celebrated. They offer employment, coffee, and a shop full of merchandise, but people come in for the unique customer experience. Reid, my mom, and I wanted to see it ourselves.

The tiny Charleston shop is smack in the middle of the French Quarter of this historic city. Dodging horse-drawn carriages and walking-tour groups, we slipped in the storefront to find a long line snaking through custom merchandise—tee shirts, onesies, playing cards, coffee mugs, growlers, bumper stickers—to get to the register. A young man on the spectrum took our order. We had his energetic script down by the time it was our turn. "Welcome to Bitty & Beau's. Where are you from?" We overheard customers in front of us who were from Utah, Arizona, and other parts of South Carolina. Many more were represented by pinpoints on a map behind him. "May I take your order? What size? Any flavors for you today?" He was more consistent than many Starbucks baristas.

To eliminate the need to make change, the coffee house takes only credit cards. We were given a playing card as an order number. Two other employees prepared the coffee with push-button espresso machines and plated the muffin. One of them had noticed Reid step out of line and belly up to the bar out of turn when we first entered. Concerned and helpful, he asked, "Are you looking for something?" Now I heard this same employee tell the female manager, "Benjamin is having a breakdown back there." She kept a low profile, not engaging with the customers but supporting the staff. A few minutes later Benjamin, a young man with Down syndrome and teary eyes behind his glasses, came out from the back having partially recovered. A little sulky, he resumed his position at the front door greeting customers as they entered and handing them a descriptive postcard. During a lull, the concerned coworker went over to cheer him up with a sock puppet from the merchandise display. My mom befriended them both and learned that Benjamin was the newest hire. Before we left he was chipper; Reid asked him to pose with him for a photo.

I think the greatest contribution Wright has made to the employment landscape is the high level of professionalism she lends to the cause. The shop is slick with black signage, captivating photo wallpaper, matching aprons, and suggested hashtags as you leave. She has created a high-profile space at the crossroads of culture where adults with disability can be seen as employable and capable.

OTHER FOODIE PROGRAMS

On that trip to Jupiter, Florida, we encountered Foodies4Autism. This food truck travels to different events and autism-related venues serving wraps and Chick-fil-A sandwiches. Adults with autism interview for job openings and obtain valuable job experience in food preparation, ordering, stocking, and cash register sales. The program was developed by the Renaissance Learning Academy and the Autism Project of Palm Beach and uses the tagline: "Engage. Empower. Employ. Eat." Similarly in Los Angeles, Joanne Lara with Autism Works Now is developing a food truck business called Glorious Pies.

Shari Hunter opened Two Café in our hometown of Chagrin Falls, Ohio, with a similar vision of creating a neighborhood place where individuals with mild to moderate exceptionalities, like her son Derek, could receive job training, coaching, and placement in an integrated work setting. They use local farms for produce and meats, so their menu changes seasonally. Their big message is: "We are all just people who belong together." Proceeds from the Two Café and boutique fund the Two Foundation.

Ruth Thompson, a passionate and determined cooking teacher with experience doing in-home and respite care, founded Hugs Café in Dallas in 2013 as a retirement project. They have expanded with a greenhouse as well. Tim's Place was a restaurant in Albuquerque, New Mexico, from 2010 until 2014. Tim has Down syndrome, and his parents helped fund the restaurant he owned and operated. Tim's Place was dubbed the "world's friendliest restaurant" by local media and they kept a running total of the number of hugs he gave to customers. The restaurant closed when Tim announced plans to marry the love of his life, but it will reopen in Denver in the near future.

KINDNESS ON DISPLAY

At all these businesses, customer service and kindness are magnified by virtue of the unique personalities of the owner/operators. Trader Joe's works to create "WOW" moments by enhancing the customer experience. These places do it naturally through a surprising workforce. Both places look for staff with great personalities. Unabashed kindness is their competitive advantage. People come in out of curiosity, but they return because of the connection they experience that restores their faith in what's possible.

Could these super ideas be implemented in your town? I challenge local restaurateurs to use their expertise as social activism and start one. Believe me, there are families praying and dreaming about just such an opportunity. If I had to guess, they lack the know-how and experience of owning a café. The supported employment food establishments that are the most successful are those that have someone with a track record of experience working as their driving force. Nonprofit leaders and country agencies know the demand and have the intentions, but they are not experienced at making these enterprises profitable, so they fold. We need

Children's Books to Start a Conversation About Disability

You can increase understanding of disability in your home by reading these titles to your children. Also, ask your local library to stock them.

Andy and the Yellow Frisbee by Mary Thompson
Orlando's Little-while Friends by Audrey Wood
Ian's Walk by Laurie Lears
A Friend like Simon by Kate Gaynor
Be Good to Eddie Lee by Virginia Fleming
My Brother Charlie by Holly Robinson Peet
The Autism Acceptance Book by Ellen Sabin
All My Stripes by Shaina Rudolph
Rules by Cynthia Lord
Fish in a Tree by Lynda Mullaly Hunt
Chester and Gus by Cammie McGovern
Different Like Me by Jennifer Elder

to join forces for businesses like this to thrive, and savvy business people are the missing link. Do me a favor—when you open your doors, book live music too!

SEABISCUIT[50]

We live three miles from the famed Del Mar Thoroughbred Club and racetrack, where the turf meets the surf. My interest in horses began when I discovered that the morning workouts during race season in late summer were free and open to the public. When Allie and Reid were about nine years old, we would wake up early, pick up bagels, and head over to Jimmy Durante Blvd. Parking was easy at 7:00 a.m., and the attendants were relaxed. We found ourselves among trainers, jockeys, owners, and stable hands rather than off-track bettors, high rollers, and mad hatters. Much more my speed. It was like having a walk-on role in *Seabiscuit*.

Based on a true story, *Seabiscuit* is about an unlikely champion racehorse that became a national symbol of optimism and possibility during the Depression. Charles Howard (Jeff Bridges) buys the horse for a song, recognizing that he is a long shot. But after winning at every track on the west coast, "The Biscuit" defeats the invincible "War Admiral" in what was dubbed the "match of the century" at Pimlico Race Course, proving that success is more about heart than skill.

At the beginning of the movie, Howard throws himself headlong into his new equestrian hobby after losing his young son in a car accident and his first wife to depression. He and his new wife are shopping for a horse. Tenderhearted, Howard asks about an old cowhand who is alone in a field tending an injured horse. Over his campfire and some lousy coffee, they have a profound conversation about horses that I think applies to people too. Kindness between men is direct and simple.

Tom Smith (Chris Cooper), the rugged loner, has an intense stare and a definite point of view. He is wary, studying Howard's

---

50 *Seabiscuit*. Directed by Gary Ross. Universal City: Universal Pictures, 2003.

every move as he explains why he nurses horses back to health. Some won't race again. Still, he believes that every horse is good for something. The line that haunts me is, "You don't throw a whole life away, just 'cause he's banged up a little." Knowing that truth personally, Howard stokes the fire, and their lifetime partnership begins. Together they rebuild their own lives along with the life of their horse, an unlikely jockey, and Americans down on their luck.

Smith finds scrappy Red Pollard (Tobey Maguire) swinging a bucket to take on five guys in a barn fight. Behind him, an ornery Seabiscuit is resisting restraint from three handlers. Smith doesn't know it, but Red was abandoned as a young boy by his parents who had too many mouths to feed during the Depression. The juxtaposition gives Smith an idea. Pollard and Seabiscuit might just make a perfect match.

Not afraid of anything, Pollard is willing to take a risk. He's already experienced a lot of people's worst fears. He knows trust is hard to win. Leading with kindness and empathy, he takes half of an apple with him as he approaches the mettlesome Seabiscuit. The apple is tinged brown, but still represents kindness to the horse.

If Smith's hunch is accurate, Seabiscuit has forgotten what he was made to do. They take him out to an open countryside and let him run until he stops. Pollard understands Seabiscuit's fight-or-flight response. They have the ride of their lives over hill and dale, picking up steam as they go.

Pollard turns out to be an encourager now that someone believes in him. He is welcomed into the Howard's home and allowed to eat his fill instead of having to "make weight." As the country attempts to make a comeback through soup kitchens and relief programs, Pollard also discovers that people really care, and he's not alone anymore.

We don't throw a whole life away because it's banged up a little.

People with disabilities may not be able to do some tasks, but they can all do something. We don't throw them into institutions just because they can't do as much as the majority of people around them. We can modify jobs so that they can do them and find jobs they are equipped to do. We don't leave them alone; we care.

This caring is more than a choice to see life through rose-colored glasses; I'm telling the truth as plain and simple as Tom Smith. I know adults who are beautiful orators but can't write or comprehend what they read. I know one who can't drive but is an excellent navigator. In fact, he's got a photographic memory and has memorized whole sections of Google maps. Another can't speak but types profound poetry about her reality and aspirations. Everyone is good at something. Radical as it sounds, when we identify what they're made to do, we all thrive.

WRAPPING UP CHAPTER 9

Life is hard. With or without disabilities, we all face challenges that wear us down. We despair and grow weary. At the same time, the human spirit is resilient. We have an enormous capacity to do hard things. Our attitude and beliefs determine which will prevail: the difficulty or our resilience. As we show kindness to each other, we keep our spirits up and encourage each other to do the hard things. Kindness matters.

We often hear how resilient children can be. In fact, that is the trait I most admire about Reid. He has retained a childlike exuberance about each new morning and little things like garage sales and popsicles. Difficulties don't seem to accumulate for him. He lives in the moment.

Our podcast guests enter into Reid's present moment. They take him seriously. Many sit poised listening for a common thread. They give Reid compliments and encourage him. Research confirms that witnessing acts of kindness produces oxytocin—the "love hormone"—that lowers blood pressure and improves heart-health, self-esteem, and optimism[51].

Dan Bane of Trader Joe's cultivates kindness through the core principles and ethical traits that make his business successful. Kindness isn't reserved for interpersonal interactions. It translates to corporate environments and can be applied to customer service, employee relations, and embossed nametags. You and I can be like the "helmsperson" at Trader Joe's, roaming our town and improving our neighbor's experience that day. When we show kindness, we are serving up comfort food for the spirit. Kindness convinces us that we can do more than survive; we can thrive. Life is good again.

Acts of goodwill are not dependent on other people's responses. We can just spread them like Johnny Appleseed scattered seeds. Goodness isn't controversial. The vote is unanimous in favor of as much kindness as possible. We all like to be on the receiving end of generosity. The hard thing is making and keeping a resolution to give time and grace away. How can we remind ourselves to show more kindness?

Visiting a place like Bitty & Beau's Coffee is uplifting and aspirational. Friendliness and sociability are hallmarks of adults with Down syndrome. They show affection and grace more than the norm. Just as the legacy of Trader Joe's founder trickles down to their employees today, the founders of places like Bitty & Beau's set the tone for what happens in their stores. In these businesses, diversity is celebrated. Kindness including hugs and smiles is exaggerated. Participating in this celebration interrupts our unconscious

---

51 Inc. "Science Says Random Acts of Kindness Week has Astonishing Health Benefits." Inc.com. https://www.inc.com/scott-mautz/science-says-random-acts-of-kindness-week-has-astonishing-health-benefits.html (accessed June, 2018).

routines. We step out of an automated state to embrace a new, better "normal." Something about hanging out with friends who have intellectual disabilities recalibrates our perspective and reminds us that love—and its offshoot, kindness—are the greatest aspects of life. Is there a place near you where you can go to be reminded of this reality?

In *Seabiscuit*, Tom Smith is an unorthodox horse trainer. He couldn't "throw a whole life away just because it's banged up a little." He believes there is a job for every horse. He may have had more faith in horses than in humans, but you get the gist. Watching the underdog struggle and succeed against all odds restores our faith in humanity, whether it's a horse, an individual, a sports team, or a demographic of people. The victory of heart over talent motivates us to be our best. Acts of kindness along the way build fortitude and persistence.

Kindness between men is simple, direct, and practical. Charles Howard gave the orphaned jockey Red Pollard a job, food, and a roof over his head. His kindness mirrored the relief programs our country created during the Depression. Smith and Howard offered people—and horses—a second chance. Sometimes like the Biscuit himself, we just forget what we were born to do. Kindness restores our faith in each other.

10

Render Time Priceless

In our sleepy beachside town in a row of restored Quonset huts sits a small music venue called the Belly Up Tavern. Tasteful as nightclubs go, it draws big-name acts to an intimate stage. How convenient for Reid you might think, as I did. He interviewed Keb' Mo' there and performed a sound-check jam with Dave Wakeling of the English Beat. Jungle Poppins, Reid's band, has played there twice. It is a familiar and favorite place. When Reid turned twenty-one and could get in, we celebrated his birthday at the Belly Up. He serves on their volunteer street team hanging posters around town. Nobody loves a brochure rack more than Reid, so distributing handbills is near and dear to his heart.

We check the Belly Up marquee every month to see if someone is coming who Reid might know. One summer, Ladysmith Black Mambazo was on the docket. The distinctive sounds of the South African choral group were made popular in the U.S. by their collaboration with Paul Simon, and their music and dancing had captured Reid's attention years before. Paul Simon's *Graceland* was on the playlist of Reid's childhood.

HIS FATHER TAUGHT HIM WELL: THULANI SHABALALA OF LADYSMITH BLACK MAMBAZO

The group that tours now is the next generation, and many of them are the sons of the founder, Joseph Shabalala. Their manager granted Reid an interview with one of the singers. I've learned that the typical band routine is to load-in, run a sound check, then break for dinner before the evening show. Scheduling the interview right after the sound check was perfect, better than the concert itself for Reid. He resists going places where crowds are given to hearty and unexpected applause. When Reid performs, he starts the applause himself so he knows when it is coming. If he is ready for the assault on his perfect-pitch ears, it is tolerable. But once he has heard a whistle or hootenanny of screams at a place, forget about returning.

We arrived about 5:00 p.m. before the lights were even on. In the dim nightclub, we sat at a high table facing Thulani Shabalala, son of Joseph. Getting the pronunciation of his name right was half the fun. Short, compact, and youthful for fifty, his round, ebony face animated the jovial interaction. He and Reid took time to understand each other's pronunciation of familiar words. At several points, Reid repeated his question and Thulani his answers as they adjusted to each other's accents. The extra effort shifted us into slow motion so we could cherish the exchange even more.

Reid: Welcome to the Belly Up in San Diego.
Thulani: Thank you so much for welcoming me. My name is Thulani Shabalala.

Shabalala treated Reid like he was an ambassador sent to welcome him to southern California. Perhaps we might have brought him a bar of locally made surf wax or something. Everything he said sounded like music. His voice was gentle like a shepherd talking to his sheep.

Pronouncing his name involved a short lesson. Reid said it perfectly after the third attempt.

Reid: So, Thulani, who taught you to sing?

Thulani: When I was growing up with my father, he taught us to sing at the early age. I started to sing with Ladysmith Black Mambazo at the age of eleven. Most of the songs that he was writing, he would teach us the songs first, before teaching the older group.

Reid: Alright, that's amazing! So, music and dancing is kind of my first language. When you were a boy, what made you first sing?

Thulani: Everyone at home sings. My sisters, my mom, and everyone in the village ... we grew up singing. The singing is always around us. So, it's not like ... everyone ... at the weddings.... Anything we do, we sing.

His bright smile made a sound all its own.

Reid: Okay. *(whispering)* I think your music sounds like what music will be in heaven.

Thulani: Wow.

Reid: How do you create your sound and your songs?

Thulani: Most of the songs ... my father ... he took the songs from the animals. He grew up in the farm. He was a herd boy looking after cattles, and also chasing birds .... So, he took all the sounds from those kinds of animals, the birds, the cows, the goats.

Reid: Amazing! I love how all of your voices sound like one voice. What is one secret to singing in tune and together?

Thulani: It's the rehearsals. When you rehearse, and also keep rehearsing and stay together .... Trying, always trying to find the right tone, the right harmony. It takes a lot of time. It takes a lot of energy, a lot of dedication. Focus. I think that is how we get the "one sound."

Reid: What makes choral singing so powerful, in your opinion?

Thulani: I think it's the spirit. You know and also love. When you love what you do, and you know you put your whole energy in it. Before we sing, we pray. We try to get together spiritual and mental.

His English was impressive. Still, the broken bits didn't matter to Reid. He caught the keywords and was not concerned with tense or suffixes.

Reid: Okay. So, do the cool sound effects in your music translate into English words or are they explanations of joy?

Or did the question say "exclamations"? It made sense to them either way.

Thulani: BRrrr. Brrrr.

He demonstrated the distinctive trills of their music.

Reid: RRRR. RRRR

Reid could do it! They both chuckled.

Thulani: That's got no explanation, because my father, he took that while he was driving the span of oxen. So, he would be talking with the oxen. When it touches the oxen's ear, telling the oxen what to do, he'd go like: Brrr Krrrr kkr, do this. That's how he was talking to the oxen. There's no really explanation in English or any other language.

Reid: Alright. Is "Amen" the same in Zulu as English?

Reid whispered his question as if trying to help Thulani understand him. They were connecting heart to heart.

Thulani: The, what?
Reid: Amen.
Thulani: Amen? Amen. Amen! *By moving the accent to a different syllable, he figured it out.* Amen is the same and hallelujah is the same everywhere.

Amen to that. Reid and Thulani had to concentrate to understand each other's speech. Have you ever been in a foreign country and needed to do the same? You lean in thinking *I took French. How come I can't make out what they're saying?* "Say it again, slower. Can you write it down? Aha! Got it." What would we better understand if we listened that intently to our children or neighbors and also took the extra time to read their body language? We would likely hear more. And doing so requires an action of the heart. Imagine how valuable that would be! Priceless.

Reid: Isicathamiya is hard to say.
Thulani: Isicathamiya.

He added the dental click.

Reid: Tell me your favorite memory of a capella tradition in Zulu.

Turns out Thulani didn't compete in the traditional isicathamiya singing competitions as his father did. Having learned from the master, Thulani coaches them. Zulu dancing songs involve vigorous foot stomping. He told us that most often, he encourages the young competitors not to stomp too hard. They tend to sing very loud, too. He reminds them that singing is like talking to a person. You wouldn't shout at the person. Thulani's best music teacher was his father, Joseph, who was always singing, writing, or humming. He had music in his blood.

Reid: Thulani, the last question is: Can you teach me one of your dance moves?

Thulani: Yes! *Up from the stools they hopped and over to an open space, arm in arm.* I will teach you the dance moves as well as the song: "Tim-leet-us" *They started snapping their fingers in time. Reid snaps louder than anyone I know.* Let's go like this.

Thulani began stomping his foot in a forward movement. Reid followed.

Reid: Ahhaha, okay.

He copied Thulani. Over the loudspeaker, we could hear the technicians doing sound check with their own snaps and clicks of the tongue. Thulani added the singing:

Ala tim lis
Ala tim lis *(stomp)*
Ala tim lis
Ala tim lis *(stomp)*

Thulani: Ah no, you cheated!

Reid: Hehehehe, you're funny.

Thulani: Very nice. You learn very quickly. When are you coming to visit us in South Africa? *Yikes, I could only imagine that flight.*

Reid: When am I coming to South Africa? I'll consider it. Maybe in a couple of weeks.

Reid has always appreciated kinesthetic, interactive teaching. That's how Thulani taught and likely how he learned too, from his dad in a hot, dry field of South Africa. At least that is how I pictured it. Thulani's gestures of kindness were universal. Patience, smiling, and compliments are understood across cultures.

Similar to the studies on laughter, significant research has been done on the science of kindness. According to the Random Acts of Kindness Foundation, kindness is teachable and contagious. Their website offers stories and specific ways to spur you on to practice kindness.[52] "It's kind of like weight training. We found that people can build up their compassion 'muscle' and respond to others' suffering with care and a desire to help," says to Dr. Ritchie Davidson at University of Wisconsin.[53]

Also to promote kindness, the Choose Kind campaign was launched on the heels of the movie *Wonder*. Based on the book by R. J. Palacio, *Wonder* is an inclusion story about a boy who is born with a severe facial difference. Choose Kind offers a classroom curriculum and encourages educators to take a pledge and certify "kind classrooms."

Small gestures like offering someone water, helping with a heavy grocery bag, or giving up your seat matter. The more we dole out these niceties, the more habitual they become. Virtue spreads like the runners of a spider plant infiltrating your yard.

Last month, I had to wait an hour at the Apple store for service.

---

52 RandomActsofKindnessFoundation.org.

53 Random Acts of Kindness Foundation. "The Science of Kindness." RandomActsofKindness.org https://www.randomactsofkindness.org/the-science-of-kindness (accessed May, 2018).

Reid was on a computer Googling *The Backyardigans* cartoons. I stood near him people watching. The scene made the movie *Wall-E* look prophetic. Everyone was on a device—clients and clerks—disconnected from each other, except for one young employee who saw me as he was helping someone else. He acknowledged me with a sweet smile and asked, "Would you like a stool? I can bring one over for you." Kindness; it's that easy.

We can show kindness in a million tiny ways—through music or manners, with words or actions, to friends or strangers. Showing kindness doesn't take very long, but it can make a big difference. The way to render time priceless is to give it away doing something money can't buy. How will your town change when you choose kindness?

> *"I think kindness is like oxygen. It's something*
> *we can't live without."* —Morgan Neville,
> director of *Won't You Be My Neighbor?*[54]

---

54 Variety. "Director Morgan Neville on the Mr. Rogers Movie That Will Make You Cry." Variety.com https://variety.com/2018/film/features/morgan-neville-mr-rogers-wont-you-be-my-neighbor-1202851648/ (accessed May, 2018).

GIG BUDDIES
Sussex, United Kingdom
GigBuddies.org.uk

Have I told you how often Reid wandered off as a child? He wasn't lost; I just didn't know where he was. Nine times out of ten, we would find him beside a stage listening to a band playing or on the lap of a harp player in a park. Any sort of music was a siren wooing him toward it. In my experience, one cannot have too many music programs.

Started in 2013 in Sussex, United Kingdom, Gig Buddies is a nonprofit that has music, inclusion, and belonging at its core. They solve the isolation problem of adults with autism who can't go out on their own to socialize and enjoy music. Gig Buddies are volunteers rather than music therapists, which gives the program a power all its own. You can feel the difference when people spend their time with you out of choice rather than because it is their job.

Founder Paul Richards was working as a support worker when he answered an advertisement to play bass in a band. The band, Heavy Load, formed in 1977. Two of the members had developmental disabilities and one, now deceased, was exceptional at cursing. Richards says, "Punk found us." As they played out and developed a fan base, they puzzled over why the crowd thinned out at 9:00 p.m. Richards thought, "There could only be two reasons: either the band was crap, or they were tired." They knew it couldn't be the former. Turns out, audience members had to leave when their support workers' shifts ended.

So Richards launched a Stay Up Late campaign to foster a more natural social life for his friends with disabilities who loved music, wanted to go out, and weren't tired at 9:00 p.m. He knew lots of people going to shows who had empty seats in their cars and thought,

"What if we fill those seats with people who can't go out alone?" The simple solution gave birth to Gig Buddies. The organization now has eight locations around England and a satellite in Sydney, Australia.

Volunteers with Gig Buddies invest their time in friendship supported by and focused around live music. It's genius, like a platonic dating service through which you can be matched with a vetted friend. By design, these volunteers share a common interest and can help their friends navigate being out in public whether by driving, ordering food, finding a place to sit, or taking a break.

Gig Buddies are set free from the confines of social service, yet volunteers are screened and matched by gender, age, sexuality, and geographic location. Organic friendships form over mutual interests, whether the "gig" is fishing, church, punk rock, or classical music. Gig Buddies have plenty of volunteers, but a wait list forms because they take the matching process seriously.

Volunteers participate in a full day of training that covers the social model of disability, communication tools and idioms, how to safeguard from seizures to drunkenness, and ongoing support issues like administering medications. The day ends with an experiential component. In a free dancing situation, volunteers practice dealing with potentially awkward social scenarios that might occur on a dance floor. Being willing to step outside your comfort zone and take a risk is as vital to the program as having a vehicle. Learning to improvise cannot be taught as much as practiced.

Richards' favorite story is about a night he substituted for a volunteer who was double booked. He and a friend with different abilities named Tom headed out to hear a Depeche Mode tribute band. Arriving at the venue, Tom introduced Paul to everyone he saw: the bartender, bouncer, and other patrons. The tables were turned; Tom knew everyone in the place. He was a genuine part of their tribe. "That is what it's all about," for Richards. He believes, and I agree, that if communities were really working, Gig Buddies wouldn't be needed. Richards acknowledges that, "A community that sees people as individuals with particular interests will see past any disability and get to know the person."[55] His vision for a better world is to make Gig Buddies redundant.

Imagine that you have autism. From the age of three, you have had twenty to forty hours a week of intervention from speech therapists, occupational therapists, and play therapists. You don't have time to play in the cul de sac or your backyard because you have appointments with adults who bring their own toys, whistles, or bag of tricks with them. They pull up to your curb, open their trunk, and wheel in a case of games targeted to meet your early intervention goals. Maybe some typical peers are involved because your mom recruited them from down the street. Their mom may even be paying them as a reward for being your friend.

Reid grew up with this kind of structure. His "friends" were highly trained adults. They taught our entire family a lot. Allie, Jim, and I learned tools and ways to interact with Reid, generate more language, motivate cooperation, and engage him. I am grateful, yet in waves, I rebelled against this. A structured childhood seemed like a prescription we had to take rather than how we wanted to live. I recall one summer looking out the window of a spare bedroom we called the "office." We had turned it into a therapy room with a child-sized table and chairs where therapists worked with Reid. Out that window one July day, I caught a glimpse of kids playing in the cul de sac at the end of our street. The contrast shocked me. Reid was being contained and made to play with Pooh and Tigger figurines while kids his age were racing bikes and Razor scooters up and down the street. It was absurd, like an existential children's book. I cancelled his

---

55   Paul Richards. Personal interview. July 18, 2018.

therapies for a month and announced to his case manager and powers that be that, "He needs a summer break."

Living with autism is a balancing act between what works and too much structure. The scaffolding needs to be there, but how much is enough? Fast forward to Reid's teenage years. He would come home from a huge high school campus where he was sequestered in a special day class and protected from bullying by a one-on-one aide. He would get off the bus and go into the house for a quick snack while I heard an update of every move he made from the bus driver. Then we headed out to horseback riding or music lessons. The irony of his difficulty making friends was that he didn't have any free time to spend with them.

I remember the awkwardness of the first unpaid "friend" who came to visit Reid. It was Tobias Haglund, a Young Life Capernaum leader. Young Life is a faith-based youth ministry that has chapters all over the world. Capernaum is designed to include students with disabilities. Young Life is built on three pillars: club, camp, and contact work. Contact work refers to the quality time the leaders spend with students. Most often this involves after-school sports, going for frozen yogurt, or hanging at Starbucks. As is always the case in the special needs division, contract work was different in Capernaum. Mom is never far away— explaining, reminding, supporting. Poor Tobias arrived with a guitar instead of an agenda. He wanted to hang out with Reid.

I looked at him and he looked at me while Reid was upstairs in his room practicing his deeply entrenched avoidance strategies— taking off his clothes, taking a bath, and watching videos in his head. As we had done for well over a decade at that point, I began to make a visual schedule. I promised Reid a reward if he came down and sang with Tobias. Trying to be helpful, I told Tobias what he should say and how to approach this time to make it productive and worthwhile. "Maybe make a list of songs you're going to play.

You can tell him this time what the desired action is for next time." I was trying to turn it into a music lesson. We had no precedent for a friend coming to visit. The distinction struck me the week Tobias said, "Well, we can't make him want to come down here." *Can't we?* I thought. *That's what I've been doing all his life: providing incentives, modifying behavior, and reinforcing the desired action.*

Without intending to be overprotective parents, the intensity of early intervention and best practices for our kids on the spectrum dictates that we keep them busy. Inadvertently, we create over-programmed, prompt dependent young adults who have been supervised, insulated, and evaluated like greenhouse plants. Worse, they haven't experienced organic friendship. They don't know how to be a friend.

It was a huge transition for us to receive the gift of time Tobias gave. We began to realize he wasn't watching the clock, leaving after fifty minutes (a clinical hour), or sending me session notes. I wasn't getting a statement at the end of the month, either. He was being a friend. He was rendering time priceless by giving it away.

Tobias was a local, organic "gig buddy" for us. I can appreciate the value of meeting more through an organization like Gig Buddies. Tobias was the first to use this mantra when recruiting Young Life buddies and leaders, "Disability ministry is easier than you think." You don't always need a lot of special training, just a heart to care. Having hired tutors, sitters, and coaches for two decades, I concur that chemistry and attitude are more important than skills that can be taught.

In the interest of spurring on change around the country, I will suggest another idea I heard about recently. Most churches have a worship band who rehearse during the week or early on Sunday mornings. One church invited adults with special needs to these rehearsals so they could worship with fewer people and less commotion. I bet a lot of bands or choirs would be willing to allow

> ### Ten Ways to Add More Risk Taking, Humility, and Kindness to Your Life
>
> 1. Invite a neighbor for a walk.
> 2. Take up a new pastime that takes you outside your comfort zone.
> 3. Learn the name of a clerk where you shop most often.
> 4. Humble yourself to ask for help daily—maybe pumping gas or carrying in groceries.
> 5. Start laughing more at yourself.
> 6. Swear off defending yourself as a way to cut off the fuel to pride.
> 7. Start a habit of smiling at people in traffic.
> 8. Compliment a stranger.
> 9. Treat everyone like a celebrity.
> 10. Watch a movie that will broaden your outlook, like a Sproutflix or one from this book.

adults with special needs in their rehearsals if they understood the difference it makes for some individuals.

Like Rising Tide, the staff of Gig Buddies want to pass their model on and partner with other organizations to set up a similar program in their town. So they developed "Gig Buddies in a Box," a set of resources backed up by ongoing support. What if you started a Gig Buddies program in your town? I bet you could find a dozen participants with one phone call to a group home or county agency. Where would you take them? Who would go with you?

"A kind word never broke anyone's mouth." —Irish proverb

SAVING MR. BANKS[56]

I've mentioned our family's obsession with *Mary Poppins*. When Allie and Reid were little, before the internet was available, I transcribed the words to the song "Stay Awake" to sing to them at bedtime. Reid's seventh birthday party had a *Mary Poppins* theme. Jim smudged his face in soot to be Bert; Allie as Mary carried an umbrella, and I wore a suffragette "Votes for Women" sash as Mrs. Banks. We invented games like the Spoonful of Sugar race and sent everyone home with "Let's Go Fly a Kite" favors.

Our life resembled the movie for many years, but never more than during an adolescent medication crisis. Arriving like Mary Poppins out of the clear blue sky to meet needs we didn't know we had, a passionate prayer warrior entered our life. She prayed in new ways with me, and for all of us, challenging our notions of faith and purpose "in a most delightful way." She "stayed until the wind changed" as a balm through that difficult season.

My five-year friendship with "that Poppins woman" culminated in 2016 when *Saving Mr. Banks* was released. Feeling that the movie might foretell the rest of our story, I took her on a mystery trip to the Disney Burbank Studios for the premiere of this movie about a movie. We pulled into the studio lot expectant. Disney magic filled the air.

Walt Disney (Tom Hanks) spent twenty years on a quest to get the movie rights for the book *Mary Poppins* from its the obstinate British author, P. L. Travers (Emma Thompson). Disney's persistent whimsy, ambition, and conviction clash with Travers' guarded, opinionated, and stubborn protection of her painful childhood.

Walt invites Mrs. Travers to Los Angeles and indulges her with gifts, outings, a hotel, and driver. She objects to everything the

---

56 *Saving Mr. Banks.* Directed by John Lee Hancock, Jr. Burbank: Walt Disney, 2016.

Disney team shows her—the penguins, the color red, even the smell of chlorine in Los Angeles. Disney and his writers bend over backward to accommodate her every demand, but she continues to be a pill.

After a spat over how Mr. Banks (the father in *Mary Poppins*) should be depicted, Travers rushes out of the rehearsal room through the studio lot. Ralph, her unassuming chauffeur (Paul Giamatti), sees her flop on a patch of grass behind the soundstage as if she were a little girl. Close to tears, she picks dandelions and arranges stray twigs, and we see flashbacks of her childhood in remote Australia.

Travers and Ralph connect in a poignant scene of great kindness. Ralph hands her a cup of tea in a take-out cup. The British woman is disgusted by the Styrofoam. So she pours out the tea to make a moat in her imaginary fairy world. Ralph is confused and awkward yet undaunted that his gentleness has been rejected because he realizes that refusal is instinctive for her. When he offers to drive her somewhere and asks about her family, she calls him impertinent. He laughs at himself, which shortens the distance between them.

Ralph then joins Mrs. Travers (she doesn't allow anyone to call her Pamela) fiddling with the sticks. She lets him play. Or rather hands him a stick and motions directives of what to do with it. It's then that he confides in her. He has a daughter at home in a wheelchair, which is why he cares about the weather. He likes the days when she can enjoy the fresh air. Mrs. Travers listens without a word, then she does the final honors, pouring steaming tea into Ralph's trench and watching it run all the way around their mud-and-twig park. Together, they take an odd comfort in the little utopia they created.

Ralph takes a risk; this woman is intimidating. He humbles

himself to play in the dirt with her. He hits the trifecta by extending kindness to her in a chivalrous move of vulnerability by opening up about his own problems.

In the closing scene, Travers returns uninvited to Hollywood for the premiere of *Mary Poppins*. Dressed to the nines, she heads out of the Beverly Hills Hotel to catch a cab. But before she can get one, Ralph, "her only friend in America," appears. She rushes to hug him. Arriving at Grauman's Chinese Theater, they find a spectacular hullabaloo of photographers, British bobbies, reporters, oversized dancing penguins, and a band of Pearly Kings and Queens. Mrs. Travers is overwhelmed and alone. But Ralph sends her into the fray with the affirmation that none of this would have been possible without her. As she tiptoes down the red carpet, Mickey Mouse, Walt's alter ego, bounds over to her and extends his pudgy gloved hand. She takes it.

Ralph taught Travers how to receive kindness by being present. His engineering prowess with twigs did not win her over, but his thoughtfulness in taking time was priceless and transformative.

WRAPPING UP CHAPTER 10

The kind little things we do make a world of difference. Their value and impact can far outweigh the amount of time they take. For example, allowing pre-show access at a music venue makes Reid's attendance possible. Allowing this access is fairly easy for entertainers because they have to be there anyway. But for Reid, their kindness creates a priceless educational opportunity. *Talk Time* is essentially built on the kindness of each interviewee.

Meeting Thulani Shabalala at the Belly Up was a thrill. His South African accent transported us to another culture. Reid's interview with him slowed us down enough for Reid to learn a few Zulu words and dance moves. Thulani and Reid connected on what is universal: focus, determination, discipline, spirituality, kindness, and joy. They were dancing brothers, arm in arm, if only for a few minutes.

Organic friendship is built on kindness. Giving away time to another involves a different motivation than getting paid. Gig Buddies volunteers invest their time getting to know people based on their shared interests, not their disabilities. The viewpoint of these volunteers can change the way adults of all abilities interact. In high demand in England, Gig Buddies is ready to be replicated in your town.

Sometimes people reject kindness. P. L. Travers had many reasons to push people away. But Ralph the chauffeur persisted in being who he was—a kind man—in spite of her nasty response. Ultimately, he became her only friend in America when he made himself vulnerable. Sharing our own pain and vulnerability can be a kindness that melts someone's resistance. Sometimes the gift of time, invested wisely, is the only thing that heals.

Do you know someone who needs the gift of your time? Can you show them kindness at no charge? Doing so will satisfy you both, will make your life richer, and may even start a domino reaction.

11

Extend Grace to Others

A vital part of kindness is giving people the benefit of the doubt. We never know what someone else is going through. They may be overwhelmed with having just lost their parents to suicide. Their daughter may not be speaking to them. Their bank account might be in the red. You just never know. In the last week, I have interacted with people in each of these scenarios. But we don't actually need to know someone's personal story to be kind. Almost everyone is dealing with something, and we can extend grace regardless of the details.

You've probably heard the adage attributed to Plato: "Be kind, for everyone you meet is fighting a harder battle." Giving people the benefit of the doubt is a way to show kindness and offer unmerited favor that is similar to what God extends to us.

People extend grace to Reid all the time, even though his "invisible disability" of autism is not as obvious as a prosthetic leg or blindness. Navigating the world with him has shown me how much we rely on the grace of others. For example, we would be sunk if people never extended grace when we wait in line at Panera. Or if people insist that Reid sit down, not laugh, be quiet, not rock, or fill in the blank with any number of perceived misbehaviors. I recently began to wonder, *What if we extended this grace to everyone, not just to people like Reid?* Wouldn't the world be a better place?

When we practice extending grace to people with disabilities, we keep the attitude and skill on call, warmed up and ready to show to anyone who needs it for various reasons. Hopefully as a recipient of lots of grace, I have some in my back pocket to share. Like glitter, grace would be a good thing to rub off and sprinkle around.

WHEN AN IRISH ROCKER LEADS WORSHIP: CHRIS LLEWELLYN OF REND COLLECTIVE

Rend Collective is a folk worship band from Northern Ireland. They have gained popularity in recent years by touring churches and participating in international festivals. We are fans of their adamant praise music that includes tin whistles, clapping, and shouts in unison. Jim describes the band's music as the "Pogues go to church." (The Pogues were a Celtic punk band that formed in 1982.) Rend Collective pumps up the volume on corporate worship with an authentic insistence on the good news that makes you want to dance a jig.

Rend's lead singer, Chris Llewellyn, is married to my college roommate's daughter, Gabriella. Gabby and I were connected through social media when she seemed to be reliving my time with her mom at the University of Wisconsin-Madison. She lived at Chadbourne Hall, studied journalism, and strolled home on State Street after the farmer's market every Saturday, just as we had. Gabby and I had a lot in common until she married a rock star.

When Rend Collective's tour came to southern California, I reached out to Gabby to ask for an interview with her husband, Chris. What could she say? This was one of the few interviews that came about because of a personal connection. Jim, Reid, and I drove to Irvine to a large church that met in a warehouse adjacent to the runway of the John Wayne Airport. Unsure whether Reid would stay for the concert or not—the volume would be loud and the audience pumped—we arrived early. Band load in and sound check were more our speed.

Chris had lots to do. We waited with Gabby until he could slip away. Reid took several bathroom breaks. We explored the entire church campus, including the parking lot, tour bus, bulletin boards, a coffee shop, and classrooms. The anticipation made meeting Chris seem like an illusion. Could this really be happening? I thought Reid was losing interest, but when Chris appeared, freshly showered, Reid slid right back on task.

Reid: Chrisssss!

Chris Llewellyn's Irish brogue either pulls you in close to concentrate or sit back and enjoy its musical lilt. Twenty-something, he has a ruddy complexion, broad upper arms, and tattooed forearms. Chris has the edge of a rugby player and the openness of a disciple, so he is equally comfortable on the streets of New York as on the stage of a postmodern millennial megachurch. He smiled readily, warming up to Reid.

Reid: You're doing a concert tonight.
Chris: Yeah, sure are.
Reid: I'm gonna watch your concert.
Chris: Fantastic.
Reid: Oh, the questions.

Reid was actually nervous for this one. Maybe it was the sustained anticipation, or the fact that he knew Rend Collective's music so well. Chris Llewellyn was famous in our living room whereas other podcast interviewees are remote. Seeing him in the flesh, Reid was breathless.

Reid: Let's get started.

Chris: C'mon.

Reid: This is Chris Llewellyn from the Rend Collective band. I'd like to ask him a couple questions, just four of them. And then, because he has a performance. And so, here we go. Chris Llewellyn, how did you prepare for our concert?

Our very presence likely interrupted Chris's routine, so he was extending grace already.

Chris: Well, most of the time I do warm-ups outside the bus. So, they sound kind of silly. They sound a little bit like this. BRRRRRRRRrrrrRRRRRrrrrrr.

Reid: They're silly?

Chris: That's it. Yeah. But it's what you need to do, so that you can sing every day. 'Cuz I sing six days out of seven, every week.

Reid: You do six and seven days a week. That's awesome!

Being on tour always sounds more glamorous than it is.

Chris: Yeah, that's part of it. And then, sometimes we listen to this song together to get us prepared for the concert ... get us excited. It's the theme tune to the old *Transformers* cartoon from the '80s.

Reid: Yea, I do remember. *Of course Reid wasn't born yet in the 80s, but his memory and imagination were linked.* What's your favorite American music?

Chris: Wow. I really like a band called Switchfoot. They're pretty great.

They have a lead singer called Jon Foreman who writes really excellent songs. I really like his words in particular.

Reid: Yea, Mark Forman is the pastor at North Coast Calvary Chapel.

What Reid didn't clarify is that he is our pastor and Jon Foreman's dad. Reid had interviewed Mark.

Chris: You're a hundred-percent right.

Reid: What's your favorite Irish music?

Chris: Favorite Irish music? Well, there's a band called the Frames who're my very favorite there. They're from Dublin. And I have been very inspired by them. Particularly the way the guy sings. He's called Glen Hansard.

Reid: That's amazing. So, can you tell me about your homemade instruments?

Chris: Yeah, sure. We play anything that we can find. So one of our special instruments is called the Jingling Johnny. It's basically just a big stick that's got pie pans, and a spring, and a bell, and a woodblock, and all sorts of things attached to it. You'll see that tonight. Also, we have instruments that are made out of suitcases. They used to be old suitcases that we had, but now, they're guitars, banjos, and stuff. You kind of need to see them to understand what they are.

Reid: I do remember.

Reid was agreeable to whatever Chris said. Rend Collective's homegrown aesthetic was appealing, as were their videos Reid had watched online. In one, they perform on a fishing boat that is crossing the Irish Sea to a lighthouse. In another, they host a campfire gathering. In our research, we happened upon a video of Chris busking on a sidewalk as a one-man band, and he was the spitting image of Dick Van Dyke at the opening of *Mary Poppins*. Chris and Reid went on to cover the high points and lows of being on the road. Gabby was videotaping the entire thing, presumably for her mom. Then Reid had an unexpected brainstorm.

Reid: Oh! How was the one-man band costume?

Chris knew immediately the one!

Chris: You know, I've still got that one. We're gonna try to use it sometime, but not on this tour.
Reid: Not on this tour. But someday?
Chris: Someday, it's coming out. I can tell.
Reid: Where did you get it?
Chris: Oh, I got it from the internet. I think it was from Amazon. It was very, very cheap.
Reid: I do eBay instead of Amazon. It's even better. But you have to pay a bid for the thing that you want.

Reid wasn't exactly correcting Chris, just sharing related intelligence on the topic. We had spent a lot of time around our kitchen table distinguishing between Amazon and eBay pricing when collecting Disney titles and replacing television remotes. Chris took it all in stride. When you're full of grace, things flow easily off your back.

Reid: Okay, how much do you practice guitar or banjo each day?
Chris: Well, I don't practice very much, whenever I'm out on the road. I hardly play at all—maybe thirty minutes every three days. Maybe, something like that, because I'm playing so long at night. Actually, I have a problem with my tendons ... my arms, my wrists ... so I can't play very much. If I practice too much, then I can't play the show. And they don't like that.
Reid: That's too bad. Oh, okay. When you were a boy, what did you want to you be when you grew up?

254

Chris: Well, we have a sport called rugby back at home. And it's a really violent sport. It's a really rough sport. I wanted to be a rugby player right up until I was seventeen, but then I got injured. I became a Christian a month later, and everything changed for me.
Reid: That's awesome.

It's easier to show grace when it has been extended to you, and you have experienced how life changing it is. Chris embraced a gospel of grace, so it was easy for him to pay it forward to others.

Reid: Oh, here's a good question you might like: what is your favorite Bible story?
Chris: Yeah, that's a hard one. I really like the story of Gideon. It's about a guy who ... he isn't very brave at the start of the story. He needs a lot of confirmation from God about what direction to take in his life. He needs God to tell him time and time again to do things before he will actually do them. But in the end, they actually manage to—with God's help—he conquers a whole army called Midianites. It's kind of awesome because I don't think I'm that brave. But God can use anybody and can make anybody brave.
Reid: I like Noah.
Chris: That's a good one, too.
Reid: So, who was your best music teacher?
Chris: Wow. Well, I didn't get along at all with my music teacher. He didn't think I was very good at all. Because I didn't play the piano and I wouldn't play the recorder.

Jim and I laughed, appreciating Chris's teenage rebellion vicariously. I loved his honesty.

Reid: You didn't play the recorder?
Chris: Well, I actually am quite good at the recorder. That was the problem. He

> wanted me to play the recorder for my exams, but I wasn't into it. I liked to play the guitar. So we fell out for a little while. My dad was my best music teacher. He left me alone and let me learn to play the guitar. Yeah, that's –
>
> Reid: Yea, that's amazing. He teached you how to play guitar?
>
> Chris: Not really. He just left them lying around. He plays guitar himself. So I used to just find them afterward and try and copy what he had done. I didn't really like getting lessons, but I like playing the guitar.

A wise father uses a little psychology, which is also extending grace. I think letting go of our need to be in control opens a floodgate for power from a higher source. That is what I mean by grace. Something beyond us flows through us to encourage, bless, forgive, and expand others. We become a vessel for benevolence that is greater than what is humanly possible.

> Reid: Oh, and the last question is, could we sing something together ... next time... when you're here?

I had thought of this idea on the car ride up and hand wrote it at the bottom of Reid's printed questions. Apparently, that was not enough advance notice for Reid.

> Chris: Well, what do you want to sing? Why do we have to wait?
>
> Reid: Do you know any worship songs?
>
> Chris: I know *lots* of worship songs!

He had a self-deprecating sarcasm that made us all laugh at ourselves. Not only did he know them, he wrote the ones we sang in church.

> Reid: My favorite is "Mighty to Save," and yours might be "Joy" or "Burn Like a Star."

These songs were on Rend Collective's recent release.

Chris: *(chuckling)* That could be right. I like "Mighty to Save" though. If
    you start it, I could sing it with you.
Reid: It's too bad, no... I'm too nervous.

Chris let Reid off the hook.

Chris: It's good to see you, Reid.
Reid: And I'll see you at the concert tonight, okay?
Chris: Yeah, c'mon.

Acquainted with grace, Chris Llewellyn sings about the one who
offered forgiveness to prostitutes and tax collectors, ultimately calling them friends. Chris holds out that same authentic grace from
the stage for anyone to grasp and proclaim. Allowing for grace is
like setting your life to music. The scene changes completely when
you turn on a soundtrack.

    We left Chris to his vocal warm-ups and went to find dinner. We
returned at show time, but Reid stayed mostly in the foyer. It was
spacious and had multiple video monitors and quality speakers. We
could almost see more of the show from there than inside. When Reid
got tired of pogo-jumping as high as he could, we shared a sofa with
a father and toddler. Jim and I made friends with the ushers and took
turns crossing the threshold into the actual crowd. Rend Collective
puts on an energetic, worshipful show (and Jim has seen the Pogues).

"A single act of kindness throws out roots in
all directions, and the roots spring up and
make new trees." —Amelia Earhart

L'ARCHE INTERNATIONAL
International
Larche.org

L'Arche is a federation of 152 intentional communities around the world in thirty-seven countries. More than ten thousand members with and without disabilities share life together in these L'Arche communities. L'Arche means "the ark" in French (and rhymes with "marsh" when pronounced correctly).

The first community was established in 1964 when a young philosopher named Jean Vanier visited asylums in France where people with intellectual disabilities were hidden away. Overwhelmed by the sadness he saw, Vanier determined to do something. Friends helped him buy a small, run-down house in Trosly-Breuil, France, where he lived with several men from the institution. As this "humble prophet" invested his time and energy, Vanier discovered a lot about human nature and about God.

Vanier's urge to help the men turned into a commitment to be with them and be a friend to them. A core belief of L'Arche communities is that for all of us, our strengths are revealed through weakness and vulnerability in a trusting community.

Vanier experienced how through their vulnerability, people with disabilities have a special gift for touching our hearts. They invite us into relationship, which reveals our humanness. L'Arche communities live out the Beatitudes—Jesus' call to simplicity, gentleness, compassion, justice, and peace—by creating environments where people with and without disabilities enjoy mutual friendship.

Henri Nouwen, a Dutch Catholic priest, was also associated with the movement. After leaving Harvard, Nouwen spent a year with Vanier and was called to L'Arche Daybreak in Toronto as their pastor. Nouwen wrote *Adam: God's Beloved*,[57] a moving account of his friendship with a core member at Daybreak and how this friendship transformed his own life.

Each L'Arche community is one of faith rooted in prayer and trust in God. Their spirituality is grounded in their belief that each person is unique and has sacred value. Caregivers or assistants as they are known in L'Arche, come from a variety of backgrounds. In the United States, many are recent college graduates who commit to community life for one or two years. Though drawn to the time of service, these people often discover the transformational nature of authentic community and extend their stay.

What's the same about each L'Arche community is their mission to make known the gifts of their core members, and these gifts are revealed through mutually transforming relationships. What's different is the local expression. Each L'Arche community has a unique culture based on the gifts and interests of their members and the geographic area in which they live. So a community in Germany looks different from one in Alabama. The wide diversity of L'Arche communities can be is seen in a web series of short "As I Am" films.[58] Each film introduces you to a core member from Africa, Poland, Australia, or Egypt.

All L'Arche communities seek to provide meaningful living for their core members and assistants. Some have an art gallery or workshop for creative expression. Some operate organic farms, growing and selling plants and produce. Others include day programs for the core members or have extensive woodworking shops. L'Arche communities often have a gathering site where people

57 Nouwen, Henri, *Adam: God's Beloved*. Orbis Books, 1997.
58 L'Arche USA. "As I Am Web Videos." LArcheUSA.org. https://www.larcheusa.org/category/as-i-am-web-videos/ (accessed July, 2018).

from the local area can interact with core members in addition to a residence or cluster of homes.

The L'Arche mission is complete in their call to be human: Relationship. Transformation. Sign. As relationships form between human beings of all abilities, people are mutually changed, and that transformation becomes a sign to others in the community.

PARENTS WORKING TOGETHER

Several years ago, a group of my friends—other moms with special needs teenagers—and I started touring residential living options. Ever on our radar is what will happen to our children when we're gone. One mom promised her daughter that she would have a plan worked out for her brother with Down syndrome before she left for college. Another has no family in the area who are familiar enough with her boys with ASD to care for them. Together, we made lists of the features that are most important for our adult children. Some moms prioritize lifelong medical care. Others want safety and security cameras. Some want social opportunities, others prioritize location. Every parent is different, as is every individual.

We keep our ears to the ground and watch our friends who are farther down the trail. We swap stories of options. Some families purchase condos for their adult son or daughter to live in with support. Others remodel a granny flat for the same reason. Some parents even become certified as group home operators. For a time Reid and his friend Tobias led music at a group home near us, and I took these sessions as an opportunity to check out that option. However, different agencies operate group homes with different standards.

As we continued to research, we discovered some exciting models for adult living, both near and far. I offer this list of a few places where the founders and staff have a passion for quality support,

People First Language

When we use people first language, we put the person first—not their condition. Like gender and ethnicity, disability is just one of many human characteristics. Would you want to be known by one trait or your medical diagnosis? People first language is not being politically correct. It is using language to show respect, dignity, and good manners. Here are a few ways to recalibrate your thinking and vocabulary to use people first language:

- People with disabilities—NOT handicapped/disabled
- Cognitive disability—NOT mental retardation
- Mike has autism—NOT Mike is autistic
- Joann uses a wheelchair—NOT Joanne is wheelchair bound
- Bob has a mental health condition—NOT Bob is mentally ill
- Kay communicates with a keyboard—NOT Kay is non-verbal
- Accessible parking—NOT handicapped parking

productivity, and belonging. This list is certainly not all of them, nor nearly enough. But perhaps one is close enough for you to visit or get involved with.

Sweetwater Spectrum, Sonoma, California
Noah Homes, Spring Valley, California
Casa d'Amma, San Clemente, California
Berkshire Hills Music Academy, South Hadley, Massachusetts
The Camphill Association of North America
Bittersweet Farms, Whitehouse, Ohio
Quest Farm, Georgetown, Kentucky
First Place, Phoenix, Arizona

Far and away our single greatest desire is that our adult children are in a place where they are loved. Not just safe. Not simply busy. Not merely supervised and productive. We dream they will have care-givers who *want* to be with them, rather than *have* to be because their only option is this minimum-wage job. Initially, we weren't sure this was a reasonable expectation. Now we know that finding love is possible since it is the L'Arche distinction. L'Arche is not a residential housing solution; it is an intentional spiritual commu-nity whose time has come in San Diego.

BEING THERE[59]

Jim and I watched *Being There* movie decades ago, before our kids were born, before *Rain Man* came out, and before autism was trending. Something about this movie stayed with me. While the main character is never labeled, he seems to have a form of autism.

Chance the Gardener (Peter Sellers) has lived his entire life as the gardener for a wealthy recluse. Watching television has been Chance's only exposure to the world beyond the garden walls. When the old recluse dies, the cook makes Chance his last breakfast and leaves. The estate attorneys find no mention of Chance in the wealthy man's documents, so they tell Chance that he must also leave. Dressed in the old man's double-breasted suit, hat, and cane, Chance sets off to fend for himself. He is blissfully unaware of the dangers outside the garden walls, and a mystifying grace protects him whether he walks down the center of a highway median strip or through a gang-infested ghetto.

When a slow-moving limousine injures Chance's leg, the wealthy owner (Shirley MacLaine) takes him home for medical attention rather than to a hospital, because she happens to have a full medical staff caring for her ailing husband. Chance is good company and a breath of fresh air for this dying business tycoon and insider in Washington politics. Impressed by Chance's urbane dress, cultured manners, and deliberate speech, the tycoon introduces him to lobbyists, decision makers, and even the president of the United States (Jack Warden) who begins to seek Chance's counsel on policy issues. Shaking hands and emulating interactions he has seen on television, Chance speaks about gardening which gives him an aristocratic air of expertise. He shares what he knows about the seasons, watering, and fertilizer, and the politicians begin to

---

59 *Being There*. Directed by Hal Ashby. Los Angeles: Lorimar Productions. 1979.

quote him and apply what they think are his metaphors to policy decisions in the White House. Chauncey, as they mistakenly call him, is trying to please them, not deceive them.

Being There is an interesting example of the principle of "presuming competence" taken to the extreme. When we presume someone is intelligent, our assumption can change how he or she acts. For example, children become to an extent what we expect of them. If we presume they will go to college, they often do. When we presume they will achieve greater things than the generation before them, they often do.

Alternatively, if we presume someone cannot read or is unintelligent, we do them a disservice and change their reality. For example, teachers might misjudge someone and not include them in a lesson. Or peers might talk down to someone who is presumed to be incompetent. Through a natural progression, these people are isolated from intelligent conversation. Presuming incompetence can also explain systemic poverty and generational addiction because expectations have a formative influence on us.

Think of what happens when we presume incompetence in people with a disability. We tend to err on the side of expecting little of these labeled people. The danger of this thinking is that we dilute teaching or don't present new material, so they achieve low results. This outcome is tragic for everyone. I know several adults with autism whose high intelligence was only revealed late in life when they learned facilitated communication (FC) or the rapid prompting method (RPM). They are now writing books and speaking to underscore the tragedy caused by years of falsely presumed incompetence.

In the closing scene of *Being There*, the president of the United States gives a eulogy at the graveside of the business tycoon. Chance blithely wanders away and steps onto a lake, but he doesn't sink.

Instead, he steps casually across the surface and sticks his cane below the surface showing the depth of the water. Does he not know about gravity? Does it not apply to him? This obvious reference to Jesus walking on water suggests that Chance's simple wisdom might have been supernatural.

Often Jim and I catch a glimpse of Reid from a distance and say the same thing at the same time, "He looks like the guy at the end of *Being There*." Reid walks like a man on a mission. We don't always know what his mission is, but he struts at a determined clip with a long stride and his shoulders pinched back. When he is intensely focused, I have seen Reid step in front of backing cars and remain unscathed. Neither the fenders nor the snickers faze him as he crosses a parking lot. Within his simplicity is a definite brilliance.

When I was a teenager, my mom taught me to "walk in like you own the place." She used the expression to impart in me a sense of confidence and assertiveness in new situations. Her words still ring in my ears when I enter a fancy hotel in a big city, an awkward holiday party, or a contentious meeting. But Reid does this confident walk without ever being told. Not to be confused with arrogance, "walking in like you own the place" conveys a sense of responsibility. When the owner of an establishment sees litter on the floor, she picks it up. If you own a property and people are trashing it, you stop them. The owner pays attention to details and makes improvements. When you own the place, you also welcome others.

Whether Chauncey was simple, profound, or delusional, he made it through life thanks to the sheer kindness of others. A community—the old recluse, the cook, the limousine driver, the wealthy woman, the tycoon, and the president—claimed him. Chance belonged with them. They looked after him when he needed food or help. They respected what he had to say. They presumed his competence. They retrieved Chance when he wandered off. I think we all hope for this sense of belonging and community, no matter how many faculties we have or lose with age. We want to be presumed competent, and we hope for a safety net of grace extended from people who are connected to us.

WRAPPING UP CHAPTER 11

Extending grace to others is an act of kindness that begins with humility. In a spiritual sense, pride sets us up as our own little gods. When we pretend to know it all, we pose as omniscient. Closed off and self-sufficient, we don't leave space for any higher power to flow through us. I believe God is waiting to inhabit the praises of his people and fill us with his grace when we yield to him. Like a vehicle in traffic, we can let him take the lead. Stepping out of our own way opens the floodgates for God's grace to surge through us. As we yield, we join a mysterious spiritual current.

Chris Llewellyn of Rend Collective extended grace to Reid by fitting him into his pre-show schedule. Like so many of the other podcast guests, Chris let unpleasant things flow easily off his back. When grace has been extended to you, it is easier to show it to others. You follow the example of your parents, teachers, audiences, or others who have been gracious in your life.

Founded by a humble prophet, L'Arche communities are places where grace flows. As people share life together in radical and countercultural acceptance, they create an image of how God wants to befriend each of us and dwell with us. Being human together changes our perspective.

By taking the concept of presuming competence to the extreme, the movie *Being There* shows us a man who relies on the goodness of strangers to survive. Being at the mercy of others is a tough place to be, but if the strangers are willing to extend grace, it can be a safe and generous place. Unbeknownst to Chance the Gardener, a mystifying grace protects him—and maybe Reid and you and me—from many a danger and snare. Chance reminds me of the village idiot in Van Morrison's lyric, "He is onto something, but he's just not saying."[60]

Be aware of how grace has been extended to you in your life. Recognizing that a gracious hand or unsolicited action saved you from danger or guided you may require hindsight. But seeing how this grace has benefited you will motivate you to extend grace to another, whether or not they ask for it. And remember that grace ultimately comes from a higher and infinite source. How can you yield today to allow this grace to flow in your life?

60 Morrison, Van. Hymns to the Silence. "Village Idiot," Polydor, 1991, compact disc.

267

12

Bring Heaven Here and Now

Reid's trajectory in our Sunday morning church routine was unorthodox. Though he ducked in and out of the children's choir, children's worship, and the youth group, he plugged in most often to the nursery. Until his late teens, the familiar nursery workers and collection of familiar *Veggie Tales* and *Beginner's Bible* videos were irresistible.

We tried, really we did. For a time he volunteered as the sound guy in the preschool room cuing up their video lesson. For another time, he sat in the sanctuary with us and took notes on the sermon outline. For a season, he assisted the worship director breaking down music stands and band equipment at the end of the service. For a long time, he browsed the defunct church library reviewing illustrated stories about Noah, Jonah, and Zaccheus or rewinding VHS tapes.

Eventually I accepted the fact that individual people modeled Jesus to Reid, rather than a disability ministry per se. People, not a program, ensured that Reid had a rich faith journey. When we sat in the left transept in the second pew, he bear-hugged the pastors whose names were in the bulletin that week. One Easter Sunday he asked to be baptized in the ocean as Allie had been a few months prior. He was the first to say, "You have to go to church, Allie. You're part of the family." He got the majors, so we let go the minors.

After twenty-three years at the same church, we changed churches when Reid and Allie were seventeen, and Allie was in her senior year of high school. This may not have been the best time, but we had reached a frustration point with following Reid around the campus. We had put out one too many all-points bulletins only to find him—all five feet, six inches of him—crouched in a cupboard in the nursery sorting videos by label and production company. I nearly had a coronary more than once trying to find him in the adjacent shopping center when he wandered to the CVS drugstore. Sunday morning was turning into a search-and-rescue exercise rather than a worship and fellowship time.

This change wasn't all because of Reid. We were also ready for some new teaching that I had tasted at neighboring churches. One blessing of being in southern California is that practically every freeway exit has another active congregation with an amazing preacher and worship band. We migrated up to North Coast Calvary Chapel where Mark Foreman is the senior pastor. Humble and kind, he resembles Jesus as a servant leader and friend to all.

The first week we attended, we sat in the *very* back row of the auditorium-style sanctuary. We were prepared to follow Reid if he got up, and we wanted to distract as few people as possible. In time, these became our regular seats. We befriended a few other back-row sitters and Reid wandered, but he came back and found us easily.

Despite Mark's unassuming nature, he gets around. He epitomizes the old Tom Peters philosophy of management by walking around. Before each service, Mark is often milling around the foyer and the back rows enjoying "your church," as he likes to call it to emphasize that the church doesn't belong to him.

The second time we attended, Reid understood who Mark was the main coach even without a printed bulletin. Reid's intuition and visual observation skills are stellar. He spied Mark moving through the crowd shaking hands and greeting everyone in his path. Before you can say, "'Scuse me, pardon me," Reid was on his feet making a dash to Mark like a linebacker with an opening for the goal post.

Mark was unprepared yet undaunted. I watched from a few paces behind as I apologized to everyone Reid had bumped into along the way. Reid was only an inch from Mark's face with a message to deliver, "Mark Foreman!" They locked eyes. Reid grinned, creasing his young face into crow's feet. "You were talking about the test." Reid rested both his hands on Mark's shoulders. Mark reciprocated the demonstrative action in a moment that could only be described as good.

This first encounter was over as fast as it began. *What just happened?* I thought to myself once we were contained in the car. I figured Mark must have been wondering the same. I hadn't given him much backstory on who we were, but he didn't need it because kindness was his reflex. And he didn't need any explanation or forewarning to show love.

It took me a week to decode Reid's comment, but I eventually did. The Sunday before, Mark had preached about Abraham and his son Isaac. God tested Abraham's faithfulness by asking him to sacrifice Isaac on an altar. The intense story registered in Reid's memory. Reid and I sent Mark a Facebook message to explain. Do you know, that man replied? He's a public figure with a million responsibilities, including a book to finish and sermons to prepare. Our message may still have been puzzling to him, but he showed the graciousness of a reply.

Mark and Reid connected. If Reid belonged at North Coast Calvary Chapel, then so did Jim, Allie, and I. We knew the head pastor, and from him trickled down acceptance. That meant on any

Sunday morning, Reid could get up and down, stand in the aisle, sit in the foyer, or write lists in the coffee shop because he was part of the family.

FACE-TO-FACE WITH YOUR PASTOR: MARK FOREMAN OF NORTH COAST CALVARY CHURCH

A few months later—no surprise—Reid wanted to interview Pastor Mark. Reid asked Mark on the sidewalk where we tended to pass him on our way to the parking lot. We scheduled after he returned from having shoulder surgery. He was scruffier than usual but his beard underscored his reputation as a scholar. In his sixties, Mark is a small man of great intellect with a compassionate heart. I've seen his eyes well up in front of two thousand people when his heart is broken by a tragedy in the news. I'm tickled every time he pantomimes God taking us under his wing to give us advice, "C'mon, little buddy." He unlocked an empty office, and the three of us pulled up chairs under a framed map of Narnia.

Reid: Alright! We're here to interview the head pastor at North Coast Calvary Chapel, Mr. Mark Foreman. What board are you surfing now?

Mark: Great question. *He has a gentle voice of conviction.* Well, the board I was surfing, before my surgery, is shaped by Ed Wright. It's a nine foot by three inch longboard.

Reid: Ok. Yours is a longboard?

Mark: Yep, but once I get back in the water, I'll be on my five foot by nine inch fish.

Reid: Okay, Mark Foreman, what's one thing everyone should know about God?

Mark: That He is an artist.

Reid: He's an artist?!?

Reid giggled in surprise. This was not the answer he expected. Mark almost expected the question Reid had "bounced him before," as they say of Tigger.

Mark: He's an artist who made the world ....
Reid: That's amazing, Mark.
Mark: ... and it's beautiful.
Reid: Okay.

Reid continued with a number of questions. With each answer, Mark aimed to make theology simple enough for a child to understand. Reid asked about Mark's favorite Bible story, and Mark explained the story of Jesus with his disciples on the road to Emmaus in a nutshell. Recognizing the details, Reid's eyes opened with a snap.

Reid: "That's the story of Easter. I know that!" *It all segued naturally.* Do you have a favorite Easter memory, Mark?
Mark: Oh boy, I think sunrise service when the thousands of people show up at the beach. And I don't know where they all come from. Each year, I think they're not going to come, and there they are again. One year, a whale showed up, and all these thousands of people were looking at the whale while he was spouting. And I was trying to keep their attention—on the sermon—but the whale was winning.
Reid: That's funny. Mine is when you let the doves go, Mark.
Mark: Of course. Yeah. Is that mind-blowing? It's just amazing.

They talked about Mark's favorite hymns and his classical piano training.

Reid: What job do you think you'll have in heaven?
Mark: Ah, well, one of them will be washing your feet.

Reid: Washing feet?
Mark: Your feet.
Reid: Yeaaha! That's great.
Mark: I will be your servant.
Reid: Okaay!

Reid asked Mark what his favorite live recording was. Mark had that answer at the ready

Mark: Switchfoot's "Dirty Second Hand" because of the intricate time signature.

That would have to sink in when Reid replayed this podcast in the future.

Reid: I love it when you mention movies in the sermon. What movie have you watched the most times?
Mark: It's probably not good to say, I think it's a movie like *Princess Bride*.

They covered *Mary Poppins* and *The Sound of Music*. Then Reid asked Mark where he would take him first if they could go to the Holy Land. Ever relevant and personal, Mark said he would buy Reid an ice cream at the Western Wall of Jerusalem. Then Mark asked Reid what flavor it would be. This was a man who knew the value of imagination.

Reid: Okay, interesting.

I made a mental note to pick up on this later and educate Reid about the Holy Land with a Dorling Kindersley book.

Reid: What's your high point of being a dad or a low point, Mark?

Mark: My high point was probably ... night after night ... reading to my sons, *Narnia.*

Reid: You read them *Narnia*? It's right there!

Mark turned around to see the artwork—a framed map of the fictional land C. S. Lewis created for the *Chronicles of Narnia.* Mark had forgotten it was there to illustrate his point.

Reid: If you were one of the *Narnia* characters, which one would you be?

It was as if the transitions were planned for us.

Mark: Well, I can't be Aslan, so let's see .... You know, my heart goes out to Edmund in the first one, *The Lion, the Witch, and the Wardrobe.*

Reid: Of course!

Mark: ...'cuz I think he feels so shamed, and he doesn't know how to get back to being right. Once he's made right, he becomes a real hero.

Reid: Okay, Mark Foreman.

Mark: But I also might be Lucy. I love Lucy.

Reid: You love Lucy?

Mark: Yeah, she's so innocent, and she's so trusting. She's the littlest, but perhaps the most courageous.

Reid: Hey, remember Lucy met Mr. Tumnus?

Mark: Yes.

Reid: I do remember that.

Mark: Yeah, and she went to have tea ... with Mr. Tumnus.

Reid: You'd be perfect for Mr. Tumnus. *I think this was a reference to the beard Mark had grown; Tumnus is a faun.* Alright, we have one more question.

Mark: We should have a drum roll for this.

He and I made one by tapping on our knees.

Reid: Alright, Mark, can you summarize the Bible in one sentence?
Mark: Yes!

He didn't even hesitate.

Reid: Go ahead.
Mark: For God so loved Reid that He gave his only begotten son that whoever believes in Him would not perish but live forever.
Reid: Thank you, Mark. That was niice!
Mark: High fives?

They tapped each other up high.

Reid: It was nice talking to you.
Mark: Reid, you are the man!

I was wowed. This little social experiment of ours—making a podcast—was becoming Reid's continuing education. In lieu of college, he was having tête-à-têtes with different people in his areas of interest. Reid was learning from experts in the field which ensured an emotional intensity that held his attention and ensured long-term memory, because what we hear in relationship, we remember. Little did Mark—or any of the other guests—know how many times Reid would listen to them on repeat, memorizing and internalizing each of their personal messages to him.

In true form, we were in and out of the interview with Mark Foreman in twenty minutes. I thanked Mark profusely as Reid bounded down the stairs to the car, "You are so sweet to do this," I said. "Thank you for making time in your schedule."

"Are you kidding? Of course," he replied. Kindness is a given for this man. His nature is to be agreeable; the title of his book on parenting

How Can My Church Become More Inclusive?

1. Ask parents about their goals for Sunday morning.
2. Attend an annual IEP meeting for morale and prayer support.
3. Offer to hire an aide who is already trained and familiar with a child who needs a buddy.
4. Look for relevant service opportunities from ushering to folding chairs to leading worship.
5. Make an intentional effort to value siblings.
6. Put existing visuals to use including bulletins, sermon outlines, and campus signage.
7. Add families to the prayer chain and meal trains during diagnosis and crisis times.
8. Create social stories and visuals for the Lord's Prayer and other fundamentals of faith.
9. Feature the special needs community in announcements, testimonies, and performances.
10. Cultivate a ministry of presence. For example, even sitting and doodling can be relational.

is *Never Say No.* While I'm sure Mark would say "no" if doing so was in someone's best interest, he actively looked for ways to say "yes" to his children, his wife, the Lord, people in need, and unlikely conversations.

> *"Practice kindness all day to everybody, and you will realize you're already in heaven now."* —Jack Kerouac, author[61]

---

61 Kerouac, Jack. *The Portable Jack Kerouac.* Penguin Classics, 2001.

CREATIVITY EXPLORED
San Francisco
CreativityExplored.org

The month I started writing this book, I saw an image on Facebook that I loved enough to screen grab and save on my phone. We were in the midst of creating mood boards for Reid's business as part of the brand and identity program with Celebrate EDU. The drawings on the post— confident, black-and-white, organic lines and quirky color-washed images—grabbed me.

On further investigation, I discovered that the picture was of an art gallery installation at Creativity Explored, a nonprofit visual art center in San Francisco where art changes lives. "Quintessentially José Nuñez" was a one-man show of the work of this native of El Salvador who had moved to California as an adult. In time, I licensed the art to use on the cover of this book.

Creativity Explored is a studio art program giving adults with developmental disabilities opportunities to express themselves by creating art. They offer instruction in printmaking, painting, drawing, sculpture, ceramics, media arts, and textiles and support their clients' quest to become artists who sell their work and earn an income. The staff of Creativity Explored also promote their clients' work as significant contributions to the contemporary art world. The program has five aims: to foster artistic development, inspire connection, enhance personal identity, change attitudes, and lead responsibly.

In 1974 after the Lanterman Act, thousands of adults with disabilities were released from state institutions. In 1983, Florence and Elias Katz, an artist and psychologist respectively, attempted to meet the resulting needs by founding Creativity Explored and three similar places in the Bay Area. The Katz's vision was fueled not only by the social service it provides; they also created the program to foster the creation of art. Any parent can feel the difference between a program that is primarily child care and one that cultivates a specific area about which the teachers are passionate. Creativity Explored is a marriage of the two, like the founders themselves. And this marriage distinguishes the program.

The Katz's believed that all people have the ability to create and that artistic expression is a viable way to enhance personal growth. Creativity Explored successfully straddles two worlds—the social service sector and the contemporary art world. With county and state funding, it functions as a day program. But the program has also secured a spot on the art-scene map by attracting staff from both folk art and outsider art museums.

The staff of Creativity Explored are concerned with the process as well as the outcome of making art, and they respect their clients as professionals. Instruction is tailored to each individual and is not therapy. Instead, clients are establishing an art practice as studio artists, and the first priority is teaching art. If behavioral specialists are needed to accomplish that end, they are available. Creativity Explored is not a recreational parking place; it is a working studio. Behavior is not the curriculum, making art is.

A visit to Creativity Explored begins in their storefront gallery space in the Mission District of San Francisco. The building was a dance studio in the 1920s and retains the ethnic flavor of this Latina neighborhood. The gallery is a valued cultural center among neighboring boutiques and restaurants. Creativity Explored is consistently voted "Best Art Gallery" in the Bay Area and welcomes more than fifteen thousand visitors a year.

The "aha" moment comes when you pass through French doors to behold a surprising expanse of sixty-some artists all working at once in individual spaces. This is a collective social experience of artists. A constant stream of teaching artists and volunteers move throughout greeting visitors, offering advice to artists, showing an interest, and providing feedback loops to fuel the creative process. Presentation of work and critique stimulate the artists' studio practice. The volunteers of Creativity Explored are models of kindness who make a commitment to maintain consistent relationships, both of which are vital to the program's success.

Visitors may browse for work to buy from bins or talk with an artist. The creative synergy in the building is palpable. You might observe a workshop on wire arts or animation. Every couple of months at Thursday night openings, the space becomes even more social than during the work week. I intend to do my Christmas shopping in the gallery this November.

In this supportive environment, artists with developmental disabilities receive quality art materials, individualized instruction from mentors, and opportunities to exhibit their work. Through their art, artists express thoughts, emotions, and experiences with their peers, instructors, patrons, and art lovers. As they create a body of work, artists expand their sense of self and establish a place in the world. They belong.

Creativity Explored uses art to challenge assumptions about disability. The beauty, depth, and humor of their artists' work offer fresh perspectives and show inherent value. When I inquired about José Nuñez, his diagnosis, and how he arrived in California, the licensing director I worked with didn't share much, which was appropriate. Even though my curiosity begged, her response made me respect the organization even more. "We don't discuss our artists' personal lives," she said. "We want to let their work speak for itself and stand on its own merit." *Right,* I thought.

My interest in purchasing this art was not a sympathy vote, but I had a lot of empathy and wanted to make sure José received as much of the proceeds of the licensing as possible. The situation reminded me of when the *Purple Party* CD was released. Reid's very first music therapist, Michelle Lazar, insisted on paying him for a box of fifty CDs. She planned to give them as recital gifts to all of her clients. I had to correct my own perception and get comfortable accepting money for Reid's music for the same reasons Creativity Explored licenses their artists' work. This work has value. Those who create it have innate talent, education, and experience, the same as other artists.

I did learn that José Nuñez came in one Sunday when the studio was closed to paint directly on the walls for the installation. His extended family came with him after church and sat for hours watching him paint each stroke, and their perception of him changed. Nuñez came to life as a capable artist, a man worthy of respect who was selling his own work and preparing for a solo show. Artists are selected for solo shows after they have established a specific style and collector base. José worked with a curator and his teacher to prepare new work for the one-man show.

When Jim, my resident designer, asked me, "What are you thinking for the cover of this next book?" I remembered my screen grab.

"Hey, let me show you this." I pulled up the photo of José's installation. He had painted black and white climbing foliage on the walls of the gallery depicting the flora and fauna of his home country—including crops and animals in a sunbaked-baked landscape. Inside the foliage border were José's works on paper in multiple colors. In this art I saw radical inclusion—a scaffold holding everyone together and making room for diversity. The work reminded me of how our quality of life shifts from black and white to full color when we are safely contained. The figures José arranged near the baseboard represented a community of diverse individuals. All different sizes and shapes, yet they fit together in the larger structure.

I negotiated a licensing rate based on the number of books I would sell, and the staff at Creativity Explored reshot the images to Jim's specifications. José Nuñez had a deal. As a licensee, I am in good company with CB2, Recchiuti Confections, and others who have licensed work by the Creativity Explored's cadre of artists. Their work has been reproduced on throw pillows, bed sheets, chocolate, and apparel and commissioned by numerous corporations. You can scroll through the Creativity Explored website and select artwork based on color, artist name, or size. It's a fabulous resource.

The culture that Creativity Explored has created over the last thirty-five years is a model worldwide. I am aware of a few similar programs: Vibrant Palette Arts Center in Seattle, Dresner Foundation Soul Studio in West Bloomfield, Michigan, Creative Growth Center in Oakland, Nurturing Independence through Artistic Development Art Center in Richmond, California, and Able ARTS Works in Long Beach.

ABLE ARTS WORK
Long Beach, California
AbleARTSWork.org

Allie and I took a tour of Able ARTS Work when she was applying for music therapy internship programs. Founded by music therapist Helen Dolas, this program includes visual arts as well as the performing arts. It is a magical place because of what happens inside.

Greeting us in the lobby was a yarn-bombed bicycle. The staff clued me in to this new phenomenon. The yarn bombing project had engaged many Able ARTS Work clients at once. Those who could braid created handlebar fringe. Those who could wrap decorated the spokes. Others cut pom-poms. This finished textural vehicle could have been entered in the Whitney Biennial. I wanted one. That's what real art does, right? It challenges assumptions, changes perceptions, and stretches worldviews. I learned something new on that tour. When I went home, and I pulled out my basket of half-finished knitting looking for something to bomb.

In the front hallway of Able ARTS Work hung a one-woman show by one of the clients whose mother had just died. It was compelling to see her process of grieving and grappling with real-life events through art. She had not been told to "paint this side blue" or "put a tree in the center with birds on it." Her journey and expression of her difficult year processed in paper and ink was treated with respect as a legitimate exhibition of unmistakable style. It was real artwork.

The guiding principle at Able ARTS Work is drawn from Maslow's hierarchy of needs: first love, then learning. Within a safe, caring, and kind environment, artists can learn new skills—both life skills and creative art skills. The staff members believe each client is an artist with unique expressive potential. Instead of painting pre-cut birdhouses or cookie-cutter crafts (as I've seen elsewhere), we saw adults in wheelchairs who could not speak creating splatter paintings on a large communal canvas. One batted a paint bottle that was suspended from the ceiling by string. The love and respect from the staff meant each client had a way to contribute, and creativity was fostered in both students and staff.

We left out a back door where artist-clients arrive by bus each morning. Colorful murals had been painted on a cinderblock wall. The art made me think of Mary Poppins as she unpacks her carpetbag and declares, "A thing of beauty is a joy forever." Able

ARTS Work had made this corner of Long Beach a beautiful place to belong.

One of my dreams is to have a creative arts day program in San Diego like Creativity Explored or Able ARTS Work. Not that Reid paints or creates visual art. But if the performing arts and music are involved, it would be a place where he could belong long after I am gone. Is there one in your town?

THE JUNGLE BOOK[62]

The first feature-length movie that Allie and Reid ever watched was the original animated *The Jungle Book*. They were two years old, and we were living in the Chicago area for a year. Friends of ours who had no kids but loved ours invited us to their apartment to barbecue. Nikky insisted we bring the kids because she was overjoyed to introduce them to her all-time favorite Disney movie.

I had never seen *The Jungle Book*. "You're kidding me," she exclaimed. "It's so good. The music's incredible. *I wanna be like you hoo hoo* …. You've gotta see it." So with a glass of cabernet in hand, even the adults ended up on their sofa watching Baloo the Bear befriend Mowgli, save him from the ssssinister Kaa, and groove in the ancient ruins to King Louis' beats.

The Jungle Book has an adoption theme. Bagheera the Panther finds human baby Mowgli in a basket. Knowing the baby needs food, Bagheera carries him to a wolf pack to raise as their own. But after "the rains come and go ten times," there is a problem. Shere Kahn, the insidious tiger, has returned to the jungle and will surely kill the boy and all who protect him. Bagheera must take Mowgli to the man-village where he will be safe. Carefree Baloo the Bear lends a hand.

When we owned the movie on a VHS tape, Reid would fast forward and rewind to particular scenes that resonated with him. As an intuitive and attentive mom, I noticed what he was doing. He identified with Mowgli who didn't quite fit in with the wolf cubs, yet wasn't safe in the man-village either. He was betwixt and between and missing something he couldn't define. Reid's main language as a child was not a language at all but music and movie scenes that encapsulated what he couldn't say. He would jump up

---

62 *The Jungle Book*. Directed by Wolfgang Reitherman. Burbank: Walt Disney, 1967.

and down with a vengeance at certain scenes that underscored a particular abstract concept. Reid got the gestalt, and movies were his best way to articulate it.

My friend Nikky was right. *The Jungle Book* has everything. Risk. Humility. Kindness. And music. The wolves take a risk by adopting Mowgli into their pack as one of their own. Bagheera and Baloo humble themselves and put aside their own rank in the jungle to help this little man-cub who is oblivious to danger as well as logic. As Bagheera and Mowgli set off for the man-village, Mowgli doesn't want to go. Claiming he can take care of himself, he runs away. It isn't long before he runs into Baloo who has a thing or two to teach him—from how to eat ants and prickly pears to resisting Kaa the Snake's hypnotic coils. Baloo and Bagheera play good cop, bad cop with Mowgli. One toughens him up through play; the other keeps him safe by thinking ahead.

Baloo and Bagheera exhibit a lot of grace and patience. Baloo enjoys Mowgli's company as they float down the lazy river, sparring and tickling each other. But this makes it harder for Baloo to let Mowgli go. Baloo has more trouble than Bagheera, so they help each other.

Walt Disney struggled with how to end the movie. He took a departure from the Rudyard Kipling story and created a distraction to get Mowgli into the man-village. After a close escape from Shere Kahn, the trio hear a young girl singing in the distance as she collects water in a jug. Mowgli is intrigued. He's never seen another human, let alone a girl. Not ready to part, Baloo tells Mowgli to ignore her. But Bagheera sees a strategy that might work for getting Mowgli to where he belongs. Then the little girl drops her jug, half on purpose. Her mock vulnerability might just win Mowgli over. He forgets all the fun he had eating ants and follows her. Lamenting their loss but knowing this outcome is for the best, Baloo and Bagheera dance back to where they belong.

Is there a place where you belong? I hope you belong in a village that has water and safety. I hope this village includes young men and women of all abilities who belong there too. If you know someone with special needs, where does he or she belong? I hope they are connected with people who are willing to take risks, act with humility, and show kindness in their man-village. People with special needs deserve to use their unique abilities in a context of community. And they deserve you as their champion.

Whatever labels we carry, we actually have more in common with each other than we have differences. Whether we are more akin to the wolves, the panther, or the bear, each of us has unique qualities and skills to share in our man-village. When we offer them graciously to each other, earth becomes a bit more like heaven.

WRAPPING UP CHAPTER 12

One might assume that if we want to find heaven on earth, we'd head to church. But for us, even though we went every Sunday, church attendance when our children were young was difficult. The time felt more like a scavenger hunt or a wild-goose chase. If we define heaven as being in God's presence, then I have found that the interpersonal relationships Reid has with his podcast guests bring heaven into here and now. When he sits down one on one with someone he loves and who loves him back, the experience feels like heaven to me.

Pastor Mark Foreman doesn't just work at a church; he is a man who lives like the kingdom of God has already begun. Mark enjoys serving others right now and looks forward to washing Reid's feet in heaven. Humility and kindness are a given in Mark's interactions as a teacher, missionary, father, and neighbor. Mark taught Reid that God is an artist who created a beautiful world. Mark wants God to get the credit for anything accomplished through his pulpit or on the streets he travels. I am so grateful that Reid's continuing education included a private tutorial on theology from this man that was customized to Reid's comprehension level.

Creativity Explored is supporting and promoting artists who happen to have disabilities. Challenging cultural assumptions about disability, the staff give their artists opportunities to express themselves, work, and make money by creating art, pursuits that are central to being human. Representing all abilities in the contemporary art world is game-changing for all of us.

Kindness doesn't have to be syrupy. Baloo the bear in *The Jungle Book* shows his kindness by sparring with Mowgli and takin' five down a lazy river. This children's classic has it all: risk taking, humility, kindness, and music. Adopting Mowgli the man-cub into a wolf pack was a risky proposition. Bagheera and Baloo humble themselves and volunteer to get Mowgli to safety, even when he resists. And they count on the kindness of the man-village to receive Mowgli. I do, too.

Our house many never be an empty nest. I'm okay with that. But what I'm not okay with is doing Reid a disservice. I believe that keeping him with us forever prevents him from reaching his potential, which would be a disservice to him as well as the community. They deserve to learn as much from him as we have. Like Baloo or Bagheera (*hmmm, which will I be?*) I will have to trust my maturing man-cub to the man-village at some point.

You are that man-village. Today's man-village is more of a metropolis, and many "Reids" live in it. I hope this book has compelled you to get involved, make a difference, and improve your own life with a little radical inclusion.

The fact that we are created in God's likeness makes us all creative artists with a capacity for relationship. Some of us paint, some write, some tell jokes, some solve riddles, some invent machines, some cure diseases, and some give hugs. We live our lives here on earth being creative and developing our character—figuring out our passions and using them in community—until it's time to return to our true home. Our man-villages are campsites of sorts, temporary homes we live in until we join God for eternity. In heaven, there will be no tears, no strife, no dying, no disorders, no labels. There will be love and loads of time to create, serve, and connect with one another. But let's start practicing now.

Can we bring a little heaven down to earth now? I believe all of us can.

Thank you for reading this book and taking action.

Please join the dialogue and let me know about your favorite podcasts, programs, and movies at andreamoriarty@mac.com. You will find additional material to download for free on my website: andreamoriarty.com. And for many more *Talk Time* interviews visit reidmoriarty.com.

But before we part, I'd like to share one more story.

DOOR NUMBER FOUR

Reid had a one-on-one behavioral aide for much of his school career. We tried to wean him off this support in favor of the more efficient one-to-three or one-to-twenty ratios. The school district would have saved money, and more typical classroom possibilities would have opened up for him, but to no avail. By the time Reid reached high school, I accepted that this need for support was a gift rather than a failure. The aides—as long as they were carefully chosen and monitored—protected Reid from bullying, provided better instruction, and communicated with me. The situation wasn't ideal, but I chose to look at the bright side.

We became well acquainted with several aides over the years.

When we updated Reid's program in high school to involve more time in the community, one aide was with him for three years. This aide recounted a rule from his training that described what we were doing intuitively. I wish there was a name for it like the "village effect," but there isn't. Yet it is simple to summarize:

If you can teach it, teach it.
If you can't teach it, modify it.
If you can't modify it, teach around it.
If you can't teach around it, teach the neurotypicals in the community to tolerate it.

Some members of the village learn quickly. Others need adaptations. Some may need visuals to help them grasp a lesson or facilitated communication boards to speak their mind. Some need more time than the rest of the group. Others need ramps to get in buildings. Some need help, supervision, and partnership. The village can provide all of these things, and the village can change itself. If the villagers will take a risk, humbly serve each other, and show kindness, then even the underdog can belong. And as in *Seabiscuit*, we will have fixed each other.

Chapter Discussion Questions

INTRODUCTION

What interactions have you had with people with disabilities in your childhood or as an adult?

Where do you see people with special needs in your community during a typical week? Do you know these people by name?

When have you experienced a "disability" yourself?

RISK

Would you call yourself a risk taker, or are you more cautious?

Who or what gives you courage to step out in faith?

Can you recall a time when you took a risk and were rewarded for doing so?

What small relational risk can you take this week?

CHAPTER 1
REVEAL YOUR AUTHENTIC SELF

When or where do you remove your mask to reveal your authentic self?

If you know someone with a disability, what factors can make it awkward to interact with them?

If you had a podcast, who would you want to interview?

If you had all the money you needed and failure was not possible, what risk would you take?

CHAPTER 2
RAISE THE BAR ON YOUR PERSONAL BEST

What modifications do you make in your life to achieve success?

What motivates you when you don't want to do something new?

What is your favorite movie of all time? Why?

Is there a business or brand that you "evangelize"? Why? What core belief do you share?

How do you raise the bar on your personal best, or has it plateaued?

CHAPTER 3
COLLABORATE WITH OTHERS

Have you collaborated with others in your life's work, and if so, with whom and why?

What activities do you need assistance to do?

What ability do you have that you can offer to others?

Who are people with whom you share an affinity? Or where do you find "your peeps"?

CHAPTER 4
EMBRACE YOUR COMPETITIVE ADVANTAGE

How would you describe your uniqueness or competitive advantage?

Think of the dandelion metaphor. Where might you be considered a weed? And what environment do you thrive in?

What are you passionate about or determined to accomplish?

Who encouraged you in your pursuits when you were a child? Who can you encourage in similar ways?

HUMILITY

Do you have an arc as a parent? How did you begin? What are you like now?

How does pride manifest in your life?

When have you laughed at yourself?

How are fear and pride or humiliation and humility connected for you?

CHAPTER 5
WIN PEOPLE OVER WITH VULNERABILITY

Remember and share a recent time when you felt vulnerable.

Have you ever bonded with someone because you needed help?

Who do you know who is vulnerable and needs help?

How can you include a new person with special needs in a group, club, choir, or class?

CHAPTER 6
LAUGHTER IMPROVES YOUR QUALITY OF LIFE

What makes you belly laugh?

Has your laughter ever been awkward for others or gotten you in trouble?

Is it easier for you to laugh or cry?

Have you ever done theater or taken an improv class? If you have, what did you learn about yourself?

Can you recall a time that laughter has improved an awkward or sad situation?

CHAPTER 7
LEARN FROM EXPERIENCE

How has travel expanded your horizons?

Who is the most interesting person you've met on an airplane or while traveling?

Can you recount a time when your plans were thwarted and the adventure began?

What have you learned from experience rather than from a book or a class?

Watch a movie from Sproutflix together as a group and discuss what you see.

CHAPTER 8
BE A HERO
Who is one of your heroes? Why do you admire this person?

Are you a hero to someone? How could you become a hero to more people?

What expertise do you have that you could pass on to someone younger?

KINDNESS
What is the kindest thing someone has done for you this week?

When does kindness impress you most?

Have you ever gone out of your way to show kindness? How was it received?

CHAPTER 9
RESTORE FAITH IN HUMANITY
How much faith do you have in humanity? Why do you feel that way?

How can you restore someone else's faith in humanity?

If everyone has value, what purpose do you believe people with disabilities have in our society?

How does diversity benefit culture?

CHAPTER 10
RENDER TIME PRICELESS
Is there an act of kindness that you always make time to do (or wish you did)?

Remember and share a time when you spent extra time to encourage or help someone and experienced great rewards.

Which of the model programs described in this book would work in your town? Which one would you like to replicate?

Make a list of ways to extend kindness this week and determine how much time each of them would take.

CHAPTER 11
EXTEND GRACE TO OTHERS

What is your experience of God's grace? How do you define it?

When or where has someone extended grace to you? What were the results?

When have you extended grace to others? How did doing so make you feel?

If you had physical or intellectual challenges, where would you want to live?

CHAPTER 12
BRING HEAVEN HERE AND NOW

What do you think heaven will be like?

When do you experience heaven on earth?

If you are created in God's image as an artist, when are you most creative?

Where do you have the greatest sense of belonging? How can you help others feel like they belong?

How has your understanding of community changed after reading *Radical Inclusion*?

More Model Programs

Here are some more outstanding programs that embrace radical inclusion. This book does not allow enough space to describe them, so I invite you to read about them online.

As I Am
AsIAm.ie
A one-stop shop for the autism community in Ireland that accreds autism-friendly towns each year, hosts a conference, and offers resources for parents, autistic individuals, and professionals.

Inclusion Festival
InclusionFestival.com
A sensory-friendly, outdoor, multi-day annual event that celebrates neurodiversity and promotes understanding and acceptance in Jermyn, Pennsylvania.

KultureCity
Kulturecity.org
Rethinking accessibility in public places, Kulture City was founded by a father whose son had a meltdown at the barbershop that motivated him to create more acceptance. Their work includes life-BOKS for children who wander, Toys Aucross America sharing

program, creation of accessible technology, and a Sensory Inclusive app and certification of public venues to make them more sensory friendly for individuals with autism.

Pal Experiences
PalExperiences.org
Inclusion meets customer experience with tools that Pal Experiences creates to let individuals prepare and explore at their own pace while helping venue partners from restaurants to aquariums provide more inclusive customer experiences.

Index of Informational Text Boxes

Acknowledgments

As it was for P. L. Travers and Walt Disney, telling stories has been cathartic for me in mastering life's challenges and finding significance. I am grateful that writing enables me to be productive while Reid watches movies. Thrilled with the extra viewing time, he has begun asking, "Mom, when are you going to work on your book?" Thanks for helping me out, Reid.

Paul Eddy spends three mornings a week hanging with Reid as if he was family. I couldn't craft a fictional character as perfect as you are for the role at this stage in Reid's life. Thank you for playing it so well.

Writing is time consuming. In the final phase, I wrote at the pool while Reid was swimming. Thank you to his coaches Kay and Troy who bought me that time.

Many others in our town of Solana Beach—from the ladies in the library book sale room to Laura at Panera, Barbara at Sprouts, and Jackie at Rubio's—make every day a beautiful day in our neighborhood.

Every author needs honest readers. This time around, mine were Linda Anderson, Melissa Collins-Porter, Adryon Ketcham, Aleta Barthell, Amanda Weinberg, Paul Quinlaven, and Alessondra True. Thank you for making time to read and respond. When I was drowning in words, you threw me a line.

To Marni and Tracy, my writing coach and editor—I can't decide if you are more like midwives or medicine women. Thank you for bringing *Radical Inclusion* into this world and treating it with all your healing potions. You're a great team.

Good writers become so because of good editors. Lisa, thank you for your honesty and objectivity in the final stages. I wish you had been my high school English teacher.

My mom spent a week of waking hours in her bathrobe, poring over my manuscript, red-lining, highlighting, and compiling notes. I couldn't go on without your approval. Thanks, Mom.

Jim is chief in charge of vision, graphics, cover design, marketing, bookmarks, tee shirts, dinner pick-up, and everything except editing. Thank you for applying your significant genius to loving our family.

Allie, from birth radical inclusion is all you have known. I watch your life like my new favorite movie to see how it flourishes.

Honestly, each and every *Talk Time* guest embodied the message of this book and compelled me to share it with you. To them, thank you for being accessible and saying "yes" to an unlikely conversation. That's how it all starts.

Finally, to the heroes who run each model program, thank you for forging trails to make ways for all of us to thrive. You make the man-village a place where I love to live.

About the Author

Andrea Moriarty was born in Rhode Island and raised outside of Cleveland, Ohio. She studied art history and journalism at the University of Wisconsin-Madison. Before being a mother, she worked at the Whitney Museum of American Art and did special events fundraising for nonprofits in New York City. Cofounder of music therapy nonprofit Banding Together, Moriarty is an innovator compelled to create solutions that fill a void. Also the author of *One-Track Mind: 15 Ways to Amplify Your Child's Special Interest,* her refreshing, spiritual take on both the challenges and triumphs of parenting a son with autism offers affectionate humor and unending hope. Equal parts memoir and reference, her writing reflects her resourcefulness.

Moriarty and her husband, Jim, are the adoptive parents of grown twins: Allie is a music therapist in Massachusetts, and Reid makes music and hosts his own podcast, *Talk Time with Reid Moriarty.* Andrea hosts workshops for other parents and speaks nationally on parenting, autism, adoption, disability ministry, and inclusion, She lives in Solana Beach, California, where she accumulates books, cooks from scratch, and whistles while she works.

Join the Community

We are our own best resource when we communicate and brain-storm together. Please add your voice to the dialogue. I would love to hear from you and learn about inclusive model programs for adults with disabilities near you.

Visit me at andreamoriarty.com or on social media @ andreamoriartyauthor.